Queer Books of Late Victorian Print Culture

Nineteenth-Century and Neo-Victorian Cultures

Series editors: Ruth Heholt and Joanne Ella Parsons

Recent books in the series

Domestic Architecture, Literature and the Sexual Imaginary in Europe, 1850–1930
Aina Martí-Balcells

Assessing Intelligence: The Bildungsroman and the Politics of Human Potential in England, 1860–1910
Sara Lyons

The Idler's Club: Humour and Mass Readership from Jerome K. Jerome to P. G. Wodehouse
Laura Fiss

Michael Field's Revisionary Poetics
Jill Ehnenn

Narrative, Affect and Victorian Sensation: Wilful Bodies
Tara MacDonald

The Provincial Fiction of Mitford, Gaskell and Eliot
Kevin A. Morrison

Women's Activism in the Transatlantic Consumers' Leagues, 1885–1920
Flore Janssen

Queer Books of Late Victorian Print Culture
Frederick D. King

Forthcoming

Lost and Revenant Children 1850–1940
Tatiana Kontou

Olive Schreiner and the Politics of Print Culture, 1883–1920
Clare Gill

Literary Illusions: Performance Magic and Victorian Literature
Christopher Pittard

Pastoral in Early-Victorian Fiction: Environment and Modernity
Mark Frost

Spectral Embodiments of Child Death in the Long Nineteenth Century
Jen Baker

Life Writing and the Nineteenth-Century Market
Sean Grass

British Writers, Popular Literature and New Media Innovation, 1820–45
Alexis Easley

Oscar Wilde's Aesthetic Plagiarisms
Sandra Leonard

Reading Victorian Sculpture
Angela Dunstan

Mind and Embodiment in Late Victorian Literature
Marion Thain and Atti Viragh

Drunkenness in Eighteenth and Nineteenth-Century Irish Literature
Lucy Cogan

Philanthropy in Children's Periodicals, 1840–1930: The Charitable Child
Kristine Moruzi

Violence and the Brontës: Language, Reception, Afterlives
Sophie Franklin

The British Public and the British Museum: Shaping and Sharing Knowledge in the Nineteenth-Century
Jordan Kistler

Dickens and Decadence
Giles Whiteley and Jonathan Foster

Temporality and Progress in Victorian Literature
Ruth M. McAdams

Queer Books of Late Victorian Print Culture

Frederick D. King

EDINBURGH
University Press

Edinburgh University Press is one of the leading university presses in the UK. We publish academic books and journals in our selected subject areas across the humanities and social sciences, combining cutting-edge scholarship with high editorial and production values to produce academic works of lasting importance. For more information visit our website: edinburghuniversitypress.com

© Frederick D. King 2024, 2025

Grateful acknowledgement is made to the sources listed in the List of Illustrations for permission to reproduce material previously published elsewhere. Every effort has been made to trace the copyright holders, but if any have been inadvertently overlooked, the publisher will be pleased to make the necessary arrangements at the first opportunity.

Published with the support of the University of Edinburgh Scholarly Publishing Initiatives Fund.

Edinburgh University Press Ltd
13 Infirmary Street
Edinburgh EH1 1LT

First published in hardback by Edinburgh University Press 2024

Typeset in 11/13pt Sabon
by Cheshire Typesetting Ltd, Cuddington, Cheshire

A CIP record for this book is available from the British Library

ISBN 978 1 3995 2594 7 (hardback)
ISBN 978 1 3995 2595 4 (paperback)
ISBN 978 1 3995 2596 1 (webready PDF)
ISBN 978 1 3995 2597 8 (epub)

The right of Frederick D. King to be identified as the author of this work has been asserted in accordance with the Copyright, Designs and Patents Act 1988, and the Copyright and Related Rights Regulations 2003 (SI No. 2498).

Contents

List of Figures   vi
Acknowledgements   x
Series Preface   xiii

Introduction. Queer Books: A Multimedial Art   1

1. Concerning Golden Books and *Silverpoints*   34
2. Pomegranate Stains on the Ideal Book; or Queering
   the Hetero-Beautiful   74
3. Trans-Textuality in Michael Field's *Long Ago* and
   Whym Chow   131
4. Collaboration and Conflict: Queer Space in *Salome*   175

Conclusion: Queer Books and Their Digital Afterlives   223

Bibliography   235
Index   247

Figures

I.1 Cover of *The Yellow Book*, vol. III, with illustration by Aubrey Beardsley. Private collection. 16

I.2 Oscar Wilde's *Poems* (1890), with cover design by Charles Ricketts. Harry Ransom Center, The University of Texas at Austin. 19

I.3 Title page of Aleister Crowley's *White Stains* (1898). Harry Ransom Center, The University of Texas at Austin. 24

1.1 John Gray's *Silverpoints* (1893) with cover design by Charles Ricketts. Courtesy of the Rufus Hawtin Hathaway Collection, Identification #99102600215970516 3, Archives and Special Collections, Western Libraries, Western University. 35

1.2 Example page from a book published by the Aldine Press. Harry Ransom Center, The University of Texas at Austin. 55

1.3 Example page from the *Hypnerotomachia Poliphili*. Harry Ransom Center, The University of Texas at Austin. 60

1.4 'The Barber' and 'Mishka' in *Silverpoints*. Courtesy of the Rufus Hawtin Hathaway Collection, Identification #99102600215970516 3, Archives and Special Collections, Western Libraries, Western University. 62

1.5 'Did we not, Darling' and 'Lean back and press the pillow deep' as they appear in *Silverpoints*. Courtesy of the Rufus Hawtin Hathaway Collection, Identification #99102600215970516 3,

List of Figures vii

	Archives and Special Collections, Western Libraries, Western University.	66
2.1	Oscar Wilde's *A House of Pomegranates* with cover design by Charles Ricketts. Courtesy of the Rufus Hawtin Hathaway Collection, Identification #991026002159705163, Archives and Special Collections, Western Libraries, Western University.	75
2.2	The 'ugly' cover of a yellow-back for Wilkie's Collins's *Hide and Seek* (1872). Private collection.	83
2.3	Backside of the yellow-back for Collins's *Hide and Seek*. Private collection.	84
2.4	Dante Gabriel Rossetti's cover design for *Poems* (1870). Harry Ransom Center, The University of Texas at Austin.	85
2.5	Christina Rossetti's *Prince's Progress* (1866), with cover design by Dante Gabriel Rossetti. Harry Ransom Center, The University of Texas at Austin.	86
2.6	Title page with facing first page of chapter 1 from William Morris's Kelmscott edition of *The Story of the Glittering Plain* (1891). Harry Ransom Center, The University of Texas at Austin.	89
2.7	Example of the paper used in Kelmscott books. Note the edges where the density is visible. Kelmscott edition of *The Story of the Glittering Plain*. Harry Ransom Center, The University of Texas at Austin.	95
2.8	'The Wounded Amazon' by Charles Shannon from *The Pageant* (1897). Private collection.	105
2.9	Image of Wilde's Young King as interpreted by Ricketts on the first page of the story. Courtesy of the Rufus Hawtin Hathaway Collection, Identification #991026002159705163, Archives and Special Collections, Western Libraries, Western University.	107
2.10	An example of the medallion's urging the reader to remain silent in the face of an open secret. Courtesy of the Rufus Hawtin Hathaway Collection, Identification #991026002159705163, Archives and Special Collections, Western Libraries, Western University.	110

2.11 The reaction of the mass public to the King's beauty. Courtesy of the Rufus Hawtin Hathaway Collection, Identification #991026002159705163, Archives and Special Collections, Western Libraries, Western University. 112

2.12 Charles Shannon's drawing for 'The Birthday of the Infanta' by Oscar Wilde. Courtesy of the Rufus Hawtin Hathaway Collection, Identification #991026002159705163, Archives and Special Collections, Western Libraries, Western University. 114

2.13 Rickett's interpretation of the Fisherman and his Soul in conversation after they separated. Courtesy of the Rufus Hawtin Hathaway Collection, Identification #991026002159705163, Archives and Special Collections, Western Libraries, Western University. 115

2.14 The Star Child rejecting his mother. Courtesy of the Rufus Hawtin Hathaway Collection, Identification #991026002159705163, Archives and Special Collections, Western Libraries, Western University. 120

3.1 Front cover of *Long Ago* (1889). Courtesy of the Thomas Fisher Rare Book Library, University of Toronto. 145

3.2 Frontispiece from *Long Ago*. Courtesy of the Thomas Fisher Rare Book Library, University of Toronto. 146

3.3 H. T. Wharton's *Sappho: A Memoir and Translation* (1885). By permission of the British Library. 148

3.4 Cover binding for Michael Field's *Whym Chow: Flame of Love* (1914). Courtesy of the Rare Books and Special Collections, University of British Columbia. 159

3.5 Front matter with Whym Chow's date of birth and date of death. Courtesy of the Rare Books and Special Collections, University of British Columbia. 160

3.6 Poems IV. and V. Trinity from *Whym Chow*. Courtesy of the Rare Books and Special Collections, University of British Columbia. 163

3.7	Poem XXX. from *Whym Chow*. Courtesy of the Rare Books and Special Collections, University of British Columbia.	168
4.1	'The Stomach Dance' by Aubrey Beardsley from *Salome: A Tragedy in One Act* (1894). Private collection.	176
4.2	Gilt impressing from cover of *Salome*. Harry Ransom Center, The University of Texas at Austin.	195
4.3	Gilt impressing of Beardsley's Colophon from back cover of *Salome*. Harry Ransom Center, The University of Texas at Austin.	201
4.4	'Woman in the Moon' by Beardsley for *Salome*. Private collection.	211
4.5	'The Death of Salome' by Beardsley from *Salome*. Private collection.	215
C.1	'Death and the Bathers' by Laurence Housman from *The Pageant* (1896). Private collection.	224
C.2	Cover design for *The Pageant* (1896). Note the stains along the spine from the packing tape used by the library to hold the book together. Private collection.	226

Acknowledgements

This project is the culmination of over a decade of work. I owe a debt of gratitude to many people who mentored, supported, directed, guided, reviewed and provided access to materials during that period of time.

First, thank you to the team at Edinburgh University Press, particularly commissioning editor Emily Sharp, assistant editor Elizabeth Fraser, the series editors for Nineteenth Century and Neo-Victorian Studies, Jo Parsons and Ruth Heholt and to the blind peer-reviewers who provided valuable feedback on my manuscript. Thank you all for the enthusiasm, support, trust and opportunity.

Many librarians and library staff members at various institutions helped me find materials and navigate the rules of archival research. Others granted permissions to reprint images in their archives. I want to thank everyone who supported me and who works for the Reading Room and the Manuscripts Room at the British Library, Special Collections at the University of Leeds Library, the John Johnson Collection of Printed Ephemera at Oxford University, the University of Western Ontario's Archive and Research Collections Centre, the Harry Ransom Center at the University of Texas in Austin, the Rare Books and Special Collections at the University of British Columbia and the Thomas Fisher Rare Book Library at the University of Toronto.

Thank you to the Faculty of Arts at the University of Western Ontario for the research funding support for some research travel and conference attendance during the early stages of this project.

Thank you to the many publishers who have granted permission to reuse quoted material from important scholarship cited throughout the manuscript. I work within a community of scholarship and this book grows out of the work of those whose ideas preceded mine.

I want to thank Marvin Post and Cassandra McVicar at Attic Books in London, Ontario who gave me employment while a struggling grad student and sessional instructor and who provided me access to many of the books cited in this book, including many difficult-to-find sources discovered in their book history collection. All the images from my own collection are from works purchased at Attic Books. Much of my knowledge of bibliography and book history comes from my work for you, and I want to thank you as well for funding one of my research and conference trips to the United Kingdom. I will never forget your generosity and support.

I want to thank the many mentors who helped me along the way: Sarah Maier (University of New Brunswick Saint John Campus) for introducing me to late Victorian aestheticism and decadence as my undergraduate thesis supervisor; Michael Groden (Western) who introduced me to bibliographic and textual studies; my dissertation supervisor Christopher Keep (Western), and my second reader Steven Bruhm (Western) whom I owe much for your patience as I learned how to write as a scholar. Thanks as well to my dissertation external examiner, Dennis Denisoff (University of Tulsa) and dissertation committee members from the University of Western Ontario, Alison Lee, Mark McDayter and Grant Campbell. Your feedback and interest encouraged me to continue my work in order to create the book that follows.

Thank you to the many scholars who provided feedback at various conference presentations over the years as this project developed. Thank you particularly to Helena Gurfinkel (Southern Illinois University Edwardsville) for warning me that I did not invent the term 'textual intercourse' and to read Jeffrey Masten. I also want to thank Koenraad Claes (Anglia Ruskin University) for his friendship and collegial support, encouraging me to submit my manuscript to Edinburgh University Press. Thank you to James Miller for his work at the University of Western Ontario's Pride Library where he introduced me to the work of Aaron Betsky and the idea of queer space.

Thank you to everyone who is part of the Centre for Digital Humanities at Ryerson University, particularly Lorraine Janzen Kooistra, Reg Beatty and Dennis Denisoff, with whom I worked on the Yellow Nineties 2.0 as guest editor of *The Pageant*. Lorraine, your mentorship in particular means the world to me.

Thank you to the Faculty of Management at Dalhousie University where I have had the good fortune to teach communication, writing and visual rhetoric to Commerce students for the past five years, enabling me to finish this manuscript while creating opportunities to contribute to undergraduate pedagogical research.

Thank you once more to Alison Lee with whom I have had the good fortune to collaborate on multiple peer-reviewed journal articles after I finished my dissertation. I am a better writer and scholar because of our shared scholarship. I am a happier person because of our friendship.

Thank you to my mother, Marion King (1942–2016) and my father, Murray King for always believing in me. I love you both and am forever grateful.

Thank you to my husband James DuPlessis with whom I have shared a relationship for over a quarter century. Thank you for joining me on this adventure. I owe you everything that I am and everything I have. I love you.

Thank you to Aubrey Beardsley, Katharine Bradley, Edith Cooper, John Gray, Charles Ricketts, Charles Shannon, Oscar Wilde and the many other flamboyant authors and artists of the Victorian *fin de siècle* for the pleasurable sensations that your poems, plays, illustrations and bibliographic designs evoke when I pick up one of your books.

Thank you to everyone who picks up this book and considers the ideas presented.

To every queer reader who picks up this book, please enjoy.

Series Preface

Nineteenth-Century and Neo-Victorian Cultures
Series Editors: Ruth Heholt and Joanne Ella Parsons

This interdisciplinary series provides space for full and detailed scholarly discussions on nineteenth-century and Neo-Victorian cultures. Drawing on radical and cutting-edge research, volumes explore and challenge existing discourses, as well as providing an engaging reassessment of the time period. The series encourages debates about decolonising nineteenth-century cultures, histories, and scholarship, as well as raising questions about diversities. Encompassing art, literature, history, performance, theatre studies, film and TV studies, medical and the wider humanities, Nineteenth Century and Neo-Victorian Cultures is dedicated to publishing pioneering research that focuses on the Victorian era in its broadest and most diverse sense.

Introduction
Queer Books: A Multimedial Art

> Methinks my life is a twice-written scroll
> Scrawled over on some boyish holiday
> With idle songs for pipe and virelay
> That do but mar the secret of the whole
> 	— Oscar Wilde, 'Hélas!'

I first considered the idea that books could be queer when I read an original collection of poems by John Gray, published by the Bodley Head in 1893, called *Silverpoints*. I sat in the University of Western Ontario's Libraries Archives and Research Collection Centre (ARCC) examining this strange book with boards thicker than the total number of pages it encased. Though I could not name the pattern, the embossed design of gold latticework and willow leaves seduced me with its peculiarity. This unfamiliar book felt exotic: tall and thin with a spine, which is typically a means of identification, strangely left blank. In contrast, the front and back boards spoke loudly with their decorative gold lattice aesthetically tempting me to open the book. Inside the covers, there was no gold leaf, but the poetry's italicised type hailed the cover's elaborate aesthetic. The print strained my eyes, and I could not understand why someone would print poems in a type that measures only one sixteenth of an inch in height. It was a beautiful, but an excessive object that drew attention to the artificiality of Gray's decadent poetic style.

The book's material excess provides the poetry with a sensual value unavailable in other formats. Gray's poems, as they appear in anthologies and online databases, struck me as homoerotic and the spiritual implications of his imagery regarding late Victorian culture were interesting, but they did not move me the way, say, Michael Field's ekphrastic poems evoke sensual, intellectual and personal engagements with their subjects. However, sitting in the archives, my impression of Gray's poetry changed – the small italic type demanded my close physical interaction and made the process feel like an act of translation, as if I were decoding a secret language. I hunched forward and used my finger to keep my place and remain focused. The delicate beauty of each word demanded my attention, and poetry suddenly became a material, tactile experience. I discovered that Gray's poetry and Ricketts's book design together created a work of art: a presentation of homoeroticism, aestheticism, spirituality, theatricality and melancholic decadence as a material and poetic experience: a space where the physical book mediated a queer discourse between literary and bibliographic art.

After this subjective experience, I wanted to engage more critically with the material experience of reading, specifically in relation to queer readers. The tactile experience of reading a beautiful book suggested an aesthetic response that could engage physically with queer sexual discourse for LGBTQ+ readers. I also wondered about that experience for queer aesthetes at the *fin de siècle* who often could only engage in queer sexual discourse through the exchange of books that suggested such ideas. With *Silverpoints*, I knew that John Gray, its author, and Charles Ricketts, its designer, both had sexual relationships with other men and engaged with aestheticism, eroticism and decadence. But how did the awkward silences of everyday life influence their books, in both literary content and bibliographic form? This book will argue that such a tactile relationship exists and that it can be read as a textual and sexual discourse.

The queer book as defined in this study is not the result of an author or a designer's homosexuality, although that is certainly a factor in its composition. Rather, it is the result of collaboration between authors and artists, compromises demanded by new printing technologies, publishing budgets and contesting visions of queerness that emerge from the various hands who contributed to a particular edition of the book. The queer book also emerges from the experience of a double life that queer men and women often led in order to protect themselves from prosecution and persecution. Same-sex desire was an open secret in the nineteenth century, spoken of in obfuscating fashions: sexology used the language of pathology; the law used vague concepts of sodomy; many others simply dismissed it as something unmanly or culturally corrupting. For British aesthetes, particularly queer aesthetes, it was something beautiful to study and dangerous to experience. Where open and frank discussion was not available, discussion of same-sex desire was instead integrated into other discourses. Appreciation for the 'sexless' male form as a sign of an aesthete's true understanding of beauty; study of ancient Greek literature and the tales of Doric soldiers or the passionate 'comradeship' of Achilles and Patroclus; and celebration of Sappho's lesbian desires by men who could not speak of their desire for other men: these are myths and histories of *eros* that tell dual stories. One tale is a troubling but moderately acceptable historical and scholarly appreciation of a supposedly non-sexual aesthetic, while the second tale is dangerously suggestive of the role that same-sex desire performs both historically and contemporaneously in western culture. Queer desires, both those of men for other men as well as women's desires whether queer or simply for the male body, were hidden in plain sight, an obscured presentation of queer sexual discourse within works of literature and art. That obscurity was, in part, the result of collaboration with designers and illustrators who spoke a coded language of aestheticism, juxtaposing a desire to both hide and reveal.

These queer creative expressions are complicated by everyday experience. The epigram for this Introduction, an excerpt from Oscar Wilde's poem 'Hélas!', laments the necessity of the 'twice-written' narrative demanded of him. It is an immature, 'boyish' script that the speaker finds he no longer appreciates. While it can result in beautiful poetry or 'idle songs', it also damages the idea of the whole identity of the poet. Everything is spoken but some readers only read the story that they find acceptable. At the same time, to only examine the homoerotic in aestheticism mars 'the secret of the whole', or how a reading of both stories together results in a deeper and more complex understanding of the art created.[1] It is this twice-told tale written in the codex book that will be examined in *Queer Books of Late Victorian Print Culture*. It is also a reflection of my methodological approach. With every text explored in this project, there are two stories: the story of how discourses of queer desire are circulated, and the story of how material expressions of queer desire are both the results of, and an influence on, British aestheticism's multimedial aesthetic – an aesthetic where form and content interact and merge so that one element, such as a book's design, may not be separated from another, such as its literary content. Rather than examining the human body and equating the homoeroticism of literature with the homosexuality of its author(s), I focus on the textual body, material books, as bodies in which different stories are told simultaneously, but are too often read separately.

The beautifully produced books of British aestheticism are queer in their particular moment in time and history because of the introduction of new and affordable printing technologies aligned with the limited budgets and aesthetic choices necessary to publish the queer sexual discourses of aestheticism and decadence. Together, print culture and literature merge to create a multimedial art form with beautiful editions of poetry, fiction and drama. If, as Michel Foucault has long taught us, what we think of as a history of sex is instead a sexual discourse, a history of how we discuss, identify and integrate sexual desire into cultural practice, then the body in which that discourse lies is not a person's fleshy form where desire and pleasure exist; it is the material book's body where discourses of sexuality shared amongst a community of aesthetes can be found.

Queer for the purposes of this study is defined as a form of sexual discourse about same-sex desires as well as the complex experience of gender for those who experience such desires. A book may be queer because it is a medium of expression, giving material body to queer sexual discourse for the artists and authors who contributed to its creation. For the aesthetes, the discourse of same-sex desire is part of a larger discourse about beauty and the appreciation of art. To understand their sexual discourse, we must also understand that aesthetes did not necessarily separate sexual desire from aesthetic appreciation.

There is a long, rich history in Victorian studies of important interventions in our understanding of same-sex desire in British aestheticism. What has yet to be considered is how queer desires, and the codes used to disseminate queer sexual discourse, influenced the material construction of the books these artists published. Aestheticism, of course, is not a sexual discourse in the same sense that we would read sexology or legal discourses of sodomy. Aestheticism is largely concerned with art and art criticism. Emerging from a variety of influences including the Pre-Raphaelite movement; university-level studies of classical philosophy, history and myth (especially the Hellenic Greeks); scholarly studies of the European Renaissance by leading aesthetes

Walter Pater, John Addington Symonds and Oscar Wilde; and an emerging avant-garde that was turning away from Victorian literary conventions of sympathetic realism and seeking alternative expression in Classicism and the Renaissance.

This merging of schools of thought found its first British expression in Pater's essays complied for the first time in *Studies in the History of the Renaissance* (1873). Pater calls out to aesthetic critics to pleasurably awaken a multitude of senses simultaneously, which meant a more pleasurable experience and art that could achieve the effect on the observant aesthete was held in the highest regards. Music in particular was idealised because of how it merges form with content in a manner that will not allow the listener to separate the two. Similarly, contemporary scholarship by Richard Dellamora, Joseph Bristow, James Eli Adams and Stephano Evangelista has established the link between queer sexual discourse and aestheticism's concept of Neo-Platonism. Dellamora's *Masculine Desire: The Sexual Politics of Victorian Aestheticism* (1990) studies literary expressions of desire between men in Victorian literature from Tennyson to the dissident figures of the *fin de siècle*, paying particular attention to the language of same-sex desire unique to Victorian aesthetic culture in order to show how the sexual scandals of the 1890s led to sexology's privileging of heteronormative sexual practices and the marginalisation of other forms of sexual desire as aberrant deviations.[2] Bristow's *Sexuality* (1997) offers a detailed history of our attempts to understand same-sex desire and the complex issues of gender identity. Bristow traces nineteenth-century sexual discourse back to the work of 1860s German activist Karl Heinrich Ulrichs (1825–95) and the influence of nineteenth-century ideologies of binary opposition between the sexes, aligning the male and female genders with sexual desire for the supposed opposite sex.[3] Adams's book *Dandies and Desert Saints: Styles of Victorian Manhood* (1995) further complicated the binary differentiation of masculine versus effeminate behaviour, pointing out the changing conception of what it was to be normal – in regards to sex and gender – at different periods of the nineteenth century.[4] Most importantly, Dellamora, Bristow and Adams complicate cultural concerns regarding aestheticism's threat to accepted gender performance, specifically masculinity, within Victorian public culture.[5]

Stephano Evangelista's *British Aestheticism and Ancient Greece: Hellenism, Reception, Gods in Exile* (2009) demonstrates how same-sex desire was conceived and privileged within aestheticism's discourse of sensation. Evangelista notes that Oscar Wilde, in his more decadent interpretation of Pater's aesthetics, understood *eros* as a merging of aesthetic appreciation with homoerotic desire.[6] A new chivalry emerges from Pater's epistemological concept that the accumulation of aesthetic knowledge is tied to our physical experiences of pleasurable sensation.[7] Aestheticism's perception of sexuality is based on a materialist reading of Classicism and the western world's intellectual heritage as the multisensory response of the human body to contact with beauty. All sensations and desires become available for the critic's reflective analysis.

Decorated books emerge as queer objects of sexual discourse when they provide readers with multiple, often incongruent, voices of difference bound by the intercourse of their material presentation within the book. Like the efforts of queer theorists today to destabilise ideological constructions of sexuality, for a brief period in the 1890s, decorated books such as *Salome* or journals such as *The Yellow Book* were objects of beauty that destabilised the codex book. Reading took on tactile features associated with intercourse: touching, appreciation of physical beauty, surprising challenges to one's sense of self and the experience of beautiful moments hidden underneath the covers. These beautiful works of art establish a precedent of positioning books and journals as sites of distributed authorship and cultural heterogeneity. In these works, literature intersects with illustration and typography offering sexually marginalised writers, designers and consumers a physical location for interaction in the material book. The book changes, becoming an art object, a site of textual interdisciplinarity and an agent of sexual dissidence. I will refer to this exchange throughout this book as a textual intercourse, that is, an intimate discourse between literary and bibliographic elements of the book to create the queer sexual discourse unique to these aesthetic objects: a multisensory and intimate experience of touching, admiring and deeply penetrating the material book.

Sexual orientation and perceptions of gender's association with our desires complicate our motives and make sexuality difficult to locate within a web of complexity that even George Eliot could not weave into the larger structure of *Middlemarch*. There is no narrative of consensus. Discourses of nation-building, medical science, justice and the legal system, religion and family values, each fail to integrate either difference or play as factors in our sexual choices.

A new discourse of sexual difference becomes necessary, and aestheticism emerges as its outlet. A perception of a society without consensus, where institutionalised power cannot organise individuals into clearly designated categories, where binaries of the social and the socially marginalised are disrupted and challenged, is not a world of chaos. A world without consensus is a world of questions, debates, choices and play. The perceived disorder, the inability to marginalise difference, is the basis of what queerness celebrates.

For many of these dissident writers and artists, some stories could not be narrated within the conventions of realist fiction or narrative poetry, forms that dominated literary production in Victorian Britain because the stories they wanted to tell were forbidden. Specifically, stories of same-sex desire, between men or between women, had no place in the realist novel, an institution transformed in the nineteenth century by the middle-class heteronormative values of their writers and readers. Even among the lower classes, where homosexuality would be less shocking for its world-weary members, hypocritical moral leaders argued that subversive texts may corrupt people who were seen as morally weak. The aesthetes, however, understood and were critical of this hypocrisy. They knew that the brothels and music halls were as entrenched in Victorian culture as taxes and Tories. It was just that those former pleasures were unspoken. Instead of reality, the Victorian elite trusted realism to regulate social norms. Realism then, as a literary form defined by the serialised and three-decker novels of Dickens, Eliot and Trollope, could not speak the truth as defined by the aesthetes. Instead, aesthetes experimented with alternative literary forms: the short story, fairy tales, lyric poetry, prose poems and closet drama, obscuring their ideas in irony and paradox, and submitting their work to new forms of print circulation: avant-garde periodicals, fine-press *belle lettres*, limited editions, private circulation and the underground publishers of 'Cosmopoli' (London's demi-monde).[8]

These experiments in literary forms were presented in collaboration with niche methods of publication and circulation; together, literary and bibliographic experimentation formed a queer space for narratives of sexual dissidence in the 1890s. In addition, these experiments in form and circulation led to the discovery of new languages of expression. Textual scholarship historically studies the meaning made by bibliographic elements of the book for decades. Their work has an important influence on *Queer Books*: from Gérard Genette's study of the book's paratextuality, to Johanna Drucker's work on typography in modernist poetry, to Peter Shillingsburg's examination of the interface as a performance field, textual studies examines the ways in which bibliographic design alters the meaning of lexical content.[9] In nineteenth-century studies of print culture, Nicholas Frankel's research is an important precursor to this book. In *Oscar Wilde's Decorated Books* (2000), Frankel describes the collaborative process of publishing and the material limits imposed on creators, directing his textual criticism toward the reader's perspective of the book as a whole work of art.[10] Frankel's focus on Wilde allows him to examine closely the unique qualities of the beautifully decorated books of the early 1890s' most celebrated aesthete. In *Masking the Text: Essays on Literature and Mediation in the 1890s* (2009), Frankel provides a broader study of how material design choices at publication influence the formation of meaning for the reader for a variety of works ranging from Oscar Wilde's *A House of Pomegranates* to William Morris's *Earthly Paradise*.[11] For Frankel, typography, illustration, impressing, critical apparatus, the white space of the margins and other elements of book design merged with literature to create new expressions that authors could not speak without collaborating with visual artists. For a queer book, authors collaborated with artists like Aubrey Beardsley, Charles Ricketts and Charles Shannon, who understood and shared their desire for queer expressions.

By considering how the decorated book engages with and stimulates the reader's sensory responses, it is possible to revise our understanding of British aestheticism and decadence. More than apolitical and theoretical approaches to art, aestheticism and decadence are a means of reconceiving perspectives on existing social institutions in late Victorian Britain. Rather than offering fantastical notions of escape from reality, aesthetes and decadents such as Beardsley, Ricketts, Shannon, John Gray, Katharine Bradley and Edith Cooper ('Michael Field'), and Oscar Wilde intentionally rejected existing notions of literary and artistic realism to create a culture in which sexual diversity, more than just dissent from the norm, could be a proposition for something entirely new, as yet unimagined and unrealised outside the pages of these queer books.

Queer Books will support this thesis by exploring British aestheticism and decadence at the end of the nineteenth century and how it emerges, then departs, from tenets of the Revival of Printing. The Revival of Printing was a mid-nineteenth-century cultural movement that criticised modern printing practices that resulted in a significant deterioration of the material book's quality of production. Substandard and cheaply produced illustrations, acidic papers, small fonts in faded grey inks that privileged cost-efficiency over aesthetic experience, all meant that publicly accessible books were disposable, ugly items that reflected the ugly utilitarian lives of industrialised urban life. Men like William Morris sought to restore book publishing to the high-quality standards of the hand presses used in the past. Where he turned to medieval printing practices, others like Walter Blaikie at the Chiswick Press found ways to create high-quality volumes without sacrificing all the conveniences of the press.[12] The books studied here emerge from this revived tradition. Reading a selection of decorated editions of material books via queer theory and textual studies, *Queer Books* explores how bibliographic content intersects with lexical (or literary) content and how those material intersections reflect aesthetic theories of *eros*, Greek love and same-sex desire as sensual discernment. The books central to this study are *A House of Pomegranates* (1891) written by Oscar Wilde and prepared by Charles Ricketts and Charles Shannon; *Silverpoints* (1893) written by John Gray and prepared by Ricketts; the English translation of Wilde's play *Salome: A Tragedy in One Act* (1894) prepared by Aubrey Beardsley; *Long Ago* (1889) and *Whym Chow: Flame of Love* (1914), written by 'Michael Field' and prepared using the authors' instructions by the Chiswick Press and the Eragny Press respectively; and the aesthetic annual *The Pageant* (1896–7) under the direction of editors Gleeson White and Charles Shannon in the 1890s, and today as it transforms into a digital edition. In addition, other significant works will be referenced to place these specific examples of the queer book into discourse with aesthetic book production more broadly. The focus of the study will be on how typography, illustration, binding design, page layout, as well as paper and ink choices are not only aesthetic choices but decisions that influence and change how literary content can be interpreted. Literary practice is important, but the focus of *Queer Books* is how the material book transforms literary content and makes it queer. These unique limited editions, long buried in private collections and library archives, reveal the centrality of queer sexual discourses of same-sex desire in the material culture of aestheticism and decadence. The result is that scholarly editions and anthologies that take the literature out of their original bibliographic context erase the queer sexual discourse that, as I will argue, is a central component of the reading experience.

As a multisensory material means of communication, aestheticism reflects the movement's interests in sensual and sexual experience. As David Halperin notes, how we define the role of the erotic in our lives is unique to a particular space and time in culture and, as a result, we achieve our best understanding of same-sex desires in the past through the historical lens of the culture from which it emerges.[13] Aestheticism emerges from a revised discourse of *eros* taken from the study of Hellenism. Walter Pater tells us that the aesthetic effect of art communicates through an 'ideal' beauty – 'a distinction, like genius or noble place', found in the 'moral sexlessness' of the male body.[14] The male body remains erotic but sexless because an appreciation of the nude male form speaks to 'the finer aspects of nature, the finer lime, and clay of the human form'.[15] To be sexless, from Pater's perspective, is not necessarily to be outside of the erotic, but to be outside of the heteronormative discourse of sexuality. Stefano Evangelista explains how, in ancient Greece, gymnasia, where athletes exercised nude, also served as schools frequented by philosophers and artists alike.[16]

Art is connected to physical experience, and the body of the athlete gives physical sensation to aestheticism's ideals. While this interaction is technically sexless, the beauty of the male body offers an erotic sensuality shared between men as the basis for both art and art criticism. As we will see in Chapter 2, the same applies to the aesthete John Gray, whose audiences and comrades appreciated his recitations of poetry, as well as his masculine beauty, during his years as the 'real' Dorian Gray before his publication of *Silverpoints* in 1893. The intercourse between his poetry and his bodily beauty was a textual experience desired by his audience – technically sexless, but intensely erotic in its sensuality. The queer book is an iteration of that sensory intercourse, only the body is that of the book, not a poet, and a book, unlike a human, is made for the reader's objectification. It also offers the promise of bringing bodies together. While much research exists that details the history of queer sexual discourse in British aestheticism and European decadence, no one connects that discourse to the design and circulation of beautiful books.

Victorian studies scholarship, with its focus on cultural materialism, offers a detailed history of the book during the Revival of Printing. Lorraine Janzen Kooistra's study of the illustrated gift book of the Victorian age demonstrates how the material relationship between poetry and the medium of circulation changes our understanding of the role of poetry within popular culture.[17] Her earlier work on book illustration in the *fin de siècle* likewise argued for the role that illustration plays beyond the depiction of textual events that suggests a 'bitextuality' between word and image.[18] Elizabeth K. Helsinger's study of the Pre-Raphaelites and the role of visual art and design in understanding their poetry offers important insight into how materiality influences literary production.[19] Frankel's earlier noted analysis of Oscar Wilde's decorated books, as well as Josephine Guy and Ian Small's examination of Wilde and the literary marketplace both demonstrate the material performance of the man of letters that Wilde cultivated in his books and how that materiality helped to build his literary reputation.[20] Elizabeth Carolyn Miller's detailed study of literary radicalism and the late Victorian press explores the influence of print culture on the socialist movement and its many iterations at the turn of the century, with particular attention paid to the work and influence of William Morris whose work I will examine in Chapter 2.[21] These more recent scholarly works all owe a debt to the earlier research of James G. Nelson whose study of the Bodley Head set a standard for the study of aestheticism and book history that has continued to persist, with a focus on the materiality of books and the influence of publishing practices on literary output.[22] Nelson was himself reviving the work of Holbrook Jackson, whose *The Eighteen Nineties* (1913) is the first book-length scholarly study of British aestheticism's influence on book history.[23] Kooistra discusses both bibliographic features and the literary text with her theory of bitextuality, but her focus is on illustration rather than the material book as a creative entirety. Frankel's detailed analysis, particularly of Wilde and Ricketts's collaboration on *The Sphinx* (1894), comes the closest to what I hope to draw attention to, but his scholarship is not exclusively focused on the queer collaborative relations that I argue built these books. Consequently, no one has yet put the pleasure derived from reading decorated books of the *fin de siècle* aesthetes in conversation with the role of the book as an object of homoerotic and dissident sexual desire in aesthetic discourse.

Queer theory aligns well with postmodern approaches to bibliography in textual studies. We are living, after all, in an age when the material book is slowly being replaced by the digital interface. Jerome McGann went so far as to declare the death of book culture;[24] while in our academic institutions, the study of book history has been replaced by the study of media archaeology.[25] This shift is significant because it demonstrates McGann's clarifying follow-up: 'things that die need not, therefore, be dead'.[26] This shift in bibliographic scholarship to textual and media studies, encompassing the interface from clay tablets to the smartphone, integrates the field into a larger context that reveals the ongoing relevance of the study of the material book. The work of McGann and others in new textual scholarship, media history and the digital humanities allows for new ways of reading books as collaborative constructions and architectural spaces influence the meaning of the texts they circulate.

Shillingsburg, in his study of the interrelationship of bibliographic and lexical content of material books and digital platforms, looks at bibliographic codes and how they 'all affect a reader's sense of what kind of text is "contained" in the document' and at how these 'elements telegraph to readers how they should read the lexical text'.[27] His argument suggests that when we read a historical text, the form in which it is published, either then or now, either paper or digital, affects our interpretation of the content. Similarly, Johanna Drucker's work on the language of visuals in books, advertisements, periodicals and digital user interfaces over the past twenty years has drawn attention to the fact that literary content as printed on the page or coded for the screen is a visual art form. By looking at typography she draws attention to the materiality of language and its relationship to the context in which it is printed (such as the queer books of this study). Drucker draws attention to the materials used to record and preserve the language and how the quality of those materials speaks to the significance of what is written on its surface. The material presentation of the book provides the reader to historical and cultural experiences through tactile engagement and that experience cannot be separated from the experience of reading the book as object.[28] The printing processes, inks, paper and illustrative processes all affect the interpretation of the literature it circulates. The social and cultural implications of these materials interact and speak to the literature contained within. More recently, Drucker argues that the way we construct book history must engage in what she refers to as a meta-bibliographic practice that forgoes the subjective considerations of beauty on display in this chapter's opening paragraphs into the historical material realities of reading as physical experience.[29] To do so, scholars must formulate methods that turn from traditional printing and reception history, toward a means of tracking changes and differences in material practice changes that move away from the narrative of linear progression that book history traditionally embraces.[30]

While decorated books of varying quality were numerous throughout the nineteenth century, the decorated books of *fin de siècle* London were sites where British aestheticism and European decadence intersected with cultural discourses of sexual dissidence and the revival of printing, creating multimedial literary discourses inspired by, and about, same-sex desire.[31] *Queer Books* proposes that books are queer because of how the material aesthetic of these select works is in textual intercourse with their literary content on aestheticism's specific rhetoric of same-sex desire.[32] By placing British aestheticism and decadence into conversation with current approaches to queer theory and textual studies, *Queer Books* will show how a group of beautifully decorated books challenges our understanding of art and literature, positioning each as an element of media design. The body of the book brings the two together, in textual intercourse, to create something new that is the sum of its contributing parts.

Queer books are very much a decadent component of British aestheticism. Critics of aestheticism and decadence such as Max Nordau disparaged the aesthetes for their morbidity and degeneration. Nordau and others were uncomfortable with the aesthetes' interest in cultural and ideological decline. Decadence, for both its critics and practitioners, was associated with the decline of empire and political power. 'Healthy', Arthur Symons cautioned, 'we cannot call it, and healthy it does not wish to be considered.'[33] Decadence is an 'unreason of the soul', an 'unstable equilibrium, which has overbalanced so many brilliant intelligences into one form or another of spiritual confusion', a *'maladie de fin de siècle'*.[34] Max Nordau directly associates the movement with the decay of the species, claiming that decadence 'denotes a state of society which produces too great a number of individuals unfit for the labours of common life' and unable to contribute to the social 'organism'.[35] These single cells that have decayed 'cease to . . . subordinate their energy to the total energy of [society], and the anarchy which takes place [as a result of this failure to contribute use-value to society] constitutes the decadence of the whole'.[36]

Nordau, among others, assumed, in his idealisation of the social organism, that modern society was a normal, even ideal cultural development: linear progress from savagery to civility. Any deviation from that ideal or civilised social norm, any art or political position that offered a demonstrable critique of ruling social and political convention, was a failure of diseased individuals to contribute to the progress of society's existing power structure and cultural ideals. Medical science transformed dissenting sexual and gendered behaviours into diagnosable pathologies (homosexuality) and diseases (female hysteria) that were harmful, not so much to the afflicted individual, but to the health and well-being of an imagined social organism.[37] Decadent aesthetes labelled as unhealthy dissenters from the social order embraced a pose of degeneracy with ironic presentations of ennui and self-destruction. The difference between them and Nordau was how they applied the term 'unhealthy'. For critics like Nordau, it was a condemnation of aestheticism and decadence as socially and culturally destructive: hysterical, perverse and deadly. However, those who called themselves decadent, and many who didn't but still integrated its ironic play with morbidity, did so to defy those who condemned them for failing to understand their desire. Decadent works of art planted seeds of doubt regarding the health of the ideals celebrated by the social organism's existing structures such as reproductive futurism, patriarchy, plutocracy and an empire based on white supremacy.

Holbrook Jackson lists the chief characteristics of decadence to be 'Perversity', 'Artificiality', 'Egoism' and 'Curiosity', insisting that 'all inquisitiveness is in the nature of life asking for more' because 'the accumulated experiences and sensations' of culture are not enough.[38] Decadent aesthetes wanted more, demanding 'wider ranges, newer emotional and spiritual territories, fresh woods and pastures new for the soul', rejecting the limits of society, literature and bibliography, imagining new ways to live, think and perform.[39] The decadent is unhealthy, but that unhealthiness emerges from ennui – a dissatisfaction with the way things are, and an attempt to enact some resistance to the collective conventions of Victorian culture that induces their ennui. Decadence is a more acute search

Introduction 15

for new sensations than typically associated with British aestheticism, resisting and provocatively shocking social order. However, it emerges in the queer book because of the way that bibliography and literature interact.

Take for example *The Yellow Book* (1894–7), a periodical presented in hard-bound collectable editions, giving it the character of a beautiful book. Aubrey Beardsley, as art director for the first four volumes, highlights the dissidence of the literary content, with sexual suggestions and portrayals of sexual desire in his presentation of actresses, aristocrats and a strange coterie of unnatural companions. The book presents works of aestheticism, decadence and New Woman fiction alongside images like that found on the cover of volume III (see Fig. I.1), which depicts a woman preparing her face with a cosmetic brush while wearing an elaborate and impractical robe. She is aided by the light from modern gas lamps that surrounds her mirror, and a table of perfumes and cosmetics that allow her to create an artificial version of herself for public consumption. By showing readers behind the scenes of that preparation, Beardsley draws attention to the artificiality of social conceptions of women as a gender. What she presents is not real or natural, but performance and an aesthetic ideal created with the aid of the paints and scents that modernity makes available. As cover art for a quarterly periodical, the image suggests that the literature inside will also explore the role of artificiality in 1890s culture. What is perceived as normal, including the heteronormative, is reconceived as an unnatural masquerade, an artifice created through a layer of cosmetics. Modern womanhood is presented as a text created by the technologies and innovations of the industries of the nineteenth century.

Queer books, too, are products of the modern world, created from the same tools and techniques that any heteronormative reader would have access to, but used in a manner that subverts the facades of the so-called natural that organise heteronormative society. Like this cover that shows the artificiality of the unmade woman, elaborately flaunting the intimate space of her vanity, and by suggestion, her bedroom, *The Yellow Book* will explore those parts of the world that heteronormative ideologies usually refrain from considering. Queer books embrace the unnatural as modernity's common characteristic – arguing not for the natural existence of queer lives, but for the unnatural condition of modern sexual discourse.

Figure I.1 Cover of *The Yellow Book*, vol. III, with illustration by Aubrey Beardsley. Private collection.

Taking theories of aestheticism and decadence as a starting point, *Queer Books of Late Victorian Print Culture* is, in part, an attempt to stimulate the aesthetic reader's desire for new sensations in the tradition of Walter Pater's conception of an aesthetic critic who

> regards all the objects with which he has to do, all works of art, and the fairer forms of nature and human life, as powers or forces producing pleasurable sensations, each of a more or less peculiar or unique kind.[40]

The physical sensations of reading with its visual and tactile influences were particularly important for works of the aesthetic movement. British aestheticism, beginning with the work of Walter Pater, reconsidered how art could be understood as a cultural experience through individual perceptions instead of being defined by the artist's intention or the work alone. Art was understood as a critical experience, of going to a museum or opening a book, that allowed aesthetes to feel and express their response to the sensations that art stimulated. Sensation and perspective redefined art for the aesthetes so that beauty, at least according to Pater, was relative.[41] Aestheticism placed abstract philosophical theory about art in discursive contact with the physical experience of sharing space with art: reading, observing, reacting and even touching art's beauty. Pater advocates for a definition of beauty 'in the most concrete terms possible' to find 'the formula which expresses most adequately this or that special manifestation of it'.[42] In other words, the art critic and the creative artist are readers, and as such, they must recognise their influence on the art object and specify their unique experience of sensation in response to that work of art. Walter Pater's theory is a form of reader response, so it is not surprising that reader-response theorist Wolfgang Iser researched and was influenced by Pater's work.[43]

Aestheticism's sexual discourse is concerned with the individual's pleasurable intercourse with beautiful objects. Such a relation between the critic and artwork privileges textual intercourse between the critic and the work of art whereby the object of beauty stimulates all the aesthete's senses. To that end, a work of literature must be read, not as an abstract concept disseminated through the medium of the book, but as the reader's physical experience of interacting with the work disseminated by the many hands that contribute to the creation of the edition that stimulates many senses at once.

Beyond the legal or medical discourses, desire is something that occurs in response to beauty. Desire is a response to what is observed by the senses. By embracing an acute knowledge of their senses, queer aesthetes could code their same-sex desires in the language of sensation and share their unconventional desire for their sex in their art, despite the condemnation and suppression from the world in which they lived. That knowledge still needed to be hidden from view, at least from the view of those who do not see the world in the same way. However, through the language of aestheticism, like-minded queers could find community, at least in the pages of a queer book, and imagine a world, or a future, not yet possible, but as real and as tangible as any cultural value found in Victorian economic and political ideologies.

Consider the example of Oscar Wilde's *Poems*, reprinted by John Lane and Elkin Mathews at the Bodley Head in 1890.

The collection had been previously published by Bogue and Company in 1881. According to James G. Nelson, years later after the firm went bankrupt, 220 copies were remaining. Mathews and Lane purchased these remainders and, with a new binding and title page, and the autograph of Wilde himself, the book was a success and sold out entirely.[44] Designed by Charles Ricketts, one of Wilde's queer colleagues and a celebrated book designer and publisher in his own right alongside his lover Charles Shannon, the book's new cover realigns the text with Wilde's newly infamous reputation as a subversive figure in London society. The cover (see Fig. I.2) features a series of artificial plants in a row, stylised and integrated with the author's name and 'Poems' as part of the impressed design. The gilt blends with the tan-coloured binding to create a rich and glowing new appearance. More importantly, it draws attention to Wilde's unique character, as well as the character of his works, inviting readers to consider that, just maybe, the poetry within will also contain something queer. The word 'PO | EMS' is fragmented as is Wilde's name as they squeeze between the plants. A trinity of symmetrical tulips dominates the cover, suggesting an intoxicating decadent body in which to explore Wilde's poetry. What a reader will find inside, may be inspired by nature, but is decidedly unnatural – a poetic sensibility and potentially a sensuality that finds its voice in the unnatural arts of modernity. The artifice of the image challenges the beauty of nature because it is suggestive of an improvement upon nature. As Vivian declares in Wilde's 'The Decay of Lying', 'My own experience is that the more we study Art, the less we care for Nature. What Art really reveals to us is Nature's lack of design, her curious crudities, her extraordinary monotony, her absolutely unfinished condition.'[45] Nature is incomplete for Vivian because he is a queer reader, art improves upon nature because it takes the conditions of what is natural and does something new – creating unnatural spaces for allegedly unnatural readers.

The boundary between the poetry and the book is blurred and the artist is subsumed by the promise of a decadent discourse of artifice awaiting the brave reader. The binding enriches the meaning of the book and by extension, the meaning of the literary contents. As per 'Hélas!', which appears in this volume, the book is written over twice. There is the book that came before and failed, and the book that is reborn and reimagined as a work of self-conscious artifice. It did not work in its previous form

Figure I.2 Oscar Wilde's *Poems* (1890), with cover design by Charles Ricketts. Harry Ransom Center, The University of Texas at Austin.

because it was no different from any other work. Certainly, the pagination and interior of the book remained the same, but it was the body of the book that suggested queerness – a self-conscious embrace of artificiality, and the existence of unnatural sensual and sexual expression that the public already associated with Oscar Wilde as a public figure. Instead of allowing the poem or story to transport the reader away, the queer book's physicality draws the reader in to explore sensation and touch with homoeroticism and a queerness found in the artistic quality of the book in the reader's hands.[46] Queerness emerges from the book's juxtaposition of nature with unnatural artifice. Wilde's suggestive desires are diseased, according to cultural critics like Nordau, but he and others find the means to express them in the artificial arts of bibliographic design. The unnatural artifice of this diseased poet then becomes unconventionally beautiful by embracing the artificiality of modernity. While drawing on nature with the depiction of tulips, suggesting each poem within is a beautiful flower, its beauty is unlike any tulip encountered before.

Repurposing convention with the queer imagines a possible future where dissident desires need not be hidden from the cultural majority. The aesthetes are a historical precedent for more contemporary studies of futurity and relationality in the field of queer theory. This return to a hopeful creative space in queer theory is thanks to the forward-looking approach of José Esteban Muñoz (1967–2013) who places queer relationality into conversation with 'queer-aesthete art consumption'.[47] He claims that 'queer cultural workers are able to detect an opening and indeterminacy in what for many people is a locked-down dead commodity'.[48] He is referring to Frank O'Hara's poem 'Having a coke with you' (1960) and Andy Warhol's paintings of coke bottles (1961, 1962). Like the aesthetes before him, Muñoz explores how queer people adapt heteronormative spaces and practices – for him, the consumption of soda and its relationship to the cultural zeitgeist – and explores how those moments are reimagined for queer people seeking relationships with each other in the same space. Rather than exploring queer people in opposition to heterosexuals, he considers what homosexuals do among each other in spaces erected for heterosexual life, architectural, artistic and institutional, with each other when only other homosexuals are around. We must all exist in these spaces – we cannot exist outside of the commercialism of capitalist society – but small moments of intimacy, meaning and desire can emerge when engaging with one another in a shared experience of hope for the future. The aesthetes saw hope for the future in their reimagining of the past with Hellenism and Platonism and non-realist artistic expressions. They also found it in the space where bibliographical and literary arts merge in the space of the book. Joseph Freedman (1990) has established the relationship between commodification and aesthetic culture, noting the role that objects perform in establishing social status while simultaneously critiquing the system of capitalism.[49] We are complicit in commodification because of the role they play in our experiences and because we cannot escape their influence. The experience of sharing a commodity imbued in these creative expressions allows the speaker of O'Hara's poem to imagine a world not yet in existence but possible in the future based on the everyday pleasure of shared queer relations over a sugary beverage. The past for Muñoz is 'potentially imbued within the object, the ways it might represent a mode of being and feeling that was then not quite there but nonetheless an opening' and 'indispensable to the act of imaging transformation'.[50] The queer book is both a site of queer relationality and a means of imagining what Muñoz calls a 'queer futurity that is attentive to the past for the purposes of critiquing a present'.[51]

Dustin Friedman more directly argues that the concept of queer relationality has a historical relationship with late Victorian British aestheticism.[52] Aesthetes, according to Friedman, used art and literature as a means to create an abstract space where existing models of same-sex desire, legal concepts of sodomy and medical concepts of homosexuality were not binding and same-sex desire could be imagined in a way hitherto unrealised in late Victorian society.[53] He asks for further consideration of aestheticism's 'attenuated idealism as an attempt to maintain a sense of autonomy in the face of discourses intent on reducing queers to mere bodies, possibly in thrall to diseased impulses beyond their control'.[54] By exploring the shared interest in utopian thinking by both the British aesthetes and contemporary queer theory, Friedman opens up new opportunities to study aestheticism, not simply as a form of dissent against normative social expectations, but as an early attempt at queer theory.

The aesthetes, like queer theorists today such as Friedman and Muñoz, who seek to understand the means of circulating queer sexual discourse, were deeply concerned with the material arts – furniture, fashion, architecture, interior design, bookmaking and print culture – all of which were the means of revealing queerness available in everyday life's beautiful objects and affecting the social relations. These beautifully designed books circulate a queer sexual discourse with multiple, often incongruent, material expressions of difference bound by intercourse between creative outputs. This multimedial discourse is the direct result of aesthetic concepts of experiencing sensation (whether sexual, social or artistic) as a physical interaction, offering intercourse between words, images, material construction and decorative design – a tactile engagement with the reader's senses.

Queer books are a space where the linguistic interacts with, and is interrupted by, the codes of the codex to create *queer space*. The concept of queer space comes from the work of architectural scholar Aaron Betsky who claims it as a form of appropriation from nature, and, turning to Wilde's idea of art changing nature for the better, suggests that queerness changes material structures for the purpose of pleasurable experience, which he calls a 'freespace of orgasm that dissolves the material world'.[55] Betsky refers to architectural spaces, often urban and designed for one purpose but then repurposed for queer lives. For example, a warehouse on the docks designed to store commodities for import and export is transformed into a nightclub where gay men meet to dance, have sex, develop friendships and build community. However, the act of sex is not necessary for the space to be made queer. Sexuality, after all, is a discourse, and physical acts are only an expression of it. The book can be a queer space because it is a pre-existing space within a heteronormative culture. It does not stand in opposition but reimagines heteronormative structures to express queer desire modelled, in the late nineteenth century, on a discourse of *eros* in aesthetic and decadent circles. While children's books, Christmas annuals and *belle lettres* remain important means of circulating heteronormative sexual discourses of family, reproduction and capitalist wealth, the same spaces can be altered or queered to create spaces where discourses of same-sex desire can be exchanged.

Queer futurity, even as it exists in the past, is always an as-yet-unrealised goal. To achieve queerness, imaginative works must look to everyday objects and find opportunities for ecstatic realisations of pleasure, a pleasure that does not fit into heteronormative concepts of sexual and social norms. Such an approach fits well with a historical study of the book as a space for queer imaginative expressions of desire; books in which not only the contents evoke the ecstatic pleasures that Muñoz imagines, but books that physically embody those pleasures. It is a discourse that emerges from the heteronormative; so, rather than opposing conventional concepts of sexuality and gender, queer books demonstrate a relationship between queer voices and the heteronormative.

Take for example the use of subtitling and paratextual content in Aleister Crowley's *White Stains* (1898). This small collection of poems, published by Leonard Smithers at Crowley's expense, features sexually explicit and decadent poetry. Crowley (1875–1947) is typically studied as an occult figure of the *fin de siècle*, but this little studied collection of poems provides an example of his literary contribution to decadence. For example, his poem, 'The Ballad of Passive Pederasty' celebrates the joys and sexual pleasure of anal intercourse from the perspective of a receptive man who enjoys being penetrated by another man. As a poetry collection, it is unpublishable, endorsing what Victorian sexual discourse labelled criminal sodomy. What makes it possible for Smithers to publish such an explicitly homosexual poem is the bibliographic context it is published within. The book's subtitle is 'The Literary Remains of George Archibald Bishop, a neuropath of the Second Empire'. As we will explore further in Chapter 4, homosexuality was seen within heteronormative culture as something foreign to the British experience and alien to its culture. By presenting the book's 'author' as a French figure under the rule of Napoleon III, a period that ended in 1870, and as a Catholic, with the not-so-subtle use of 'Bishop' as his surname, the book's status changes to that of a historical document, presented for elite and educated men who would read it for intellectual or scholarly purposes.[56] The text positions Crowley as an 'Editor' who 'hopes that Mental Pathologists, for whose eyes alone this treatise is destined, will spare no precaution to prevent it falling into other hands' (see Fig. I.3).[57] Readers are positioned as above the influence of the text. In other words, it is claiming to not be a queer book. And yet, this editorial caution is followed by 'Une nouvelle Phèdre a lui moins dure'.[58] Bishop is presented here as a new, but less harsh, Phaedrus, elevating the book *White Stains* to the status of classical knowledge. The book can be published and circulated because it is not widely circulated and declares itself as an object of scholarly study for scientists and intellectuals. Certainly, it is clear upon reading that there is little scientific material to study within the poetry, but the queer content can be distributed, at least on a limited basis, because of how it engages with heteronormative concepts of sexology and claims to fit within the same category as the work of Richard von Krafft-Ebing or Havelock Ellis. By understanding the subversion of the bibliographic code, queer readers can find a space where their desires are displayed, discussed and disseminated.

It is knowledge hidden from a broad readership unfamiliar with Greek literature, or for that matter the French language. The book's paratextual referents are an aesthetic pose, a fiction created by the poet to signal to the reader that what the volume contains are ideas and dissident sexualities disavowed by middle-class cultural authorities. Its title, a vulgar reference to ejaculation, becomes more apparent on close inspection. The queerness it contains is not secret, but coded through bibliographic intervention, giving it a second meaning that obscures its queer relationality with a heteronormative frame of historical medical pathology.

Queer Books is divided into four chapters with a brief conclusion. Each chapter then is further subdivided, giving each chapter two tales, mimicking the dual nature of these books. The first

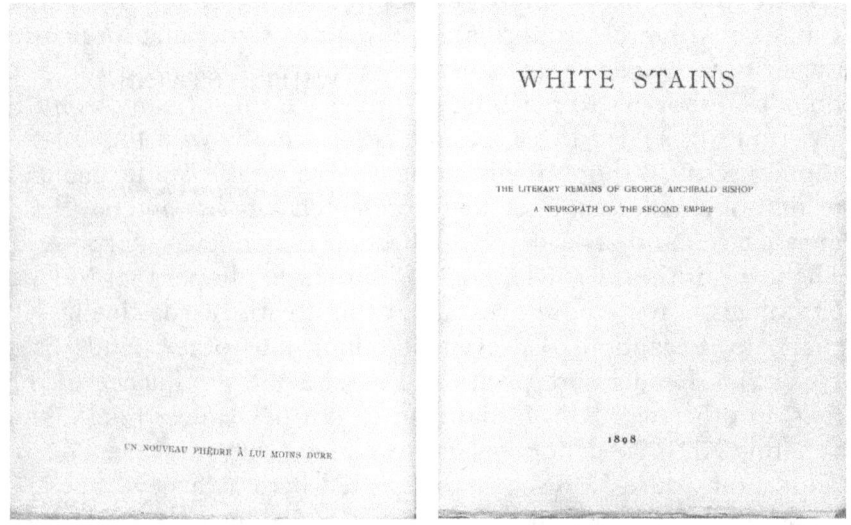

Figure I.3 Title page of Aleister Crowley's *White Stains* (1898). Harry Ransom Center, The University of Texas at Austin.

chapter, 'Concerning Golden Books and *Silverpoints*', explores the role that the material book plays in aesthetic and decadent culture. It begins by exploring the book as an object of desire in aesthetic fiction: Pater's *Marius the Epicurean* and Wilde's *Picture of Dorian Gray* as a space to express and explore dissident and queer desires. The chapter then focuses on John Gray's *Silverpoints* (1893) as it was designed by Charles Ricketts to explore how the queer book circulated a discourse of same-sex desire amongst this aesthetic community. By studying the book's small italic type and wide white margins in relation to the poems presented, we see textual intercourse between the literary and bibliographic content. A close reading of the book in relation to Muñoz's theories of queer relationality and queer futurity reveals how bibliographic design facilitates intercourse between sexual and spiritual desires, a merging of the sacred and profane, unwelcome in conventional Victorian literature, except in the coded discourse of queer textuality.

Chapter 2, 'Pomegranate Stains on the Ideal Book; or Queering the Hetero-Beautiful', proposes that the queer book is a deviation from the ideals of William Morris that defined his work at Kelmscott Press. His neo-medieval revival of the handmade book demanded unity of vision: black ink, antiquarian recipes for papermaking and decorative margins that together had to speak as one in support of the literary content. This singular vision that Morris called the 'ideal book' created a normative conception of what makes a book beautiful. This chapter carefully traces the development of what I term Morris's hetero-beautiful book to then consider how the queer book emerged from the same tradition. The hetero-beautiful, like a queer book, is the result of an intercourse between bibliographic and literary content, but that reinforces heteronormative sexual discourse. Unlike Morris, Charles Ricketts and Charles Shannon did not have the money or the influence to create an ideal. Instead, they had to take what they could from both the handmade book tradition as well as innovations in modern technology like photomechanical illustration processes and modern grey inks to create a new beauty that acknowledges the past but also imagines a new future of open queer communities and relationships only possible because of these changes. Morris saw these changes in bookmaking as a degeneration in quality, whereas for Ricketts and Shannon they were new opportunities to create a queer beauty if managed carefully. The bibliographic innovations of Ricketts and Shannon are examined to better understand how they affect the reader's interpretation of Oscar Wilde's literary experiments with the fairy tale in *A House of Pomegranates* (1891). As a queer book, *House of Pomegranates* is a text that must survive in two worlds: one of the marketplaces for children's books and expectations of heteronormativity, and another of queer books and same-sex desire.

Chapter 3, 'Trans-Textuality in Michael Field's *Long Ago* and *Whym Chow*', takes an alternate approach to the work of lesbian authors, Katharine Bradley and Edith Cooper, who take on the queer identity of their aesthetic contemporaries to reconsider their first and last collections of poetry as bibliographic trinities defined by an intersection of feminist, queer and trans* criticisms of binary sexualities, genders and bodies. Weaving their desires into discourses of history and beauty, Bradley and Cooper's choices and influence on the design of their books reflects and enriches the complex shifting of identity, gender and sexuality that defines both works. *Long Ago* (1889), the earliest queer book studied here, offers fine examples of the authors' poetic expressions of their lesbian desires in conversation with Sappho's recently translated poetic fragments. The book's binding is designed on vellum to give it the appearance of ancient Greek marble, its paratextual references to Sappho's historical significance, and the decision to conceal their queer desires in the figure of a male aesthete they called 'Michael Field' complicates the poetic experiment in the form of a material expression. As a queer male poet, their trans* gendering of identity becomes a means for these women to join a discourse of same-sex desire that largely excluded women and lesbianism. Moving from this early collaboration, the chapter then turns to *Whym Chow: Flame of Love* (1914), which explores their spiritual lives in transition in the wake of the death of their pet chow who serves as a conduit for Bradley and Cooper's conversion to Catholicism. This book presents their paganised Catholic faith and simultaneously reimagines queer intimacies between women, between humans and their pets, and between author and poetry.

Chapter 4, 'Collaboration and Conflict: Queer Space in *Salome*', takes Foucault's idea of the *ars erotica* and recognises its cultural appropriation to consider how the 1894 English edition of Wilde's *Salome*, as illustrated by Aubrey Beardsley, takes inspiration from eastern influences to create a queer space in the book where heteronormativity can be criticised and replaced with queer alternatives. Wilde did not want Beardsley to illustrate the play; he wanted

Ricketts to illustrate it because he thought their visions were more closely aligned. Beardsley found out and their conflicting perspectives on sex and sensuality produce a gender non-binary Salomé (complete with an Adam's apple in 'The Stomach Dance') who defies the limitations of women as objects of desire and, despite Salomé's death at the end of the play, the dream of fulfilled queer desire. From Salomé's intersexuality to her pairing with Oscar Wilde as both moon and Herod, Beardsley's illustrations are an interpretive dramatisation of the play's English translation. Too often the images are dismissed as disconnected from the play, usually because of Wilde's criticisms of Beardsley's drawing. But, following Elliot L. Gilbert's interpretation of Beardsley and Wilde's edition of *Salome*, I consider how publisher John Lane's decision in collaboration with Chiswick Press to merge Wilde's play with Beardsley's work creates the book's unique queer expression – one that neither artist could have imagined separately.[59] The chapter is also an opportunity to explore the influence of white supremacy and scientific racism on the queer imagination in the late nineteenth century to highlight *Salome*'s important inversion of those tropes.

Queer Books concludes with 'Queer Books and Their Digital Afterlives', taking a brief look at *The Pageant*, a Christmas annual edited by Gleeson White and Charles Shannon (1896 and 1897). Its openly aesthetic and decadent content contrasts with the conventions of Christmas annual publications. The pairing of queer sexual discourse with a flawed printing process, which did not meet the standards of the fine-press model established by publishers like John Lane at the Bodley Head, suggests that even though the publisher could not replicate the quality of fine presses, even after Wilde's imprisonment, a market for queer discourses was seen still seen as a possibility. Its failure also suggests hope for a future queer relationality that I will explore through my experience as a guest editor for a digital edition of *The Pageant* for *The Yellow Nineties Online*. The shift from codex to digital interface brings up the issue of queer spaces today and the role that historical text, particularly queer historical texts, may perform as queer cultures shift into digital spaces. What can be taken from print culture's early examples that will resonate with queer students of literary history today?

I would also like to address and explain my use of modern terms for sexuality that may seem anachronistic for a study of late nineteenth-century literature and book history. First, let me be clear that the focus of *Queer Books* is on the objects published, circulated and now archived in libraries and private collections. I make no claims about the sexual practices of any author or artist here that have not already been established by other scholars. In addition, it is important to me as both a researcher and a teacher in the higher education system to address the relevance of studying historical literature to contemporary readers. The very use of queer theory, feminism and textual studies introduces discourses that did not exist in the nineteenth century. That, to me, is not a flaw of presentism in my work, so much as a critical intervention that we in the field only have access to now. The interdisciplinary languages of queer theory, transgender theory and postmodern bibliography enrich our understanding of the literary and bibliographic past and provide an argument for the continued study of *fin de siècle* literary and publishing cultures.

In addition, other terminology introduced here, including the monograph's title, *Queer Books*, is introduced in order to provide clarity and differentiate various forms of aesthetic beauty from a queer perspective. For example, in Chapter 2 I introduce the term hetero-beautiful to describe the beautiful books of William Morris in order to acknowledge the importance of his work with the Kelmscott Press but to also address how even something beautiful can systemically isolate and marginalise other voices. Today's discourses of identity have their historical roots in the Victorian age – issues of race, sex, gender and identity had a different language in the nineteenth century, but as Ronjaunee Chatterjee, Alicia Mireles Christoff and Amy R. Wong have recently argued, there is a need to 'undiscipline' Victorian studies in an attempt 'to challenge the multiple rigidities, cultural and conceptual, that have kept Victorian studies isolated from other fields'.[60] Chatterjee, Christoff and Wong are particularly concerned with 'why contemporary scholarship on a period and a geographical cent[re] that consolidated a modern idea of race – the nineteenth century in and beyond Britain – lacks a robust account of race and racialization'.[61] I extend their concern to the study of the nineteenth-century history of sexuality. While there has been robust study of sexuality and gender in the discipline, most is limited to the pre-queer theory scholarship of Michel Foucault's work from the late 1970s, and the work of Eve Kosofsky Sedgewick and Judith Butler from the 1980s and early 1990s. While each of these scholars appear in this monograph, *Queer Books* turns also to scholars like the influential José Esteban Muñoz on queer relationality, Dustin Friedman's recent look at aestheticism as an early attempt at queer theory and recent trans* scholarship by Alyosxa Tudor and sj Miller. *Queer Books* challenges notions of presentism applied to contemporary reconceptualisations of nineteenth-century sexuality, gender, literature and print culture.

I am also acutely aware of the possibility that the study of material books in the post-COVID-19 world will be increasingly mediated through digital interfaces where students will no longer touch books. *Queer Books* is a meditation on both what is lost, but also what new queer spaces can be created in the sphere of digital dissemination. The queer book offers a historical precedent for such event spaces and converges with the new through the digital circulation of their historical codices. The queer spaces of the past, these queer books, are models for new sexual discourses not yet imagined, beyond our current digital moment and the world that is to come – a queer futurity, not yet available, but always imagined within what I propose is the here and now of a historically informed queer sexual discourse.

Notes

1. Oscar Wilde, *Poems* (London: John Lane and Elkins Matthews, 1890), epigraph.
2. Richard Dellamora, *Masculine Desire: The Sexual Politics of Victorian Aestheticism* (Chapel Hill: University of North Carolina Press, 1990), p. 216.
3. Joseph Bristow, *Sexuality* (London: Routledge, 1997).
4. James Eli Adams, *Dandies, and Desert Saints: Styles of Victorian Manhood* (Ithaca, NY: Cornell University Press, 1995).
5. The work of Joseph Bristow on aestheticism, Oscar Wilde and same-sex desire is extensive, and includes his most recent monograph, *Oscar Wilde on Trial: The Criminal Proceedings from Arrest to Imprisonment* (New Haven, CT: Yale University Press, 2023).
6. Stephano Evangelista's *British Aestheticism and Ancient Greece: Hellenism, Reception, Gods in Exile* (New York: Palgrave MacMillan, 2009).
7. Evangelista, p. 151.
8. Leonard Smithers's books published for the Erotika Biblion Society were presented as published in 'Cosmopoli', aligning his and other

booksellers' underground publishing practices with an imagined space where queerness could live.
9. Gerard Genette, *Paratexts*, trans. by Jane E. Lewin (Cambridge: Cambridge University Press, 1987); Johanna Drucker, *The Visible Word: Experimental Typography and Modern Art, 1909–1923* (Chicago: University of Chicago Press, 1994); Peter L. Shillingsburg, *From Gutenberg to Google: Electronic Representations of Literary Texts* (Cambridge: Cambridge University Press, 2006), p. 84.
10. Nicholas Frankel, *Oscar Wilde's Decorated Books* (Ann Arbor: University of Michigan Press, 2000), p. 9.
11. Nicholas Frankel, *Masking the Text: Essays on Literature and Mediation in the 1890s* (High Wycombe: Rivendale Press, 2009).
12. James G. Nelson, *The Early Nineties: A View from the Bodley Head* (Cambridge, MA: Harvard University Press, 1971), p. 37.
13. David Halperin, *How to Do the History of Homosexuality* (Chicago: University of Chicago Press, 2002), p. 22.
14. Walter Pater, *Studies in the History of the Renaissance* (London: MacMillan and Co., 1873), pp. 194, 179.
15. Pater, *Studies*, p. 179.
16. Evangelista, p. 26.
17. Lorraine Janzen Kooistra, *Poetry, Pictures, and Popular Publishing: The Illustrated Gift Book and Victorian Visual Culture* (Athens: Ohio University Press, 2011).
18. Lorraine Janzen Kooistra, *The Artist as Critic: Bitextuality in Fin-de-Siècle Illustrated Books* (Aldershot: Scolar Press, 1997).
19. Elizabeth K. Helsinger, *Poetry and the Pre-Raphaelite Arts: Dante Gabriel Rossetti and William Morris* (New Haven, CT: Yale University Press, 2008).
20. Nicolas Frankel, *Oscar Wilde's Decorated Books* (Ann Arbor: University of Michigan Press, 2000); Josephine Guy and Ian Small, *Oscar Wilde's Profession: Writing and the Culture Industry in the Late Nineteenth Century* (Oxford: Oxford University Press, 2000).
21. Elizabeth Carolyn Miller, *Slow Print: Literary Radicalism and Late Victorian Print Culture* (Stanford, CA: Stanford University Press, 2013).
22. James G. Nelson, *The Early Nineties: A View from the Bodley Head* (Cambridge, MA: Harvard University Press), p. 37.
23. Holbrook Jackson, *The Eighteen Nineties: A Review of Art and Ideas at the Close of the Nineteenth Century* (1913); new illustrated edition with an introduction by Christophe Campos (Brighton, UK: The Harvester Press, 1976).

24. Jerome McGann *A New Republic of Letters: Memory and Scholarship in the Age of Digital Reproduction* (Cambridge, MA: Harvard University Press, 2014), p. 10.
25. For a detailed look at this shift to media archaeology, Shannon R. Smith and Ann M. Hale's special issue of *Victorian Periodicals Review*, 49.4 (2016), 539–736, surveys the changes that digital media has brought to the study of the Victorian periodical press.
26. McGann *A New Republic of Letters*, p. 10.
27. Shillingsburg, *From Gutenberg to Google: Electronic Representations of Texts* (Cambridge: Cambridge University Press), p. 16.
28. Johanna Drucker, *The Visible Word: Experimental Typography and Modern Art, 1909–1923* (Chicago: University of Chicago Press, 1994), p. 45.
29. Johanna Drucker, 'Distributed and Conditional Documents: Conceptualizing Bibliographical Alterities', *MATLIT: Revista do Programa de Doutoramento em Materialidades da Literatura*, 2.1 (2014), pp. 11–29, p. 22.
30. Drucker, 'Distributed and Conditional Documents', p. 22.
31. Decadence was a term used almost interchangeably with both movements and, as a result, they can become conflated in a problematic way. Decadence and British aestheticism both emerge and are influenced by French Symbolism, a movement that used symbols, originally 'identifying sign[s]' in subversive ways (see Pierre-Louis Mathieu, *The Symbolist Generation, 1870–1910* (New York: Skira Rizzoli, 1990), p. 9). Symbolist artists, such as painter Gustave Moreau, novelist Joris-Karl Huysmans, and poet Stéphane Mallarmé, 'sought to communicate to the reader or viewer a personal message of a spiritual, moral, or even religious nature' by playing with slippage of meaning in sign systems and signification (Mathieu, p. 9). While Symbolists understood the social contract implied in established symbols – they were supposed to mean what everyone within that culture agrees they mean – 'they often ignored the traditional explanations given in them, preferring interpretations of their own' (Mathieu, p. 10). Decadence, a strain of Symbolism, emerges at times, within British aestheticism, differing in the tone because of how decadence locates beauty in places where beauty is difficult to pinpoint (even misinterpreted as ugly by the public). Arthur Symons uses 'decadence' as a catch-all for both Symbolism and Impressionism. What is critiqued as unhealthy or destructive becomes beautiful because it offers the observer a means of changing his or her conception of socially constructed limitations imposed in everyday life.

32. I borrow the term 'textual intercourse' from Jeffrey Masten who defines it as the 'intersection of the sexual and the textual' in *Textual intercourse: Collaboration, Authorship, and Sexualities, in Renaissance Drama* (Cambridge: Cambridge University Press, 1997), p. 5. Thank you to Helena Gurfinkel who many years ago, over pints at a pub in Exeter, suggested this book to me, rescuing a new scholar from falsely attributing the term to himself. For that, I am very grateful.
33. Arthur Symons, 'The Decadent Movement in Literature', in *Aesthetes and Decadents: An Anthology of British Poetry and Prose*, with an introduction and notes by Karl Beckson (Chicago: Academy Chicago Publishers, 1981), p. 136.
34. Symons, p. 136.
35. Max Nordau, *Degeneration*, 7th ed., trans. from the original German (New York: D. Appleton and Company, 1895), p. 301.
36. Nordau, p. 301.
37. The idea of the social organism comes from the Social Darwinism of Herbert Spencer (1820–1903) who misread Charles Darwin's theory of natural selection and evolution and applied it to artificial concepts of cultural progress and social civilisation.
38. Jackson, *The Eighteen Nineties*, p. 64.
39. Jackson, pp. 64–5.
40. Walter Pater, *The Renaissance: Studies in Art and Poetry*, ed. by Adam Phillips (Oxford: Oxford University Press, 1986), p. xx.
41. Pater, *The Renaissance*, p. xxix.
42. Pater, *The Renaissance*, p. xxix.
43. Wolfgang Iser's books, *The Act of Reading: A Theory of Aesthetic Response* (Baltimore: Johns Hopkins University Press, 1978) and *Walter Pater: The Aesthetic Moment* (Cambridge: Cambridge University Press, 1987), demonstrate his knowledge of Pater's aesthetics and their influence on his own theories of reader response.
44. Nelson, *The Early Nineties*, p. 79.
45. Oscar Wilde, 'The Decay of Lying', in *The Artist as Critic: Critical Writings of Oscar Wilde*, ed. by Richard Ellmann (Chicago: University of Chicago Press, 1982), pp. 290–1.
46. Byrne R. S. Fone describes the Uranians as young poets inspired by Walt Whitman's poetry and Edward Carpenter's *Narcissus and Other Poems* (1873) and his first volume of *Towards Democracy* (1883), whose poetry in the 1880s described same-sex love among men (Byrne R. S. Fone, *A Road to Stonewall, 1750–1969: Male Homosexuality and Homophobia in English and American Literature*

(New York: Twayne Publishers, 1994), p. 78). These writers 'derived their name from the writings of the German Karl Heinrich Ulrichs' who wrote pamphlets on same-sex desire and love between men 'in which he employed the word "Urning" to denote' same-sex desire between men (p. 78). For additional details on the Uranian poets see Timothy d'Arch Smith's *Love in Earnest: Some Notes on the Lives and Writings of English Uranian Poets from 1889 to 1930* (London: Routledge & Kegan Paul, 1970) and Michael A. Lombardi-Nash's translation of Karl Heinrich Ulrich's collected pamphlets *The Riddle of Man-Manly Love: The Pioneering Work on Male Homosexuality* (New York: Prometheus Books, 1994).

47. José Esteban Muñoz, *Cruising Utopia: The Then and There of Queer Futurity* (New York: New York University Press, 2009), p. 7.
48. Muñoz, *Cruising Utopia*, p. 9.
49. Joseph Freedman, *Professions of Taste: Henry James, Aestheticism, and Commodity Culture* (Stanford, CA: Stanford University Press, 1990).
50. Muñoz, p. 9.
51. Muñoz, p. 18.
52. Dustin Friedman, *Before Queer Theory: Victorian Aestheticism and the Self* (Baltimore: Johns Hopkins University Press, 2019).
53. Friedman, *Before Queer Theory*, p. 13.
54. Friedman p. 14.
55. Aaron Betsky, *Queer Space: Architecture and Same-Sex Desire* (New York: William Morrow and Company, 1997), p. 18.
56. Aleister Crowley, *White Stains* (London: Leonard Smithers, 1898).
57. Crowley, *White Stains*, unpaginated prefatory material.
58. Crowley, *White Stains*, unpaginated prefatory material.
59. Elliot L. Gilbert, '"Tumult of Images": Wilde, Beardsley, "Salome"', *Victorian Studies*, 26.2 (1983), pp. 133–59.
60. Ronjaunee Chatterjee, Alicia Mireles Christoff and Amy R. Wong, 'Introduction: Undisciplining Victorian Studies', *Victorian Studies*, 62.3 (2020), p. 370.
61. Chatterjee et al., p. 370.

I

Concerning Golden Books and *Silverpoints*

> O mayest thou take this volume in thy hand, And turn the leaves, and read, and understand!
> – Marc-André Raffalovich, 'To One of My Readers'[1]

In 1889, Oscar Wilde met a handsome young civil servant and poet, John Gray, at the home of mutual friends, artists and companions Charles Ricketts and Charles Shannon. Ricketts was indoctrinating Gray into the poetry, art and theories of aestheticism in England and Europe, a process that culminated in his introduction to Wilde. Wilde would complete Gray's aesthetic education, introducing him to some of the more decadent strains of the movement and securing Gray's reputation as 'Dorian' Gray. Wilde wrote his only novel, *The Picture of Dorian Gray* (1890) during the closest period of their relationship. During that same period, Gray briefly reimagined space for himself in this community as a mysterious new-chivalric aesthetic poet. Gray supported an extravagant lifestyle on his £200 annual salary as a Second Division Clerk at the Foreign Office, spending his nights in the West End of London or, on the weekends, in the fashionable haunts of Paris.[2] Gray happily absorbed everything offered to him by Ricketts and Wilde, as well as his comrades among the French *symbolistes*: Félix Fénéon, Jules Laforgue, Pierre Louÿs and eventually his partner in life Marc-André Raffalovich (1864–1934). During this period, Gray joined the Rhymer's Club meetings at Ye Olde Cheshire Cheese and attended various salons where he made his reputation through recitations of his poetry. He was strikingly handsome and admiration for his physical beauty merged with that for his poetic

Figure 1.1 John Gray's *Silverpoints* (1893) with cover design by Charles Ricketts. Courtesy of the Rufus Hawtin Hathaway Collection, Identification #991026002159705163, Archives and Special Collections, Western Libraries, Western University.

accomplishments, resulting in a theatrical identity, or an aesthetic ideal that Pater described in relation to music as

> a matter of pure perception ... in which the constituent elements of the composition are so welded together, that the material or subject no longer strikes the intellect only [but] present one single effect to the 'imaginative reason'.[3]

It seemed that no other poet in aesthetic circles could evoke the sensation of Apollonian beauty embodying the Hellenic male ideal of aestheticism like Gray. Arthur Symons writes how, at one of these gatherings where Gray gave a reading, Pater was so overcome by Gray's performance that he asked him to repeat his recitation. According to Symons, Pater's deep satisfaction and realisation of a moment of pleasurable sensation was marked by a 'certain expression [that] passed over Pater's face [and the] rest was silence'.[4] His aesthetic contribution was not just his poetry but the way his poetry was in discourse with his own beautiful body – performance welded to poetics – intercourse of mind and body resulting in his embodiment of the aesthetic pose as poetic expression.

In 1893, after Gray made a name for himself amongst the aesthetes of London and Paris, John Lane and Elkin Mathews at the Sign of the Bodley Head agreed to publish a collection of his poems in a single, 250-copy edition of his poems called *Silverpoints*, a small collection of free-verse poetry including both original compositions and creative translations of works by decadent French poets that he admired. Today, however, because Gray was a minor poet of the 1890s, aligned with the Rhymers' club but largely ignored outside of scholarship interested in his queer relationships with other aesthetic poets and artists, his writing is largely forgotten today. In fact, in the study of aestheticism and decadence, the book *Silverpoints* is better remembered for Charles Ricketts's work as the book's designer, serving as a beautiful example of fine-press bookmaking in the 1890s.

The tall octavo measures 8.5" × 4.5" and is a mere quarter inch thick. The green cloth boards are impressed with gilt in a pattern of thirty-three willow leaves spread over thirty curved lines, surrounded by a three-sided border opened along the text block fore-edge. Ricketts notes that the cover was often repeated, and even 'copied outright in America' influencing everything from 'binding, end-papers, wall-papers, and dress cretonnes'.[5] Inside, the printer, Folkards, used Van Gelder paper for the book's thirty-eight pages. Typographically, pagination is in roman numerals and centred at the bottom of each poem with large margins and an excessively large footer of white space on each page. The effect is paradoxical because the lexical detail is incredibly intricate while the page emphasises simplicity. The space appears to invite the reader to make notes or commentary on the poems presented, but in the various editions I have read, I found only seen one note, a 'PV' beside a poem that is identified as an imitation, that is, a loose or creative translation, of a poem by Paul Verlaine.[6] The title and text pages are clean with little decoration – only five decorative initials are included among the book's twenty-nine poems.[7] The paradoxical presentation speaks to the textual intercourse between an artist and a poet both interested in exploring the complex sensations evoked by simple aesthetic beauty.

Unlike the book, Gray's invented persona of aesthete poet had a short life. Gray joined aestheticism's circles on the arm of his lover Oscar Wilde in 1889 and walked away in 1893 on the arm of another lover, poet and writer Marc-André Raffalovich, rejecting not only Wilde, but also his own decadence, condemning his time spent with Wilde, and the aesthete poet that their intercourse created, as hedonistic sin. Wilde would turn to Lord Alfred Douglas, while Gray found himself in the midst of a psychological breakdown and a crisis of identity.[8] Gray found comfort in his new lover and companion Raffalovich. Once more, Gray offered himself as a blank canvas for another artist who helped him transform into another vision of ideal beauty: the chaste, Catholic Father Gray. Later conflicted about his association with *Silverpoints*, Gray, after becoming a priest in the Catholic Church, would 'buy up and immobilize' any copy of *Silverpoints* he found, erasing material evidence of his past.[9] Despite his efforts, the aesthete poet lives on through the material beauty of the remaining copies.

Citing its provocative designer and the conflicted and troubled poet John Gray, *Silverpoints* is a queer conception of the poet as an object of desire. He is not the poet's 'true self' because there is no such thing. His performance is itself a textual experience that performs intercourse with an audience. Ricketts's hand brings material expression, a textual poetics that helps to make *Silverpoints* a queer book, capturing an ideal of the aesthetic poet, based on his reading of Gray. This chapter examines the influence of, and desire for, Gray among the aesthetes. Gray himself admits that he was the creation of Ricketts, suggesting that his performance of the aesthete poet, as a performative realisation of Ricketts's desires and Gray's desire to please Ricketts was in part motivated by his own desire to be accepted by his fellow aesthetes.[10]

Silverpoints, as textual intercourse between creative artists merging multiple mediums of expression into a single work, does not recreate (reproduce) the past; instead, while it cites the past and its makers, its character is new. The book's multisensory presentation creates meaning; Peter L. Shillingsburg calls this presentation a 'textual semiotics' because it is not simply the type on the page, but the way the type is presented. The italics speak a rich history of the aesthetic movement, its celebration of Hellenism, and its debt to the Renaissance and Aldus Manutius.[11] This reading of typography as contributing to the poetics presents Gray's poetry as a canvas onto which the book's design paints intonation, gesture and accent. *Silverpoints*, as a queer book, manages 'to obliterate' the distinguishing line between form and content as well as the division between past and present.[12]

Charles Ricketts discovers the beauty of the aesthete poet in his connection to John Gray, though Gray will never realise that beauty seen by Ricketts and other aesthetes. The only means Ricketts has to preserve the Gray he imagined is with his skill as a bookmaker. Through *Silverpoints*, Ricketts can materially preserve who Gray was for him. At the same time, unlike Basil's painting which serves as a mirror into Dorian Gray's soul, *Silverpoints* takes on a life of its own. Whereas Hallward is determined to rid art of 'autobiography' in order to regain art's 'abstract sense of beauty',[13] Ricketts finds delight in preserving his subjective reading of Gray's aesthete poet. The momentary experience of 'Dorian' Gray, an ideal figure that John Gray performed, was translated on the pages of *Silverpoints* and became an unintentional *performative*, realised by textual intercourse between Gray, his poetic and personal influences, the ambitions of Oscar Wilde, the investment of John Lane and Elkin Mathews at the Bodley Head, and the designs of Charles Ricketts.

Named after a 'stylus which leaves on the surface of paper prepared with certain oxides a faint but indelible mark, the silverpoint was used by such masters as Botticelli and Dürer and in the later nineteenth century by Alphonse Le Gros and Burne-Jones to create the most delicate of drawing, whose silver-grey effect was especially delightful'.[14] Mimicking the drawing tool, the book traces with a fine silver point, a faint but indelible relationship to the past that bibliographically permits Ricketts to draw a line of influence between his work and the work of early modern bookmaker and printer Aldus Manutius (1449–1515) and his Aldine Press publications. *Silverpoints* connects to the history of print culture and serves as an important example of how queer sexual discourse emerges from pre-existing heteronormative cultural objects and institutions. Taking the book and his knowledge of printing history, Ricketts, together with Gray, created a space that resembles José Esteban Muñoz's notion of queer relationality, specifically in the latter's concept of the present in relation to the past. The past for Muñoz is 'potentially imbued within the object, the ways it might represent a mode of being and feeling that was then not quite there but nonetheless an opening' and 'indispensable to the act of imagining transformation'.[15] The queer book serves as both a site of queer relationality and a means of imagining what Muñoz calls a 'queer futurity that is attentive to the past for the purposes of critiquing a present'.[16] As this chapter will contend, these moments can exist between the past and present as well. *Silverpoints* is an object that captures not just an important narrative of homoerotic desire between Gray and Ricketts, and among aesthetes in *fin de siècle* London, but it is also a form of textual intercourse that imagines a cosmopolitan queer relationality between British aestheticism and the Italian Renaissance.

Silverpoints and John Gray scholarship is sporadic and relies heavily on biography. None of this scholarship considers the implications of queerness for *Silverpoints* as a discourse between bibliography and literature. Holbrook Jackson describes Gray as one of a group of minor poets 'who give expression to moods more attuned to end-of-the-century emotions, but who will command a select group of admirers in most periods',[17] offering no sustained criticism of *Silverpoints* except as an 'important' example of fine-press printing overseen by Ricketts and noting that 'a few of the initials of this uncommon but elegant volume are decorated, but the majority are simple Roman capitals, the text of the volume being in italics'.[18] After Jackson's work, it is not until the 1960s that new criticism emerges in the *Aylesford Review* from English Carmelites who, while committed to their Catholic faith, shared an interest in commemorating decadence and queer authors; not just Gray, but also Ronald Firbank, Frederick Rolfe (Baron Corvo) and Radclyffe Hall.[19] The *Aylesford Review* dedicated its Spring 1961 volume to a commemoration of Gray's career from poet to Canon of St Andrew's and Edinburgh. Patricio Gannon provides a censored history of Gray's 'sentimental life', ignoring the implications of his living most of his adult life with Marc-André Raffalovich, a self-described Uranian and author of sexology text, *Uranisme et unisexualité: étude sur différentes manifestations de l'instinct sexuel* (1896).[20] The aim of the Friars seems to be to bring attention to Gray, and other lesser-known artists with connections to the English Catholic Church, while ignoring facts about their sexual lives and the complex relationships they had with the institution. The *Aylesford Review* introduced two of Gray's most important critics, Brocard Sewell who wrote two biographies on Gray, one exploring his relationship with Raffalovich, and Ian Fletcher, whose critical editions of Gray's poetry and prose remain the only scholarly editions of his complete works.[21]

In 1977, Linda Dowling argued that critics have ignored Gray's poetry while paying overt attention to *Silverpoints*'s material design.[22] Since then, little has changed. Brocard Sewell dedicates his second biography of Gray, *In the Dorian Mode: A Life of John Gray, 1866–1934* (1983), to Jerusha McCormack who would later go on to become Gray's most important biographer, writing both an academic study (1991) and a creatively narrated popular history (2000). McCormack's work is the best attempt at understanding Gray's relationship to other *fin de siècle* writers and artists, especially Oscar Wilde. G. A. Cevasco's 1992 article for *Cahiers victoriens et édouardiens* studies Gray's significance as a poet, looking at both the book and the poetry. Like Dowling before him, Cevasco sets out to reconsider Gray's poetic value. He is interested in what he vaguely terms Gray's 'dandiacal aloofness' and the 'dreamlike mood' of the poetry that 'avoid[s] clear statement'.[23] Attention to the role of Catholicism in Gray's work continues with contributions by Ellis Hanson (1991) and Frederick S. Roden (2002), who say out loud what the contributors to the *Aylesford Review* left unspoken, demonstrating a complicated interconnected relationship in Gray's work and life between his Catholic beliefs and his expressions of same-sex desire.[24] There are brief assessments of Gray in works by Joseph Bristow and Michael Hatt, but neither gives the author sustained study.[25] While other critics make note of Charles Ricketts's design work and *Silverpoints*'s relationship to the niche market for beautiful, limited editions of new poets in the 1890s, none considers the materiality of the text as an integral part of Gray's poetic expression of decadent beauty.

This chapter examines *Silverpoints* as a queer book that provided a space where it was possible to imagine a queer relationality that merged aesthetic, spiritual and erotic desires. There are two tales to tell. First this chapter will demonstrate the importance of the queer book in aesthetic culture through seminal fictional examples found in Pater's 'golden book' in *Marius the Epicurean* (1885) and Oscar Wilde's 'poison book' in *The Picture of Dorian Gray* (1890). These examples will demonstrate how the queer book serves as a means of mediating discourses of same-sex desire between male aesthetes. In addition, it will also show how the intercourse of literary and bibliographic content serves that discourse. Placing Gray's queer spiritualism into dialogue with Ricketts's choices as a book designer, I will then examine how Gray's expression of a relationship between spiritual and sexual ecstasy finds further companionship in Ricketts's typographic duality: a style defined by the technological and monetary limits of the modern printing process in conversation with the early modern bookmaking processes used by Aldus Manutius, whose typographic work imagines a sensuality and eroticism that defied Roman Catholic norms for appreciative subscribers to the Aldine Press. In doing so, I will demonstrate that Ricketts's work realises a historic relationship between the Italian Renaissance and British aestheticism. The second part of the chapter will offer a close reading of select poems from *Silverpoints* in the context of the queer book and the many relationships that emerge from the book's enrichment of Gray's poetry, looking at Wilde's influence and mentorship, societal rejection of sexual difference, artistic alienation and the role of material space in queer relationship building, including the relationship between the queer aesthete and his God.

Golden books and queer desires

Silverpoints is an example of the role that the beautiful book played in mediating the discourse of same-sex desire at the *fin de siècle*. Aesthetes of the era provide multiple fictional examples of the book's role in sharing queer desires. Example abound in decadent fiction in the period. Jori-Karl Huysmans's *A rebours* (1884), Walter Pater's *Marius the Epicurean* (1885), George

Moore's *Confessions of a Young Man* (1886), Vernon Lee's *Miss Brown* (1888), Wilde's *The Picture of Dorian Gray* (1890), Richard Le Gallienne's *The Book-Bills of Narcissus* (1895) and *The Quest for the Golden Girl* (1896), all feature the book as something beautiful and desirable that stands in for or facilitates more unspeakable desires. The material book is also a communal space in which queer readers could converse. Such a perspective on books is important to understanding the role of reading in aesthetic concepts of beauty and intimacy. *Silverpoints* is an important non-fictional example of this experience.

To understand that experience in *Silverpoints*, first consider its expression in more familiar aesthetic texts, specifically, Joris-Karl Huysmans's *A rebours* (1884), Walter Pater's *Marius the Epicurean* (1885) and Wilde's *The Picture of Dorian Gray* (1890). Where *Silverpoints* is much lesser known, by examining the queer book in these more familiar narratives, we can find a narrative record of the experience of the book, not as beloved, but as a vehicle for accessing intimacy with a beloved of the same sex. Given the legal and social position of homosexual men in the 1890s, the book becomes a communal space in which readers interested in same-sex desire can find a material place to converse and recognise each other. Unlike Eve Kosofsky Sedgwick's homosocial triangle where women mediate homosocial desire by creating a physical distance between two men, books in aesthetic fiction serve a physical role that facilitates homoerotic intimacy by bringing bodies together.[26] Sedgwick argues that women in fiction regulate homosocial relations, redirecting the eroticism of male-to-male sociality towards a female object of heterosexual desire. In Victorian culture particularly, public life was a nearly exclusively male culture. Women's role in this homosocial culture was to regulate its sexual order, playing the role of caregiver: mother, wife, daughter or sex worker: someone who serves, nurtures and reinvigorates homosocial culture's heterosexual imperative. Her artificial subjugation to male supremacy heightens the unnatural all-male culture of Victorian public life. She is an object, robbed of agency, who triangulates heterosexual men through the homoerotic implications of homosociality.[27]

To be sure, the aesthetes certainly objectified women as well. Women are too often portrayed as empty objects of physical desire, dangerous femme fatales or hysterical lovers who fail to meet the aesthete's ideal of beauty. Dorian Gray's beloved Sybil

Vane is an important example because, after failing to perform the ideal theatrical presentation of womanly beauty for him and his queer friends Henry Wotton and Basil Hallward, she is rejected and driven to suicide.

Wilde's narrative initially criticises Dorian's poor treatment of Sybil in the part of the book where Dorian experiences an initial sense of guilt. Henry Wotton then gives Dorian a new object of desire, a beautiful book. In aesthetic fiction of the late nineteenth century, the book beautiful performs the same role that the cola beverage played in Muñoz's earlier example, circulating a different concept of male-male intimacy. Rather than homophobically suppressing same-sex desire between men, these books imagine a queer future where such desires, seemingly *verboten*, are possible through an aesthetic pursuit of sensations, regulated by *eros*, rather than misogyny. While the book and author are later unnamed in subsequent publications, in Wilde's first version of the novel, published in *Lippincott's Magazine* (1890), the book Lord Wotton gives Dorian is *Le Secret de Raoul* by Catulle Sarrazin. Nicholas Frankel suggests that Wilde's choice of inset text references the decadent novel *Monsieur Venus* (1884) by scandalous French novelist Rachilde (pseudonym of Marguerette Vallette-Eymery). In it, the female protagonist, a virago named Raoule de Vénérande, takes her dressmaker, Jacques, as a mistress, slowly transforming him into a feminine cross-dressing figure of androgynous beauty.[28] Jacques's fate, however, resembles that of Sybil in its tragedy and misogyny.

Dorian's book more closely resembles Joris-Karl Huysmans's decadent novel *A rebours* (1884). Huysmans's novel, often translated as either *Against Nature* or *Against the Grain*, is a first person account of the life of decadent recluse Jean des Esseintes, who lives in his family's estate outside of Paris, the last of unhealthy aristocrats, seeking pleasure in objects around him. He explores and obsesses over books, art, technology, furniture and other material objects of desire in the hopes of experiencing a new pleasure worth living for, fighting against an ennui that debilitates him and prevents him from integrated into modern civilisation. In *Dorian Gray*, Wilde has his titular character read an unnamed novel with the same premise:

> The style in which it was written was that curious jewelled style, vivid and obscure at once, full of argot and of archaisms, of technical expressions and of elaborate paraphrases, that characterises the

work of some of the finest artists of the French school of Décadents. There were in it metaphors as monstrous as orchids, and as evil in colour. The life of the senses was described in the terms of mystical philosophy. One hardly knew at times whether one was reading the spiritual ecstasies of some mediæval saint or the morbid confessions of a modern sinner. It was a poisonous book. The heavy odour of incense seemed to cling about its pages and to trouble the brain. The mere cadence of the sentences, the subtle monotony of their music so full as it was of complex refrains and movements elaborately repeated, produced in the mind of [Dorian Gray], as he passed from Chapter to Chapter, a form of reverie, a malady of dreaming, that made him unconscious of the falling day and the creeping shadows.[29]

Wilde's description of how the book seduces Dorian signifies a queer turn in the relationship between man and book because its qualities of excess confuse the difference between saints and sinners. The book represents a beauty that was unknown to Dorian before. Lord Henry Wotton gives him this book after their falling out over Sybil's suicide. The book renews their close relationship, and the influence of the book reflects Lord Wotton's hedonistic influence on the younger man. Dorian is captivated by the book for years following his first reading of it and it inspires his transformation into a decadent dandy. Lord Wotton and Dorian Gray share a dangerous and dissident intimacy, defined here not by a sexual act but by a bibliographic bond in the space of the book.

The queer book does not redirect homoeroticism, but fixes a subversive gaze on the book, narcissistically reflecting the reader back towards their fellow aesthetic companions. The book is not only his object of desire but the object through which he justifies the vague and diverse pleasures of his life in the 1880s. Unlike the homosocial triangle, the queer book facilitates Dorian and Lord Wotton's desires without a socially acceptable female mediator.[30] It draws attention to unregulated male intimacy, allowing the reader to imagine same-sex desire as something more than just the physical lust of the sodomite, or the supposed psychological illness of the homosexual. It is an aesthetic discourse of beauty, something to be studied, written down, appreciated and shared with others of the same ilk.

It is often Wilde's novel, *The Picture of Dorian Gray*, that introduces new audiences to the theories of aestheticism and decadence, and the movement's interests in same-sex desire, despite the limited portrayal of explicitly declared same-sex desire in the figure of Basil Hallward. In Wilde's decadent fairy tale, Basil Hallward imposed something of himself onto Dorian Gray when he painted the young man's portrait. As a result, the portrait was not an image of the young man with whom Basil is sexually infatuated, but a material realisation of Basil's sexual infatuation. Basil tells Lord Henry Wotton that he has 'put into it all the extraordinary romance of which, of course, I have never dared to speak to him. He will not know anything about it. But the world might guess it; and I will not bare my soul to their shallow, prying eyes. My heart shall never be put under their microscope.'[31] Dorian, of course, does discover Basil's secret love for him, while the reader discovers that the aesthetic ideal that Basil loved was not the real, complex, troubled Dorian that Henry manipulates, but the idealised, youthful, 'harmony of soul and body' that Basil finds so appealing in Dorian's physical aesthetic.[32] The 'real' Dorian will not endure time; only the idealised portrait of Basil's image – an aesthetic symbol of innocent beauty, an imitation – remains. Dorian realises this and contributes to the realisation of the painting by imposing his own ideals of immortal beauty onto the work. The result is a creature influenced by the characteristics of Dorian and Basil but an entity in its own right – a life form born of intercourse between the desires of two desperate men, with tragic consequences for both.

Basil and Henry Wotton, and the queer reader desire his physical beauty and objectify his beauty. Dorian mimics this objectification, first in the tragic figure of Sybil Vane, but then strangely in his obsession with the book Lord Wotton gifts him the wake of Sybil's death. The relationship he shares with the book (standing in for a physical relationship with Lord Wotton) becomes physical and he lavishes attention and luxuries on the book the way one would a lover:

> He procured from Paris no less than five large-paper copies of the first edition and had them bound in different colours so that they might suit his various moods and the changing fancies of a nature over which he seemed, at times, to have almost entirely lost control. Raoul, the wonderful young Parisian, in whom the romantic temperament and the scientific temperament were so strangely blended, became to him a kind of prefiguring type of himself. And, indeed, the whole book seemed to him to contain the story of his own life, written before he had lived it.[33]

Turning his attention away from his degenerating portrait which reflects his loss of moral compass and the increased corruption with which he lives his life, Dorian finds another mirror in this decadent book – one that romantically reconfigures his perception of himself outside the boundaries of morality and virtue, and with a philosophy that embraces beauty and artifice for their own sake. The book becomes his lover, in whose eyes he sees the picture of himself that he chooses to see. Ultimately, the book is a means for Dorian to enjoy the pleasure of his beauty without requiring his empathy the way Sybil required, without being under the control of a powerful man like Lord Wotton, and without any demand to live up to the worshipful idealisation of Basil Hallward. Dorian indulges in the full gamut of hedonistic pleasures through the body of his book, and its many material bodies, which are dressed to please his moods as he would dress a lover to please his fancies and indulge in the masturbatory self-love of his unspecified sex life.

Queer books, however, need not be destructive to aesthetic culture. Oscar Wilde called Walter Pater's *Studies in the History of the Renaissance* (1873) his 'golden book' developing his decadent theories of fiction, anti-realism and the pursuit of pleasure explored in the essay collection. Consisting of a series of academic articles on Renaissance art and culture, the throughline of the collection is Pater's call for critics to think like artists and write about their physical and emotional response to art, considering the interaction of the object of beauty with the observer of beauty, as the goal of art criticism. The book is particularly remembered today for its conclusion, a decadent call for aesthetes to 'burn always with a hard, gemlike flame' in their pursuit of new sensations and aesthetic sensuality.[34] For the purposes of this chapter, Pater's only complete novel, *Marius the Epicurean* (1885), with its historical setting of second-century AD, provides an equally important insight into the experience of an aesthete reading a beautiful book in *fin de siècle* London. As Pater's only finished novel, *Marius* follows the coming-of-age of its eponymous character from a childhood passion for books and youthful companionship with Flavian to his esoteric exploration of philosophical outlooks from Epicureanism to Christian martyrdom as advisor to Roman Emperor Marcus Aurelius. The novel offers an important example of how the aesthetes used the book to mediate queer sexual discourse:

> A book, like a person, has its fortunes with one; is lucky or unlucky in the precise moment of its falling in our way, and often by some happy accident ranks with us for something more than its independent value. *The Metamorphoses of Apuleius*, coming to Marius just then, figured for him as indeed the golden book; he felt a sort of personal gratitude to its writer, and saw in it doubtless far more than was really there for any other reader. It occupied always a peculiar place in his remembrance, never quite losing its power in repeated returns to it for the revival of that first glowing impression.[35]

Here, Marius describes his relationship with his 'golden book' as an active and intimate encounter. Unlike Dorian's codex, Marius's object of desire is a beautiful papyrus scroll featuring a handwritten copy of Lucius Apuleius's *Metamorphosis, or the Golden Ass*, the only Latin novel to survive in its entirety from ancient Rome.[36] Pater's narrative reveals reading as a multisensory and communal experience. Reading is not an activity that isolates Marius from the community; instead, the book's materiality allows an imaginative process to become a tactile moment, one in which Marius can create a communal bond with his young friend Flavian.

Marius recalls memories of

> two lads ... lounging together over a book, half-buried in a heap of dry corn, in an old granary – the quiet corner to which they had climbed out of the way of their noisier companions on one of their blandest holiday afternoons.[37].

The book is an escape from a mundane day: the tactile experience of the boys concealing themselves on top of a mound of grain and the meditative experience of a 'quiet corner' pleasantly separating them from their more boisterous playmates. Marius loves this beautiful book for both its ideas and its physical presence; the book is an object to touch, to see and to smell, 'perfumed with oil of sandal-wood, and decorated with carved and gilt ivory bosses at each end of the roller'.[38] Marius's physical memory of this scroll of papyrus inextricably connects him emotionally to Apuleius's philosophies; just as important, it also connects him to his comrade Flavian. Marius and Flavian's love is mediated by their golden book, Apuleius's *Metamorphosis, or the Golden Ass*, making it, for them at least, a queer book: a space for queer relationality to be imagined and nurtured. It is an experience that takes the readers out of time and out of the limits of their contemporary societies. Marius and Flavian share their mutual desire for one another's companionship by sharing their mutual desire for the book beautiful.

This transference, however, does not regulate gender norms. If anything, the book emphasises the homoeroticism of their relationship. Pater's novel invokes the emotional bias of an individual's subjective experience of art – in this case, the beautiful book – to draw attention to both the material and social elements of reading, and Pater presents the book as an intimate, secretive experience, full of the promise of knowledge. This papyrus scroll as an object of desire bonds these two young men together in a love connection that, while platonic, is rich in homoerotic implications. It offers a space for them to be intimate and form a community hidden in plain sight from the regulatory systems of heteronormative society.

Queer space is a site where relationships can form whether it be an intimate relationship between two queer men or an entire community of like-minded aesthetes. Heteronormative spaces do not allow for such relationships to develop because they are designed for husbands and wives, parents and children, the public sphere of men and the private sphere of women in the house.

Norms regulate erotic behaviour within those spaces along gender and sexual binaries that do not permit queer desire to thrive. That queer desire can be explicitly homosexual or, like aestheticism, explicitly dissident in its vision of material spaces as sites for beautiful expressions of difference. Once a space, like that in the book, no longer has a role to serve in regulating desire, then new desires, new relationships and new communities can form. Matthew Potolsky notes that the decadents were 'an unnatural family' bound together by their artistic interests and theories passed down through an eclectic history curated by its own members.[39] In the queer book, that fraternity is based on a common experience of same-sex desire, so that family is transformed into an even more intimate and supposedly 'unnatural' relationship.

It is important to stress that, unlike women in homosocial triangles who suffer for the desires of men, as an inanimate object, a book exists to be used, objectified by the one who possesses it. In this sense, Pater's aestheticism allows the focus to remain on male-to-male relations and the beauty that emerges from that sexually charged intimacy. In *Marius*, Flavian's book serves as a substitute object for Marius's passionate desire for Flavian.

The book allows Pater to displace expressions of desire between the two boys – a desire best described as love – onto the text.

Instead of having sex in the hayloft, a conventional sight in literature for sexual intimacy, they read a book, a choice that aligns queer eroticism with intellectual pursuit. The book makes a space for them to develop an intimacy not available in their lives away from it. Marius associates his copy of the book with love for his comrade, imbuing the object with his passionate feelings of loss and the memory of an eroticised intimacy. The association of the material book with love is important because, by the 1880s, Pater's aesthetics defined an emerging culture of what Charles Kains-Jackson called the 'New Chivalry', or 'the exaltation of the youthful masculine ideal' as 'the flower of the adult and perfect civilization'.[40] The book and the art of literature more broadly became the site of an aesthetic attitude to social practice, a chivalric duty, not to a female beloved, but to desire more broadly and to an appreciation of the beautiful male body as a new sensation that can be shared amongst fellow aesthetes through the production of literature.

Whether Marius's scroll or Dorian's large-paper codex, the book performs the role of a lover, emphasising the eroticism of homosocial intimacy. In aesthetic fiction of the 1890s, the book as an object of desire takes centre stage, not only within the literature, but within the publication of aesthetic and decadent texts of prose, poetry and closet drama. Many books that do not figure the book in its literary content became avatars of precious beauty to be desired and collected.

The collection of these queer books becomes itself a sign of coded same-sex desire. These texts were created for the publication and distribution of literature that addresses issues of aestheticism found in Pater and of decadence found in Wilde's work. Designers of these books found their inspiration in the literature that they bound. What results is a new way for same-sex desire to be expressed, and it is particularly placed into practice in expressions of love between men who were often the writers, publishers and designers of these aesthetic books. Whether the book is golden or poisonous, British aestheticism in the 1890s came to define itself as a materially sensuous experience and the books are artifacts of this community's queer relations.

Pater's exploration of the love between Marius and Flavian through the shared aesthetic experience of reading leads to a reconsideration of the book's material means of expression and circulation. The book becomes the site of physical intimacy, where bibliographical design comes into intercourse with literary content. Because of technological developments in printing, typology, illustration and book design, the material space of the book becomes a place to explore wider cultural conversations of same-sex desire and passion. However, those places go far beyond their material use value of distribution and promotion.

Silverpoints's queer materiality

As the previous section outlines, the book performs a role within late Victorian homosexual relationships, giving both a space to meet intimately and explore their desires, but it also serves as a manifestation of queer desire's expression. In *Silverpoints*, not only does Gray celebrate his queer relationships, but his literary expressions are also enveloped in a bibliographic package that reflects back on the speaker as object of desire. It is not Gray himself that we admire as readers, it is his aesthetic persona, captured in the pages of a small green volume of poems. The book's artistic value is as much Ricketts's accomplishment as a designer, but it is the realisation of the two expressions together that make *Silverpoints* a queer book.

This section performs a close reading of several key poems in the context of their physical publication in this volume. Just as Basil puts too much of himself into his portrait of Dorian, so too does Gray, Ricketts and Wilde into *Silverpoints*. The result is a volume that is more than the sum of its parts. In terms of Gray's poems, which frame this section, while some are translations and others were previously published elsewhere, what will be argued is that their material presentation here generates a meaning entrenched in queer relationality between content and form, between Ricketts and Gray, between Wilde and Gray, between the reader and *Silverpoints*.

An aesthetic education

As per Halperin's criteria for 'organizing human erotic life' in a manner unique to the historical lens of the culture from which it emerges,[41] aestheticism emerges from a revised discourse of same-sex desire inspired by the study of Hellenism. Pater tells us that the aesthetic effect of art communicates through an 'ideal' beauty – 'a distinction, like genius or noble place', found in the 'moral sexlessness' of the male body.[42] The male body remains erotic but sexless because an appreciation of the nude male form speaks to 'the finer aspects of nature, the finer lime and clay of the human form'.[43] Stefano Evangelista explains how, in ancient Greece, gymnasia, where athletes exercised naked, were also schools of art frequented by philosophers and artists alike.

It is for this reason that among the visual arts of antiquity Johann Joachim Winckelmann, eighteenth-century art critic and subject of an essay by Pater in *The Renaissance*, favours sculpture, with its interest in the idealised beautiful body, especially the male body.[44] Art is dependent upon physical experience – the body of the athlete gives physical sensation to aestheticism's ideals: an erotic sensuality shared between men as the basis for both art and art criticism. The queer book is an iteration of that sensory intercourse replacing the human body and offering the promise of bringing men's bodies together in sexual discourse.

Silverpoints, with its golden cage, stretched out over a sea of green cloth that binds the book, is an artificially landscaped garden. British aestheticism takes nature and uses art to improve upon it. Such a philosophy can be found in Wilde's own art criticism, the most famous of which is collected in *Intentions* (1891), and includes 'The Decay of Lying'. Structured like a Platonic Dialogue, Vivian in 'The Decay of Lying' tells his companion Cyril that Art reveals 'Nature's lack of design, her curious crudities, her extraordinary monotony, her absolutely unfinished condition. Nature has good intentions, of course, but as Aristotle once said, she cannot carry them out.' Ricketts, a student of aestheticism and Gray's mentor, transforms his acolyte's natural imagery into artifice, an element of irony born from the bibliographic alteration of Gray's lexical expression. Ricketts's garden of queer typography delights and transforms Gray's portrayal of his intimate relationship with Oscar Wilde into another aesthetic pose. It is not their relationship that is commemorated; instead, it is the sensations they discovered and the moments of bliss that their relationship created.

As with the other poems in the book, 'Summer Past: To Oscar Wilde'[45] is made into a typographical challenge with the small Aldine italics in a sea of white space. This white space exists within the cage surrounding the cloth-bound book. While there is room to contemplate for the queer reader or poet, such repose for queer relations is limited to the confines of the book.

Gray captures this moment of creative influence as an aesthete poet under the influence of his mentor and lover Wilde in 'Summer Past' using garden imagery – gardens being artificial recreations of nature – to present Wilde as one of the 'great trees' to pass its 'pearl' unto 'the proud leaves' below. Wilde, as the tree, becomes a sanctuary where 'the eves' lull 'song-tired birds to sleep' so that 'other things might tell their secrecies'.[46] The suggestion of intimacy shared between Wilde and Gray and his acolytes is sexualised with adjectives describing leaves curling in 'ecstasy'. The intimacy they share implies both sensual pleasure and sexual desire when we hear the speaker whisper about 'the stern gods' who 'keep / Their bitter silence' as if the sleeping birds, or the culture that allowed the tree of Wilde to flourish, may find out their secrets.[47] The end suggests that holy trees are 'song-set' as if a moral contagion, resistant to change, and will silence their secret sharing and 'unfurl eternally the sheen / Of restless green'. These are not secrets so much as aesthetic philosophies of decadence and beauty that integrate poetics with bodily senses, including the erotic.

Like those who looked up to him, Wilde was also learning and acquiring new sensations. 'Summer Past' casts Wilde as a mentor for a generation of aesthetes when he was rather their more famous colleague. Wilde as a tree, in the hands of Ricketts, becomes an artificial source of nourishment – a decorative symbol for poetic influence naively romanticised by an inexperienced young man. The sexuality of 'Summer Past' is realised through a dialogue between biographical and lexical codes. The tree is a symbol of a life of decadent hedonism that Gray embraced as one of many young men who fell at the roots of Wilde's celebrity in an attempt to share in his fame and fortune of the late 1880s and early 1890s.

As the young poet's other mentor, Ricketts 'taught Gray to see, to discriminate, to explore', allowing him to see the world from a perspective 'as wonderful now as things were in childhood'.[48] Gray's indoctrination into aestheticism's discourse of sensuality incorporated concepts of sexual desire into one of a multitude of experiences that would inspire his creativity and ability as a poet. In contrast, the perception of Gray's relationship with Wilde as hedonistic and shallow was due to his association with the fictional Dorian Gray. Gray and Wilde were in the most intense period of their relationship in 1889 when Wilde wrote *The Picture of Dorian Gray* (1890); later, Gray becomes 'Dorian', going so far as to sign at least one of his letters to Wilde 'yours ever, Dorian'.[49] McCormack resists the idea that 'the tragedy of [Gray's] life as "Dorian" Gray' was based on a sexual affair with Wilde.[50] Instead, presenting Gray's tragedy as his 'conscious exploitation of Wilde's attraction towards him', suggesting that despite his later rejection of 'Dorian', Gray was not a victim of Wilde's desires but complicit in nurturing a public persona that took on a life of its own.[51] The public persona of Gray, as the iconic aesthete poet, was a collaborative invention. Just as Basil Hallward, Henry Wotton and Dorian Gray were all complicit in creating the artificial persona of Dorian Gray, so too were Charles Ricketts, Oscar Wilde and John Gray complicit in creating what *Silverpoints* came to embody. The resulting work of art from this three-way discursive intercourse – between Ricketts, Wilde and Gray was not Gray the man, but the *objet d'art* – a portrait capturing the beauty of Gray's queer beauty in a dainty little book, the only material body where such an ideal could endure.

The poem ends by questioning the order of things. The role of nature suggests that all these figures are natural elements in the world, but for a green lawn to be unfurled is to landscape and alter nature, turning the secrets shared between tree and leaf into something unnatural, or queer. Simultaneously, then, the poem casts natural elements as artificial – an artificiality enhanced by the stylised willow leaves and green-dyed boards of the book. Nature becomes an art – an artificial imitation displaced from and improving upon the natural. The speaker suggests a beautiful intimacy, where the tree (Wilde) nourishes his acolyte (Gray) with his knowledge and wisdom regarding aesthetics, poetics and sexuality. The integration of bodies into philosophical initiation has erotic connotations without being explicitly about sexual penetration. It also suggests sexual pleasure derived from a creative bond between the acolyte and his poetic mentor. The sensuality of aestheticism and its incorporation of all sensory experience, including the erotic, nourishes Gray and his generation of aesthetes for good and for ill since, while the poem and the book propose what may appear to be a queer Eden, the reality had consequences outside of the aesthetic movement that were decidedly not idyllic.

Reminiscent of Henry Wotton's mentorship of Dorian Gray, Wilde, like Ricketts, saw Gray as a blank canvas on which to paint his vision of the beautiful aesthete poet. Gray was thirteen years younger than Wilde, so at the time of their love affair, he had not yet developed a strong enough personality to do anything but absorb Wilde's teachings and transform himself into the poet of his mentor's queer imagination. Gray found himself striving to be the thing he never was. Instead, he strives to become the ideal that both Ricketts and Wilde desired to see in his beautiful face and body. The book then is not a recreation of Gray, but an attempt to recreate the sensations experienced by other aesthetes in response to Gray as an aesthetic ideal.

Knight in shining armour

Some of the poems collected in *Silverpoints* are original compositions while others are loose translations, or what Gray calls 'imitations', of French poetry that celebrate, imitate and interrogate aestheticism as an artistic movement, as a way of life and a way to love. Many of the poems included are dedicated to some of the most important English and French poets and writers of the day, including Félix Fénéon, Jules Laforgue and Oscar Wilde. Typography gives *Silverpoints* its character. James G. Nelson notes how 'exotic, eccentric, or unreadable type' is rare in a Bodley Head book, so the choice to use such a small italic is significant.[52] The delicate Aldine italic type was named after late fifteenth- and early sixteenth-century Italian bookmaker Aldus Manutius who designed the italic for his octavo series that began with a 1501 edition of Virgil (see Fig. 1.2).[53] Before Ricketts had even begun working on *Silverpoints*, he notes that he 'was by that time, as I am still [in 1899 when this essay was published], utterly, won over and fascinated by the sunny pages of the Venetian printers', describing 'the page of a fine Kelmscott book [as] full of wine', and the page of 'an Italian book as full of light'.[54] Aldus, as scholars of his work shorten his name to, did not punch type himself. Like Ricketts, he designed type by hand, taking advantage of the skilled labour of Francesco Griffo (aka Francesco da Bologna) who punched the type for him. Neither Aldus's nor Ricketts's dependence on other craftspeople to produce their books lessens the value of their work. Rather, it demonstrates the role of collaboration and compromise necessary in the creation of the book as an art form.[55] For *Silverpoints*, it also demonstrates a collaborative response to Gray's spiritual voice in the poems.

Helen Barolini mentions that the type's other names – 'chancery hand' and 'Aldino' – are important: 'While the latter term subtly includes Francesco's name in the final syllable, 'chancery hand' is the cursive hand adopted at the Vatican in 1431 for its 'beautiful and clear formal style'.[56] The type is significant in two ways regarding Ricketts's knowledge of his profession: first, cursive handwriting does not look like print and italics mimic the slant of such a cursive hand. Aldus's use of this type took the impersonal and artless printing press and gave it a renewed relation to the illuminated manuscripts that came before print. Ricketts's adoption of the type for the entire text of *Silverpoints* suggests a handwritten document, a personal and intimate diary or account kept by Gray, providing the intimate connection Wratislaw said the poetry lacked. Second, as the official type of the Vatican, it suggests that *Silverpoints* is written by one of God's representatives

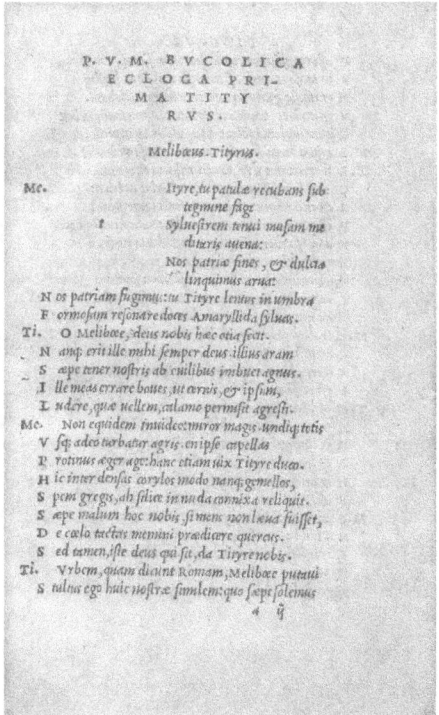

Figure 1.2 Example page from a book published by the Aldine Press. Harry Ransom Center, The University of Texas at Austin.

on earth. Because of the heavy influence of Catholicism on the aesthetes, and not forgetting Gray's conversion shortly after the release of this book, Ricketts's typeface suggests that God's hand has touched Gray's, presenting intercourse between Christ and a queer poet.

Gray's poems, as part of the book, penetrate aestheticism revealing layers of surface each with its sense of beauty and ability to trigger a sensational and pleasurable response. 'Le Chevalier Malheur' is also 'Imitated from the French' of Paul Verlaine – what Cevasco calls 'liberal translation' – Gray can 'take certain liberties' in his interpretation of a challenging French Symbolist poet.[57] The poem speaks to both the sexuality and the spirituality of the book's creative textual intercourse between Gray and his mentors. The poem, presented in an accentual Anglo-Saxon verse form, complements the medieval theme of knightly adventure. Gray uses the metaphor of penetration as the speaking knight is pierced by a fellow knight's 'unpitying lance', conquering him in battle.[58] This first penetration by a lance threatens to kill him, pouring forth his blood in an ejaculatory 'single crimson jet'.[59] The poem takes more overt sexual license as the speaker falls to the ground in defeat and his vanquisher forces on him a second penetration, that of his mail-clad fingers which 'he thrusts into the wound', reviving the speaker who declares, 'At once within me bursts / a new noble heart'.[60] The fallen knight is not dominated in his passive reception of the other knight's phallic lance and fingers; he is revived in a second ejaculatory response to repeated penetration.

Significantly, touch revives him, a tactile experience of spiritual ecstasy that suggests a communal bond with homoerotic overtones as one man's life-giving force injects new life and inspiration into another man's heart. Significantly, the conquering knight offers new life to his comrade. In this new chivalry, one knight revives his fellow knight – one aesthete brings to life another so that he can create something new – something that will not allow him to be defeated as he was the first time he jousted. Equating penetration with the restoration, or at least to new opportunities for creative fulfilment within their queer intercourse, Gray's poem presents a queer moment where the text becomes the new life that the aesthete poet may now live. The poet endures in the body of the book in a manner that it could not in the body of Gray. Presentation is relevant because the reader is drawn to the book for its material beauty just as aesthetes Oscar Wilde, André Raffalovich and

Charles Ricketts were drawn to Gray's physical beauty. His father figures, his lovers and his friends penetrate Gray, perhaps not sexually, but certainly at a spiritual level with an aesthetic tenet warning him that 'Once only can the miracle / avail – Be wise!'[61] The queer book gives their intercourse an immutable form, but for the queer individual, it is a Paterean moment and its gem-like flame will only burn briefly.

Gray struggled with the artificiality of aestheticism, in part because of his desire for a spiritually fulfilling relationship with God through Catholicism. Many of his poems in *Silverpoints* explore his spiritual path. However, his spirituality is also caught up in material experiences: lying untouched in the earth, preparing a woman's hair, being pierced by a knight's phallic sword. For Gray, spirituality comes to be caught up in sensual imagery with significant homoerotic implications. He would later explore this further under the influence of Raffalovich, with whom he lived most of his life and whose work on sexology explored the idea that same-sex desire is natural but acting on it through sexual intercourse with other men is not.[62] Spiritual ecstasy, for Gray and Raffalovich, becomes, at least publicly, the outlet for such desires, and Gray's spiritualism becomes another artificial performance, a ritualistic intercourse between queer men and God as a lover who brings a promise of ecstatic sensual gratification. *Silverpoints* can be read, then, as an attempt to find that expression through art and aesthetic community. John Gray was kind and humble, possessing a desire to please others. He evoked queer relationality because of the combination of his beautiful face, working-class body and his espousal of aesthetic ideals in recitations of his work for his coterie of queer aesthetes.

Gray's struggle with the spiritual sensuality of God was also in conflict with the material sensuality of aestheticism. That conflict was, in part, what made Gray's performative work as the aesthete so captivating. That conflict is captured on the pages of *Silverpoints* and suggests that queer *eros* or the love between aesthetically enlightened men can unite spiritual and material pleasure. In addition, the book captures the experience of queer male life in the 1890s from an aesthetic perspective: an artificial world, a space that, on the surface limits the homoerotic, but that allows queer desire to create a space for itself in the hands of the artist, under the surface of the lush green garden, and in the act of sexual penetration by God himself, textually presented in a book that merges the pagan with the Christian, the medieval with the neoclassical, and the normative with the queer.

Usage of a silverpoint, the typographer's lance or a small metal rod pressing minute metal particles onto the page, implies a one-time act that cannot be repeated because of the delicacy of the work. The knight's one-time offer of orgasmic rebirth is reflected in the book's status as a limited edition. The title reflects Ricketts's role in the creation of the text as well as the role of material design – that is, the textual poetics that complete Gray's poetry. Ricketts presents Gray's thirty poems as aesthetic designs, beautiful material objects for the reader to appreciate. Depth becomes layers of surface as the heart's blood of the penetrated speaker spurts forth into the material world. The queer book's presentation decentres our perception of poetry as representative of the poet's thoughts because the material book and its multiple authors are an inseparable part of Gray's poems.

Queer relations captured in the queer book find a lexical representation in Gray's poem 'Mishka' (see Fig. 1.4). The eponymous hero is seduced into the arms of a femme fatale, sexually submitting to her caresses. He refers to this 'beast' as 'she' in lines 12, 13, 19 and 24, and while the immediate implication of the poem is that of a heterosexual seduction, the context of *Silverpoints* complicates this association. The feminised beast dominates his male body, forcing Mishka to become the poem's sexual object of desire. Mishka, through his beauty, possesses the 'monster's eyes' and she must 'drag' Mishka into her lair with a 'net of her yellow hair'.[63] Through his own seduction, she lures him into her clutches unawares. Mishka's beauty is defined by his naïve innocence. He is forced into nature as 'his body is bathed in grass and sun', held in nature's clutches and seduced by its false, monstrous beauty. This natural landscape aligns with the artificial landscape of Ricketts's green cloth book with its golden cage; the pastoral becomes art's abstraction of nature. 'Mishka' becomes an anti-pastoral, making nature into a false trap that seduces male beauty away from exploring 'more of the ancient south'.[64] Artifice envelops Mishka in a manner that reminds the reader of how Ricketts's designs envelop Gray. In its refusal to allow the reader and Mishka to dig below the surface, the book, as with the poem, tells us that there is nothing below the surface – there is no real 'Mishka'. It is the intercourse between reader and poem, aesthete and object, a relationship visible on the poem's surface that survives.

Key to an understanding of *Silverpoints* is the historical precedent that influences Ricketts's transformation of the material book into a subversive, discursive space. *Silverpoints* portrays a struggle between sexual and spiritual ecstasy, and like the texts produced by the Aldine Press before, portrays a cultural struggle during the Italian Renaissance between the teachings of the Catholic Church and the discovery and circulation of classical pagan texts.

Bibles and prayer books were being published alongside works by Virgil, Homer and other Greco-Roman literature that influenced and changed Europe's relationship with God. In these classical texts, readers found the promise of pleasure not restricted to Christianity's promised afterlife. The beautiful books available to the privileged classes of early modern Europe promised heaven on earth. No single text was more promising than the Aldine Press's most famous and celebrated publication, the *Hypnerotomachia Poliphili* (1499). Translated as 'The Strife of Love in a Dream', this text is an elaborate bibliographic and literary experiment where lexical content, decoration and illustration are intertwined. John Dixon Hunt notes that the text was the inspiration, and sometimes a source for imitation by many late nineteenth-century artists, including Ricketts.[65]

It is not uncommon to see the interconnection of typography and authorship when the same person does both. The common source of illustration and prose for *Hypnerotomachia Pholiphili* is assumed to be that of Francesco Colonna with assistance from Aldine Press to transfer this work to the page.[66] From Laurence Housman (1865–1959) at the *fin de siècle* to the more recent work of Glaswegian novelist, artist and illustrator Alasdair Gray (1934–2019), this tradition of author-book designer continues.[67] Ricketts, as part of that tradition, brings the visual and the literary content together in his typographic presentations. In her study of Ricketts's collaboration with Wilde during his editorialship of the monthly periodical *The Woman's World* (1887–1890), Petra Clark says that 'Ricketts seems to be encouraging readers to "read" visual markers with attention equal to that devoted to the text itself, especially at the points where the two representations do not match up', allowing Ricketts's contributions to 'challenge the pre-eminence of text, and by extension, the authors whose work he was illustrating'.[68] The effect of Ricketts's contributions to the page extends beyond illustration to his work as a typographer; in a sense, he imagines a new language, a poetics only accessible in the intercourse of the two art forms. This intercourse adapts to typography that is achieved through illustration in the *Hypnerotomachia Poliphili* (see Fig. 1.3), where Colonna's illustrations take on a narrative function, 'serving to connect significant episodes, thereby producing narrative clarity for the reader lost in the wealth of Colonna's elaborately vivid, descriptive yet confusing language'.[69] Similarly, Ricketts's italics, white space and small pica are a part of *Silverpoints*'s poetic language, confusing and merging form with content to achieve what Walter Pater claimed should be the goal of all art, including poetry, whereby 'form and matter, in their union or identity, present one single effect to the "imaginative reason", that complex faculty for which every thought and feeling is twin-born with its sensible analogue or symbol'.[70] Form and content together allow both Colonna and Ricketts to imagine prose that exists solely in the text. Readers in the period that the Aldine Press targeted with the *Hypnerotomachia Poliphili*, would have struggled to decipher the text not just because of

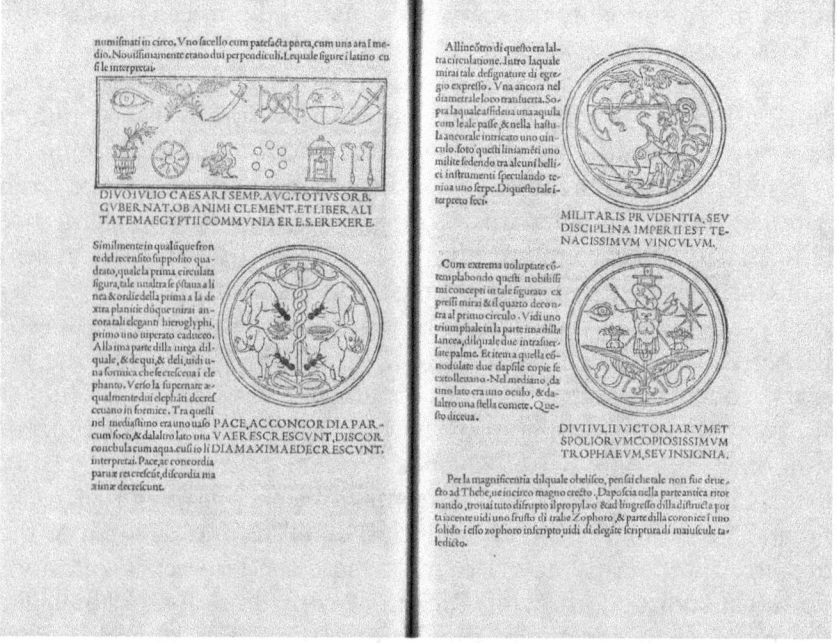

Figure 1.3 Example page from the *Hypnerotomachia Poliphili*. Harry Ransom Center, The University of Texas at Austin.

illustration, but because of his choice to write in a combination of Italian grammar and Latin syntax.[71] The result was that the book required careful attention and close study. This was not a book for casual reading, but a coded labour of love.

The story follows Poliphili through an aesthetic dreamscape of fantastical architecture, sculpture, gardens, nymphs and goddesses that leads him to his beloved Polia who, after resisting his advances, eventually admits her love, only for him to wake up and realise at the end that she has already died. The depiction of love and sex is decidedly pagan; the book offers no mention of Christianity or a monotheistic god. Instead, the gods of the *Hypnerotomachia Poliphili* are a pantheon of female goddesses who sexually stimulate and encourage Poliphili in the obsessive pursuit of his earthly love through a labyrinth of erotic landscapes. It is a heteroerotic fantasy from a male point of view with Polia, and all women in the book are portrayed as symbols, guardians or servants of Poliphili's desires, existing only to access and accept Poliphili as a suitor. That obsession is not just written in the text of the book but carved into the plaques and statuary illustrated throughout the volume. April Oettinger describes the book as a portable *studiolo*, derived from the term *studioli*, that is, a room for learning.[72] It is also specifically a place where the reader can learn about the aesthetic pleasures of human creation, art and architecture, manicured gardens and objectified women, a *'l'alta fantasia*, the imaginary space where visions were made'.[73] While decidedly heteronormative, it also sits outside of Christian convention, in a space that is circulated among an elite readership within a heteronormative Christian culture that also made space to study pagan sexuality.

Ricketts presents *Silverpoints* as such a *studiolo*; however, in his volume, the book's imaginary space queers the historical and religious implications suggested by his typographic choice.

Women are artificially beautiful, but they offer no sexual satisfaction to the speakers. The speaker is satisfied only by homosocial and homoerotic contact, contact that is more often than not reflective of Charles Kains-Jackson's concept of the new chivalry with a focus on same-sex male eroticism, but also sacred with the figure of God acting as Gray's strong chivalric beloved and companion.[74] Ricketts takes Gray's struggle with the tension between his queer desires and the spiritual ecstasy he discovers in the Catholic Church and turns it into a bibliographic experiment that makes same-sex desire a sacred, aesthetic experience that is material as well as spiritual.

A *cosmetiste*'s dreamscape

Silverpoints's typography affects a bibliographical poetic – a material stylisation of the literary that demands the reader engage physically with the book as an emotional and psychological expression. 'In a well-made book', Robert Bringhurst says, 'the letters are alive. They dance in their seats. Sometimes they rise and dance in the margins and aisles.'[75] It is an intercourse where Ricketts provides room for the reader to join in the fun. Take for example the wide swathes of white space that Ricketts leaves on every page.

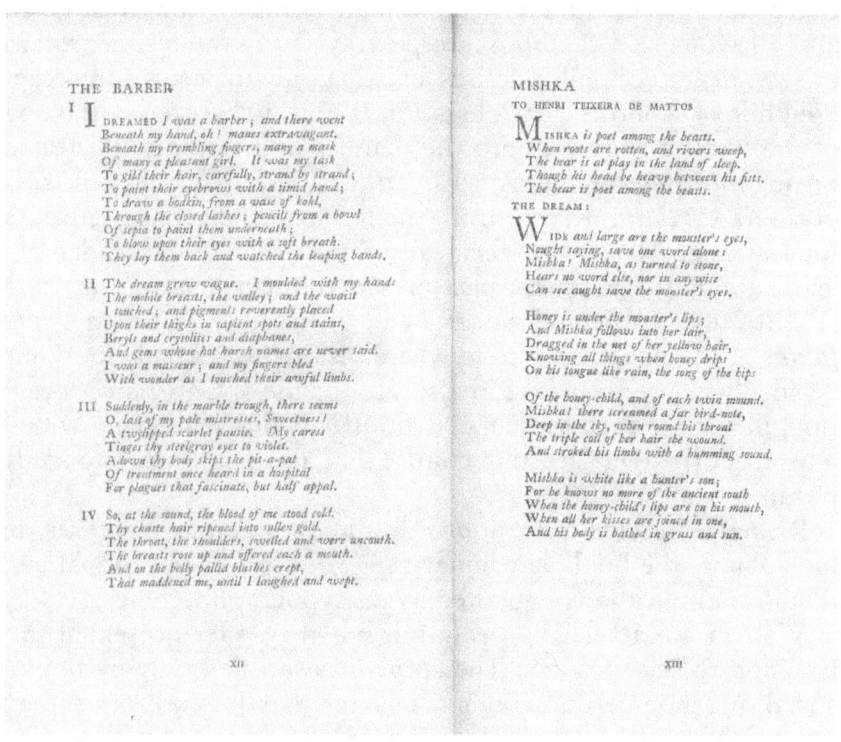

Figure 1.4 'The Barber' and 'Mishka' in *Silverpoints*. Courtesy of the Rufus Hawtin Hathaway Collection, Identification #991026002159705163, Archives and Special Collections, Western Libraries, Western University.

Bonnie Mak explains the role that white space plays when we read, particularly when reading silently. Mak states that white space 'enhances the legibility and comprehensibility of the page', offering spaces between words so that the eye can rest, both visually and cognitively.[76] 'By leaving space on the page unfilled', Mak argues, readers may 'pause' and think critically about what they have read.[77] White space is a time for contemplation, consideration and critique. In the case of *Silverpoints*, the cue to pause is transformed, and white space becomes an expressive art of discursive space – a material gap or fissure that Eve Kosofsky Sedgwick argues is the textual basis of queer reading.[78] The queer book, at least in this instance, takes the role of white space to a decadent excess.

Probably the most famous reaction to the white space of *Silverpoints*, and the most satirical, comes from Ada Leverson, who stated that she had

> suggested to Oscar Wilde that he should go a step further than these minor poets; that he should publish a book all margin; full of beautiful unwritten thoughts, and have this blank volume bound in some Nile-green skin powdered with gilt nenuphars and smoothed with hard ivory, decorated with gold by Ricketts and printed on Japanese paper, each volume must be a collector's piece, a numbered one of a limited 'first' (and last) edition: 'very rare'.
>
> He approved.[79]

The white space is part of the expression conveyed in *Silverpoints*. The book does not simply mediate between the poems and the reader; it asks the reader to consider the book's material beauty and that beauty's relationship to the poems contained therein. The white space leaves room for the material sensuality of the book to suggest new desires not yet imagined by any of the book's contributors. The reader is intimately close to the typeface, and yet psychologically steps back to see the edges of the page. The garden of typography is beautiful, but it is also artificial, a landscape born of performance and performativity. Like the green carnation that puzzled Wilde's audience and critics in regard to its meaning, the book's white space offers room to disagree, room to tease and play with suggestions, as Leverson demonstrates, and consider new means for poetry and aestheticism more broadly within the space of pages that make up the reader's own 'very rare' edition of *Silverpoints*.

Gray's poetry in *Silverpoints* is a collaborative project that hinges on the material poetics of performance and presentation. The full beauty of Gray's poetic vision is best understood within the confines of the single edition of *Silverpoints* published by the Bodley Head. *Silverpoints* is a unique art object because it is dependent upon a reading of the poetic body. Instead of trying to understand Gray as a poet, separate from the decorated book, it is important to study the book as the embodiment of aestheticism's ideal art. Gray's poems, then, are as much a material contribution to the book as Ricketts's typographical oversight. Together, they make the book queer.

Nelson pays specific attention to the relationship between Gray's poems and the beautiful book that contains them: 'the ultimate in Bodley head books achieved their exquisite beauty without either demanding the impossible from the printer and publisher or sacrificing the utility and readability of the book. Even in its extremist form – the italics used throughout *Silverpoints* – the type lends itself admirably to the subject matter and tone of Gray's exotic decadent verse.'[80] It is the decadent artificiality, imperfections and self-conscious style of Gray that makes the book design so important to understand his poems. Ricketts performs the sort of material analysis that is applicable to *Silverpoints* as a multisensory work of art, enhanced and completed by a material poetics of design and cosmetics. Gray's poem 'The Barber' demonstrates the cosmetic process and how artificiality can queer the heteronormative form. 'The Barber' consists of a highly structured series of couplets written in an iambic pentameter and organised in four stanzas of diminishing length (from eleven lines to six while totalling thirty-two) without any specific poetic purpose in its form. The speaker dreams of himself as a barber, or more accurately, a *cosmetiste*, who, with his 'marble trough' in hand, creates a vision of beauty from the body of his final mistress.[81] The Barber's art is commercial, yet profit does not motivate the speaker. His dreamed craft affords him the opportunity to compose an artificial beauty. The dream becomes tactile in the second stanza (see also Fig. 1.4):

> *I moulded with my hands*
> *The mobile breasts, the valley; and the*
> *waist I touched, and pigments reverently*
> *placed Upon their thighs in sapient spots*
> *and stains, Beryls and chrysolites and*

diaphanes,
And gems whose hot harsh names are never
said. I was a masseur; and my fingers bled
With wonder as I touched their awful limbs.[82]

The barber sculpts bodies, touching them, bleeding for them, contorting nature to create a decadent vision of artificial beauty. This discourse becomes performative through the construction of the book. Charles Ricketts takes Gray's poetry as his rough-hewn marble, stylistically distorting Gray's poetry with Aldine italic. Through the poem, Gray demonstrates his awareness of the role of the *cosmetiste* as someone who improves upon nature. Ricketts is Gray's *cosmetiste*, sculpting his poetry into an aesthetic ideal of Ricketts's imagination.

Ricketts's artifice transforms the reader's experience of poetry; it suggests that Gray's poetic language is a 'pale mistress', an aesthetic element conquered by the 'caress' and 'mask' of the book's design. It is an eroticism, not in the conventional sense of human bodies interacting and penetrating one another in intercourse, but a textual eroticism, an intercourse between the body of the book and aestheticism's discourse of a beauty. Gray and his poetry are half-lives that find completion when Ricketts imbues them with the beauty of visual artifice, giving the poetry a new unnatural pallor that 'fascinate[s], but half appal[s]'.[83]

Silverpoints's artifice speaks to the vision Ricketts offers Gray's poems. The book becomes the aesthetic poet through its artificial beauty. Like the beauty of the woman recreated by the barber, it is almost grotesque: a 'twylipped pansie' with 'steelgray eyes' that the speaker will make 'violet'. She is obscured as the 'dream grew vague' and the barber alters her imperfect, muted, natural self, making vibrant that which is 'steel-gray' (note the implications of the pun). The artifice infuses the object, the poem, and the reputation of the poet with definition and space, revealing the beautiful body as a performative parodied with subversive textual intercourse between the bibliographic and the lexical. Art reigns supreme as the book's artificial design obscures, distorts and queers the natural beauty of the poem submitting nature to aesthetics. The tools of beauty are limited, both in the barber's cosmetics and scissors, and in the book designer's ink and fount. Gray's poetry becomes a reflexive comment on *Silverpoints* as a presentation of form and style that serves to mask content while emphasising artificiality with form. Ricketts and Gray each become barbers, moulding artificial beauty that emphasises style over realism, drawing the reader's attention to surfaces and artifices – style as content. This layering of masks obscures the poem and reflects the discourse of art obscuring nature, allowing the reader to touch the 'mask' hidden in a dream of being a barber.

No pillows deep in the earth

Ricketts had quality standards that match those of William Morris, which I will discuss further in the next chapter. Like Morris, Ricketts demanded 'bold' and 'legible' type, that the 'two opposite pages form one unit' and 'that the upper margin should

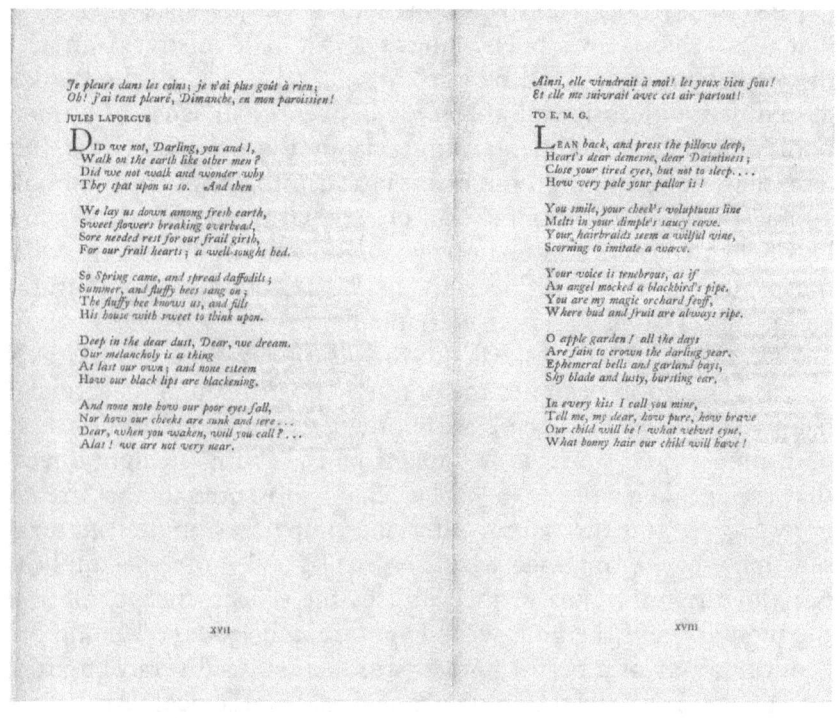

Figure 1.5 'Did we not, Darling' and 'Lean back and press the pillow deep' as they appear in *Silverpoints*. Courtesy of the Rufus Hawtin Hathaway Collection, Identification #991026002159705163, Archives and Special Collections, Western Libraries, Western University.

be a little larger than the inside margin, that the fore-edge margin would be the next in size, and the lowest the greatest of all'.[84] He also preferred papers made by 'Batchelor & Arnold' in terms of English-made papers.[85] Ricketts, however, subverts his own rules, willing to challenge and bend his designs to the limits of the technology available to him. While Ricketts insists that designers '[u]se decoration only when it can be urged as an added element of beauty to the book, let it accompany the text, and not gobble it up',[86] he bends his rule without contradicting himself. And, true to this motto, Ricketts uses little design other than typography in the pages of *Silverpoints*. Instead, he finds other ways to penetrate Gray's work.

Connection, collaboration and intercourse are crucial to understanding the queerness of aestheticism's multisensory philosophical body. The loss of that communal interaction is worse than death. In his poem to Jules Laforgue, Gray examines aestheticism's social world from the perspective of preternatural death as one dead body speaks to another seemingly silent corpse (see Fig. 1.5). McCormack notes that 'Did we not, Darling', contains imagery taken from several sources including Charles Baudelaire and Emily Dickinson.[87] Two lines from one of Laforgue's poems that originally appeared in the publication of *Des Fleurs de Bonne Volonté* (1890) serve as the poem's opening epigraph.[88] Ellis Hanson notes how the poem depicts the 'sexual dilemma' of same-sex desire: 'Confronted with the self-righteous indignation of others', Gray's lovers commit suicide only to find themselves physically separated in their graves, 'conscious, sensible, dreaming perhaps, but unable to touch each other, unable perhaps to hear each other'.[89] Hanson describes the 'blackening and rotting away of the flesh' as 'a metaphor for the repression that was all too often the fate of the Victorian homosexual', unaware whether his lover will even remember him when he is raised to the afterlife.[90] If *Silverpoints* is a garden, then outside, even underneath its landscape, there is a threat to those who voice queer desires. These men buried in the earth found no solace and lost access to their relationship. In the afterlife, they appear damned.

The poem shares the experience of losing that community by figuring the poet in isolation. Religious and social doctrine is implicated here. However, death is not an end; it is presented as a change or a queering of life that perpetuates the alienation of the poem's speaker and his implied listener. Even isolation, loss and death can be beautiful if appreciated amongst one's queer community. The dead speaker presents a social alienation, giving voice and beauty to an aesthetic audience seeking a space to discuss desire and love between men. The dead speaker is alone, 'Deep in the dear dust', and serves as a site of aestheticised isolation.[91] The death of the speaker and his beloved do not make the scene tragic; the tragedy is their physical and intellectual isolation from one another. *Silverpoints* is a space of materialised disruption, 'a well-sought bed', where same-sex desire may rest, express its fears and circulate as an aesthetic discourse.

Displayed beside one another, even in death, they are kept apart as if they are still 'spat upon' in the afterlife as they were in life by those outside their aesthetic intercourse.[92] This cruel end is contrasted with '*Ainsi, elle viendrait à moi! les yeux bien fous! Et elle me suivrait avec cet air partout!*' on the facing page. Here, love is permitted between heterosexual lovers awaiting the birth of their child. In the second stanza, the lover and the beloved are touching; the speaker seems to touch his wife or lover's pregnant stomach. At first, this reads as a return to heteronormative sexual desire and love; however, Ian Fletcher suggests that the poem's dedication 'E. M. G.' is a typo and should have read 'H. M. G.', Gray's mother's initials.[93] Fletcher's clarification then suggests that the child being born is Gray; a future lonely death is contrasted with the promise of his heteronormative birth. The promise of his parents is blighted by a world that allowed such queer children to die in 'melancholy'.[94] In both poems, we can see anxiety in Gray's work regarding identity, sexuality, the soul and even his own birth. He and men like him 'Walk on the earth like other men' but they are not like other men. An irony emerges from laying these two poems beside each other. The speaker's queer love is condemned and yet his birth is nonetheless worth celebration. The condemnation of one implicates the role that heteronormativity plays in creating queer lives and the inevitable pursuit of queer relations.

A union of content with form

Critics at the time of *Silverpoints*'s release thought little of Gray's skill as a poet. Theodore Wratislaw (1871–1933), in his 1893 review of the book for monthly periodical *The Artist and Journal of Home Culture*, argued that Gray's poetry has 'a complete want of human passion, of human sensation; an oversweet, even sickly, elaboration of beauty'.⁹⁵ His review ends with the backhanded compliment, 'Mr. Gray is often clever and occasionally an artist; and on the whole, one may say that he is a young man with a promising career behind him.'⁹⁶ Wratislaw's reading does not consider that Gray's elaborations and artifices are what give his poetry value. He also does not consider Gray's poems as fragments of a whole artwork, best understood in collaboration with Charles Ricketts's bibliographic, typographic and decorative contributions. This chapter is, in part an attempt to right that wrong – to find queerness in the intercourse between content and form.

A queer book's material existence in the late Victorian period mirrored that of queer aesthetes: it emerged and circulated in a world of institutions and social spaces that defined heterosexual practices as norms, and it altered some of those spaces so that it was possible to share a queer sexual discourse of same-sex desire. Because homosexuality was illegal in Britain in the 1890s, it is easy to interpret aestheticism's language of same-sex desire as a form of obfuscation or hiding from the public. However, aestheticism's coded discussions of queer sex signified a new vernacular that presented same-sex desire as a worthy, and aesthetically pleasurable, pursuit.

This alternate view of queerness as a communicative practice aligned same-sex desire with nineteenth-century print culture and experiments with bibliographic design and literary content. What resulted was the queer book: a space that facilitated and inspired queer sexual discourse.

Notes

1. Marc-André Raffalovich, 'To One of My Readers', *Cyril and Lionel and Other Poems: A Volume of Sentimental Studies* (London: Keagan Paul, Trench & Co, 1884), p. 87.
2. Jerusha Hull McCormack, *John Gray: Poet, Dandy, Priest* (Waltham, MA: Brandeis University Press, 1991), p. 104.
3. Pater, *The Renaissance*, p. 88.
4. McCormack, *John Gray*, p. 70.
5. Charles Ricketts, *A Defence of the Revival of Printing* (London: Ballantyne Press, 1899), p. 21.
6. I examined copies of *Silverpoints* held at Western University's Archives Research and Collections Centre, University of Texas, Austin's Harry Ransom Humanities Research Center, and the British Library.

7. Ian Small and R. K. R. Thornton, 'Introduction', in *John Gray: Silverpoints (1893), Spiritual Poems (1896)*, ed. by R. K. R Thornton and Ian Small (Oxford: Woodstock Books, 1994), unpaginated.
8. McCormack, *John Gray*, p. 97.
9. Brocard Sewell, *Footnote to the Nineties: A Memoir of John Gray and André Raffalovich* (London: Cecil and Amelia Woolf, 1968), p. 14.
10. McCormack, *John Gray*, p. 50.
11. Shillingsburg, p. 19.
12. Pater, *The Renaissance*, p. 86.
13. Oscar Wilde, *The Picture of Dorian Gray: An Annotated and Uncensored Edition*, ed. by Nicholas Frankel (Cambridge, MA: The Belknap Press of Harvard University Press, 2011), p. 85.
14. Nelson, *The Early Nineties*, p. 200.
15. Muñoz, p. 9.
16. Muñoz, p. 18.
17. Jackson, *The Eighteen Nineties*, p. 159.
18. Jackson, *The Eighteen Nineties*, p. 262.
19. These authors are listed in the ephemeral inserts from my copy of *The Aylesford Review* of 1961. There were lectures on Gray, Firbank and Rolfe/Corvo on May 17, 24 and 31 1961. The subscription insert additionally promises future numbers with articles on Gray, Hall, T. F. Powys and Oliver Onions.
20. Patricio Gannon, 'John Gray', *The Aylesford Review*, 4.2 (1961), 47–8.
21. John Gray, *The Poems of John Gray*, Greensboro, ed. by Ian Fletcher (NC: ELT Press, 1988); also, see Brocard Sewell's *Footnote to the Nineties: A Memoir of John Gray and André Raffalovich* (London: Cecil and Amelia Woolf, 1968) and *In the Dorian Mode: A Life of John Gray, 1866–1934* (Padstow, Cornwall: Tabb House, 1983).
22. Linda Dowling, 'Nature and Decadence: John Gray's "Silverpoints"', *Victorian Poetry*, 15.2 (1977), p. 160.
23. G. A. Cevasco, 'John Gray's *Silverpoints* and the Gallic Impress', *Cahiers victoriens et édouardiens*, 36 (1992), p. 107.
24. Ellis Hanson, *Decadence and Catholicism* (Cambridge, MA: Harvard University Press, 1997); Frederick S. Roden, *Same-Sex Desire in Victorian Religious Culture* (Basingstoke: Palgrave MacMillan, 2002).
25. Joseph Bristow, 'Introduction', in *The Fin-de-Siècle Poem: English Literary Culture and the 1890s*, ed. by Joseph Bristow (Athens: Ohio University Press, 2005), pp. 1–46; Michael Hatt, 'The Book

Beautiful: Reading, Vision, and the Homosexual Imagination in Late-Victorian Britain', in *Illustrations, Optics and Objects in Nineteenth-Century Literary and Visual Cultures*, ed. by Luisa Calè, P. Di Bello and Patrizia Di Bello (Basingstoke: Palgrave Macmillan, 2010), pp. 167–85.
26. Eve Kosofsky Sedgwick, *Between Men: English Literature and Male Homosocial Desire* (New York: Columbia University Press, 1985), p. 1.
27. Sedgwick, *Between Men*, pp. 2, 94, 132.
28. Oscar Wilde, *The Picture of Dorian Gray: An Annotated and Uncensored Edition*, ed. by Nicholas Frankel (Cambridge, MA: The Belknap Press of Harvard University Press, 2011), n185.
29. Wilde, *The Picture of Dorian Gray: An Annotated and Uncensored Edition*, ed. by Nicholas Frankel, 184–6.
30. Sedgwick, *Between Men*, p. 1.
31. Wilde, *Dorian Gray*, p. 85.
32. Wilde, *Dorian Gray*, p. 84.
33. Wilde, *The Picture of Dorian Gray: An Annotated and Uncensored Edition*, ed. by Nicholas Frankel, 184–6.
34. Pater, *The Renaissance*, p. 133.
35. Walter Pater, *Marius the Epicurean: His Sensations and Ideas*, ed. by Gerald Monsman (Kansas City: Valancourt Books, 2008), p. 62.
36. Pater, *Marius the Epicurean*, n39.
37. Pater, *Marius the Epicurean*, p. 39.
38. Pater, *Marius the Epicurean*, p. 39.
39. Matthew Potolsky, *The Decadent Republic of Letters: Taste, Politics, and Cosmopolitan Community from Baudelaire to Beardsley* (Philadelphia: University of Pennsylvania Press, 2013), p. 27.
40. Charles Kains-Jackson, 'The New Chivalry', reprinted in *Nineteenth-Century Writings on Homosexuality: A Sourcebook*, ed. by Chris White (London: Routledge, 1999), p. 155.
41. David M. Halperin, *How to Do the History of Homosexuality* (Chicago: University of Chicago Press, 2002), p. 22.
42. Halperin, pp. 133, 142.
43. Pater, *The Renaissance*, p. 133.
44. Evangelista, *British Aestheticism and Ancient Greece*, p. 26.
45. John Gray, 'Summer Past: To Oscar Wilde', *Silverpoints* (Bodley Head, 1893), p. xv.
46. Gray, 'Summer Past: To Oscar Wilde', p. xv, lines 15–18.
47. Gray, 'Summer Past: To Oscar Wilde', p. xv, lines 20–21.
48. McCormack, *John Gray*, p. 26.

49. Frankel, 'Introduction', in *The Picture of Dorian Gray: An Annotated, Uncensored Edition*, ed. by Nicholas Frankel (Cambridge, MA: The Belknap Press of Harvard University Press, 2011), p. 13.
50. McCormack, *John Gray*, p. 50.
51. McCormack, *John Gray*, p. 50.
52. James G. Nelson, *The Early Nineties: A View from the Bodley Head* (Cambridge, MA: Harvard University Press, 1971), p. 59.
53. Martin Davies, *Aldus Manutius: Printer and Publisher of Renaissance Venice* (Tempe: Arizona Center for Medieval and Renaissance Studies, 1999), pp. 41–2.
54. Ricketts, *Defence*, p. 19.
55. Helen Barolini, *Aldus and His Dream Book* (New York: Italica Press, 1992), p. 80.
56. Barolini, *Aldus*, p. 80.
57. Cevasco, 'John Gray's', pp. 112, 110.
58. Gray, 'Le Chevalier Malheur', *Silverpoints* (London: Bodley Head), p. xxiv, line 4.
59. Gray, 'Le Chevalier Malheur', p. xxiv, line 6.
60. John Gray, 'Le Chevalier Malheur', p. xxiv, lines 19–20.
61. Gray, 'Le Chevalier Malheur', p. xxiv, lines 35–36.
62. See Marc-André Raffalovich, *Uranisme et sexualité: etude sur différentes manifestations de l'instinct sexuel*, Bibliothèque de criminology (Paris: A. Maloine, Éditeur, 1896).
63. Gray, 'Mishka', *Silverpoints*, 1893, p. xiii, lines 6, 10, 18.
64. Gray, 'Mishka', p. xiii, line 22.
65. John Dixon Hunt, 'The Plot of *Hypnerotomachia Poliphili* and Its Afterlives', *Word & Image: A Journal of Verbal/Visual Enquiry*, 31.2 (2015), p. 134.
66. Rosemary Trippe, 'The "Hypnerotomachie Poliphi", Image, Text, and Vernacular Poetics', *Renaissance Quarterly*, 55.4 (2002), p. 1224.
67. For a detailed look at Laurence Housman's work, see Lorraine Janzen Kooistra's *The Artist as Critic: Bitextuality in Fin de Siècle Illustrated Books* (Brookfield, VT: Ashgate, 1997); for an assessment of Alasdair Gray, see Frederick D. King and Alison Lee's 'Bibliographic Metafiction: Dancing in the Margins with Alasdair Gray', *Contemporary Literature*, 57.2 (Summer 2016), pp. 216–44.
68. Petra Clark, '"Cleverly Drawn": Oscar Wilde, Charles Ricketts, and the Art of the *Woman's World*', *Journal of Victorian Culture*, 20.5 (2015), pp. 397–8.
69. Trippe, p. 1225.

70. Pater, 'The School of Giorgione', in *The Renaissance*, ed. by Adam Phillips (Oxford: Oxford University Press, 1986), p. 88.
71. Oetinger, April, 'The *Hypnerotomachi Poliphili*: Art and Play in a Renaissance Romance', *Word & Image*, 27.1 (2011), pp. 15–30, p. 16.
72. Oetinger, p. 30.
73. Oetinger, p. 21.
74. Kains-Jackson, pp. 154–8.
75. Robert Bringhurst, *The Elements of Typographic Style* (Vancouver: Hartley and Marks, 1992), p. 19.
76. Bonnie Mak, *How the Page Matters* (Toronto: University of Toronto Press, 2011), p. 17.
77. Mak, p. 17.
78. Eve Kosofsky Sedgewick, *Tendencies* (Durham, NC: Duke University Press, 1993), p. 8.
79. Quoted in Karl Beckson, ed., *Aesthetes and Decadents of the 1890s: An Anthology of British Poetry and Prose* (Chicago: Academy Chicago Publishers, 1981), p. 318.
80. Nelson, *The Early Nineties*, p. 58.
81. John Gray, 'The Barber', *Silverpoints* (London: Bodley Head, 1893), p. xii.
82. Gray, 'The Barber', lines 12–19.
83. Gray, 'The Barber', line 26.
84. Ricketts, pp. 34–5.
85. Ricketts, p. 35.
86. Ricketts, p. 36.
87. McCormack, *John Gray*, p. 134.
88. McCormack, *John Gray*, 134, n280.
89. Hanson, p. 136.
90. Hanson, p. 136.
91. John Gray, 'Je pleure dans les coins; je n'ai plus gout à rien; Oh! J'ai tant pleuré, Dimanche, en mon paroissien! Jules LaForgue', *Silverpoints* (London: Bodley Head, 1893), p. xvii, line 13.
92. Gray, 'Je pleure', line 4.
93. Fletcher, ed., in Gray, *The Poems of John Gray*, p. 297.
94. John Gray, 'Ainsi, elle viendrait à moi! Les yeux bien fous! Et elle me suivrait avec cet air partout! To E. M. G.', *Silverpoints* (London: Bodley Head), p. 14.
95. Theodore Wraitislaw, 'John Gray', in *Three Nineties Studies* (Edinburgh: The Tragara Press, 1980), pp. 14–15.
96. Wraitislaw, 'John Gray', p. 17.

2

Pomegranate Stains on the Ideal Book; or Queering the Hetero-Beautiful

The House of Pomegranates (1891) is a collection of fairy tales written by Oscar Wilde and collected for the publication, with illustrations by artist and companions Charles Ricketts and Charles Shannon. The stories have divided readers for years over their audience, seemingly children, but upon examination of its themes, decidedly adult. Ricketts and Shannon's designs and illustrations emphasise these adult qualities. Charles Ricketts's cover design for Oscar Wilde's *House of Pomegranates* depicts a luscious red garden. The vine-like trees are filled with pomegranates, some of which are cut open to reveal the seeds within (see Fig. 2.1). Of Greek and aesthetic origins, this garden of earthly delights references the legend of Persephone eating the fruit of Hades. Persephone consumes this symbol of her desire to return to the underworld and is condemned to return to Hades for half of each year. Persephone's fate is to live two lives: one in dedication to her family and earthly commitments, and one in companionship with Hades, an alternate underground world where she secretly fulfils her dissident sexual desires. Ricketts's cover tempts readers to choose a similar fate. Gathered in a golden basket, the pomegranates of this garden are left unguarded. The peacock has turned its back. No one watches as readers reach forth to open the book and partake of the temptation that divided Persephone's life.

At the end of the nineteenth century, the queer reader's life is similarly divided between the demands of the heteronormative late Victorian world and the homoerotic desires that they cannot openly discuss. *A House of Pomegranates* symbolises this struggle between social expectation and unspoken queer desires. As a book of children's fairy tales, it represents family, reproductive

Pomegranate Stains on the Ideal Book 75

Figure 2.1 Oscar Wilde's A *House of Pomegranates* with cover design by Charles Ricketts. Courtesy of the Rufus Hawtin Hathaway Collection, Identification #991026002159705163, Archives and Special Collections, Western Libraries, Western University.

sexuality, conventional gender roles and heteronormativity. At the same time, its dissident content of subversive visual symbolism and suggestive literary metaphors offer readers a space where they may access a queer sexual discourse: an underworld of dissident companionship that is hidden within the heteronormative practices of the modern literary marketplace. *A House of Pomegranates* is a book born of a culture of heteronormative ideals and simultaneously stained by the juices of Persephone's pomegranate seed. While a commercial failure, *A House of Pomegranates* remains a subversive multimedial achievement when considered within the nineteenth-century tradition of decorative bookmaking.

The purpose of this chapter is to demonstrate how queer books emerge from the Revival of Printing as sites of what Judith Butler calls 'collective contestation' – beautiful works of art that reflect neither consensus nor autonomy, whose beauty emerges from the conflicting points of view they contain.[1] Collective contestation is queer because it consists of both 'historical reflection and futural imaginings', anticipating the inevitable changes that come with time. Queer books represent the instability of queer identity in late Victorian and cosmopolitan *fin de siècle* culture. They also serve to remind readers today of the ephemerality and mutability of our own discourses of gender identity and sexual desire. In *A House of Pomegranates*, the contestation between the *historical* and the *futural* in a moment of reading the edition embodies the duality faced by queer Victorians: to plan for family, marriage, and reproductive futurity while also harbouring, and possibly acting upon, secret same-sex desires, a *queer eroticism* that does not align with such a future. In the case of the book, it is a children's book to serve the middle-class family's way of life, while also secretly exploring a homoeroticism that is quite separate from the family nursery.

Pomegranates is both a product and a subversion of the Revival of Printing's bookmaking practices. The queer book emerges from a tradition of heteronormativity, but it also inverts, twists and queers 'prior usage'.[2] *Eros* for queer aesthetes is a revival of the past as a means to imagine new forms of relationships in the present and future. The queer book self-reflexively recognises the influence of heteronormativity, a sociocultural experience that aesthetes who want to explore discourses of same-sex desire cannot escape. Instead, the beauty of their textual intercourse acknowledges the influence of the heteronormative on queer lives and desires. The resulting queer book aligns with Butler's concept of 'a necessary and inevitable expropriation' that signifies 'in spite of' its authors and designers.[3] The reader's knowledge of queer erotics in aestheticism in the 1890s will determine their interpretation of the book as a work of art. That discourse is in addition to the one between contributors, authors, designers, illustrators, printers, publishers and booksellers, who find themselves in a conversation that they cannot control, requiring adaptation to the influence of others within the pages of the book. The *boundedness* of the queer book as a codex, as a single unit, is not a work of harmony, but a complex of intersecting ideas and creations where a hitherto unknown queer space may become possible, a space that is not singular, but multitudinous, where no single hand, or creative vision, dominates.

Prior and simultaneous use of the material book by designers and artisans of the Revival of Printing is represented in this chapter by the work of William Morris (1834–96) at the Kelmscott Press. Kelmscott books were, like queer books, published in the late nineteenth century as a part of the Arts and Crafts movement. While ideologically heteronormative, these books were a discursive response to modern bookmaking culture, reviving and revising medieval bookmaking practices for modern readers. Morris's practices at Kelmscott were able to achieve an uncompromised 'ideal book', a singular vision of beauty under the controlling hand of Morris as bookmaker, author and publisher. Morris defines his ideal book as an object 'not limited by commercial exigencies of price: we can do what we like with it, according to what its nature, as a book, demands of Art'.[4] Positioning the book as an expression of art, which responds to the codex's seemingly essential nature rather than to the market, Morris outlines a number of specific details regarding the readability of the page, well-designed type and the proportion of margins. As mentioned earlier, Morris insists that all ornamentation be architectural, or part of the book's structure. In other words, the ornamentation must appear to naturally support or enhance the literary content.

Eschewing industrialised bookmaking, Morris realised handcrafted excellence that he believed had only been briefly achieved in the early fifteenth-century innovations of printers Johann Gutenberg (1400–68) and Nicholas Jenson (1420–80). After this, Morris sees compromise, what he calls a 'decline' of the book with the Renaissance-era experiments of Aldus Manutius (1449–1515), as soon as the late fifteenth and early sixteenth centuries.[5] In his critical essay, *Defence of the Revival of Printing* (1899), Charles Ricketts interprets this change to new practices differently as detailed in the previous chapter. He agrees with Morris that it is 'the duty of the typographer' to 'discard ... all accumulated debasements', and to 'hark back . . . to the finest forms of penmanship' and 'noblest founts' of the past.[6] Where Morris and Ricketts differ is that the books Morris saw as a sign of cultural decline in the early sixteenth century, for Ricketts were made with noble founts, in part because of the technological advancements achieved by Manutius. Where Morris was disappointed by these changes, Ricketts appreciated and found inspiration in the innovations that change provided.

As I outlined in the Introduction, Aaron Betsky examines how queer spaces emerge in the nineteenth century from the development of urban middle-class institutions such as the middle-class home, gentlemen's clubs and public bathhouses. There was no space for queer men in these heteronormative structures of modernity, so homosexuals adapted public spaces like parks, public washrooms or clubs to fulfil their sexual desires and create queer sexual discourse. Doing so revealed the constructed nature of architectural structures.[7] In other words, middle-class norms of heterosexuality and family were artificial or unnatural social constructions perceived as natural because they are realised through their material association with architectural spaces in the city: the church where you marry, the house where you raise a family or even the realist novel you read aloud together with your spouse and children. Queer individuals, for whom these institutions reserved no space, had to reconstruct existing structures based on their own countercultural ideologies and desires. While sex requires a physical locale, sexual discourse requires only a medium for discursive exchange. The queer space of the book becomes an example of one of the mechanisms that Michel Foucault argues was necessary for institutions and individuals to 'multiply discourse, induce pleasure, and generate power'.[8] Just as heteronormative architectures have to be reimagined for same-sex intercourse, so too does the space of the material book.

The beauty of the queer book comes from how it reimagines the 'ideal book' with a collaborative mode of creation that integrates handmade bookmaking practices with the innovations of industrial printing technologies. Ricketts and his partner, Charles Haslewood Shannon (1863–1937), certainly had more freedom when working through their own publishing house, the Vale Press. However, when working for more commercial publishers, even for small presses like the Bodley Head, they had to contend with the demands of the literary marketplace. Unlike Morris, queer men like Oscar Wilde, Ricketts and Shannon operated most often in the heteronormative space of established publishers and the demands of the literary marketplace to print and circulate their work. Their ideas of beauty dissent from established ideals to subvert and find conflict, even within the boards of a single edition. The queer books that came to market at the Victorian *fin de siècle* were not presented as a unified vision of a single author or designer but as the product of a collective effort imposed by publishers that demanded adaptability and responsiveness to the possible influences of publishing choices, printing technologies and marketing priorities. Just as queer cultures emerge in response to heteronormative structures and institutions, cultural discourses of queer desire emerge from the confines of existing heteronormative practices. Morris's ideal book did not imagine a space for queer desires. Therefore, the emergence of new bookmaking technologies was not a corruption of traditions, but an appropriation of competing practices necessary for the creation of queer books. The queer book realises textual intercourse between the normative and the queer, between the historical and the futural, and between the economics of nineteenth-century bookmaking and Morris's artisan ideals.

A House of Pomegranates is important in part because it is a seemingly flawed production. Its imperfections, however, give bibliographic and lexical voice to a creative collaboration between three queer men: Oscar Wilde, Charles Ricketts and Charles Shannon. While this book is quite different from Morris's Kelmscott book, it owes its revised conception of beauty to the incorporation of Morris's ideals into a textual intercourse with modern printing practices. It is not a reaction against heteronormative practices, but a result of understanding both bookmaking practices of the past and imagining new forms of queer relationships in the future. The new book also provides space for a queering of the fairy tale, transformed from medieval romance to queer sensuality. Together, the immersion of Wilde's stories into Ricketts's designs, and interleaved with Shannon's strange illustrations, achieves what queer theorist José Esteban Muñoz describes as an ability to see within material objects 'potentiality that is open, indeterminate, like the affective contours of hope itself'.[9] Ricketts and Shannon demonstrate in their book designs an acknowledgement of what Muñoz will describe a century later in the writings of Andy Warhol (1928–87) as a 'particular tension between functionality and nonfunctionality, the promise and potentiality of the ornament'.[10] The bibliographic design speaks to and gives readers hope for a queer space unavailable outside of the book. Ricketts and Shannon 'are able to detect an opening and indeterminacy in what for many people is a locked-down dead commodity'.[11] Where Morris interprets his project as a return to traditional artisanal practices, Ricketts sees the same books as innovative objects that generate new ideas. Morris's books are beautiful and an important challenge to the cheap bookmaking practices of the late nineteenth-century publishing industry.

His sense of beauty, however, is sentimental for an idealised past, a neo-medievalism that imagines beauty and desire in strictly heteronormative parameters. As a heterosexual man with no understanding of same-sex desire, Morris cannot be faulted. That is why I term his beautiful books as hetero-beautiful – a beautiful achievement in design, but an achievement that is based on a presumption of opposite-sex desire and the gender binary as universal experiences. For Ricketts, the beautiful book can be both a finely crafted object and a consumable good. It can also imagine beauty, sensuality and sexuality outside the parameters of Morris's imagination. The contestation between the hetero-beautiful and the queer does not diminish one beauty over another but serves to demonstrate a differentiation between heteronormative and queer conceptions of beauty in the late nineteenth century.

This chapter's two tales look first at the queer book's historical origins, and then at its bibliographic realisation on the page. The first will review the Revival of Printing, paying particular attention to the complex role of William Morris and the Arts and Crafts movement to demonstrate how his 'ideal book' is both a subversion of the literary marketplace, and a reinscription of the modern industrial economy's heteronormative ideology. The second section will illustrate how the queer book emerges from the same culture with a detailed analysis of the decorative first edition of Wilde's *A House of Pomegranates* published by James R. Osgood McIlvaine & Co. Drawing on Butler's theory of collective contestation and Muñoz's concept of queer relationality, the third and final section is a close reading of *Pomegranates* as a multimedial (literary *and* bibliographic) queering of Morris's ideal book. Persephone's seeds, the symbols of same-sex desire in aesthetic discourses of desire, stain Morris's ideals with material expressions of dissident desire, creating a new and beautiful queer book.

William Morris's hetero-beautiful books

Frédéric Barbier claims that the book's second revolution (the first being Gutenberg's press) occurred in the nineteenth century with the industrialisation of the publishing industry.[12] This industrialisation of bookmaking and the mass production of poor-quality books for a growing reading public was also the central motivation for one element of the Arts and Crafts movement in particular – the Revival of Printing. The Victorians were introduced to the work of designers Walter Crane (1845–1915), William Morris, Dante Gabriel Rossetti (1828–82) and Emery Walker (1851–1933), among others, whose design ideas and innovations helped to define the Revival of Printing, and particularly the fine-press movement.

Elizabeth Carolyn Miller aligns Morris's handmade bookmaking practices with a slow print movement associated with Socialist politics at the *fin de siècle*. Miller's research focuses on role that the little magazines performed by giving voice to socialist, anarchist and other radical groups.[13] She also looks at Morris's work with the Kelmscott Press at the end of the nineteenth century as establishing a 'utopian space', or future disconnected from the capitalist system and institutions that dominated their everyday lives.[14] This was not a queer futurity for those who felt ostracised by social conventions, but a political future based on a redistribution of wealth from the hands of capitalists into the hands of the working classes.

Morris achieves an ideal that also manages to avoid the compromises that emerged in conventional bookmaking practices. In doing so, he revitalises traditional artisan practices that flourished in medieval Britain and suggests, ideologically, that a return to the social practices of that time was in the best interests of modern workers. The heteronormative implications of his practices are problematic but important to understand in order to demonstrate a clear relationship between the emergence of the queer book and the heteronormative practices of the Revival of Printing. Morris's work at the Kelmscott Press marks a return to the traditional English arts, crafts, and architecture defined by Gothic conventions rather than the neoclassical forms that define the European Renaissance.

With bookmaking, modern industrial practices facilitated the emergence of a literary marketplace glutted with low-quality, cheaply made books that minimised costs and maximised profits. Frustrated by poor-quality printing, designers and bibliophiles, Walker and Morris saw no reason why high-quality materials could not be used in the production of books except for '[c]ommercialism', which demands not only cheap paper but 'the use of type too small in size to be comfortable reading'.[15] With economics as a design priority, printers sized type painfully small, filling the page with words and leaving only the thinnest of margins so that three-decker novels and other works of substantial length could fit into portable single-volume reprints.

Illustration was a common practice with serialised novels in Victorian periodicals as well as other works such as annuals and collections of poetry. Mary Elizabeth Leighton and Lisa Surridge examine the 'narratological function' performed by illustrations that accompanied these serialised novels for a public where reading was an uncommon practice.[16] Illustration as a decorative and communicative tool designed to attract new readers, even appealing to those with minimal literacy.

Take for example the yellow-back or 'mustard-plaster' novels of the late nineteenth century.[17] Figure 2.2 shows a yellow-back edition of Wilkie Collins's sensation novel *Hide and Seek* (1854), republished by Smith, Elder & Co. in 1872. While not clear in the figure, the book features a yellow glaze on the binding paper.[18] This colour choice had to do with the cost of printing as does the black frame that surrounds the roughly drawn image of Mary Grice, the mysterious child around whom Collins's sensational plot revolves. There is an attempt at decoration: a red framing design within the black background. The illustration is monochrome when prepared and then stamped in a three-colour-job done for this book in red, blue and black. Ruari McLean notes these stamped colour illustrations were also done in red, green and black.[19] The yellow-glazed paper adds a fourth colour to the mix at no additional cost. In terms of quality, the blue of Mary's sash does not stay in the lines and the eyes of the figures closest to Mary are drawn the same as hers. Most of the yellow-backs were illustrated and decorated by a single man, Edmund Evans (1825–1905), a printer and engraver who made his name producing colour illustrations using multiple wood blocks.[20] However, according to McLean, Evans was better known for the quantity of his work, rather than its quality.[21] The art of the design is primarily an advertisement demanding attention at railway

Figure 2.2 The 'ugly' cover of a yellow-back for Wilkie's Collins's *Hide and Seek* (1872). Private collection.

station bookstalls among hundreds of other books sold by Smith, Elder & Co. and competitor publishers.

Advertisement, not beauty, is the visual focus of the yellow-back design. The back cover (see Fig. 2.3) is a tightly printed list of books by the same publisher: all octavos, *'uniformly bound in limp cloth, price 2s. 6d. each'*. The publisher is not interested in creating a collectable book with artistic value. The 350-page book crams 200,000 words into its pages with a painfully small pica and almost no margin. The book, from the perspective of a bookmaker like Morris, is ugly, designed for no more than short-term reading, convenient advertisement of the publisher's list and disposability for the consumer. These cheap books were what Morris despised – commercial, ugly and mass-produced with utility, but without craft. The yellow-back books are but one of many bibliographic forms that offended the senses of men like Morris, but their example highlights his argument that the technical innovations

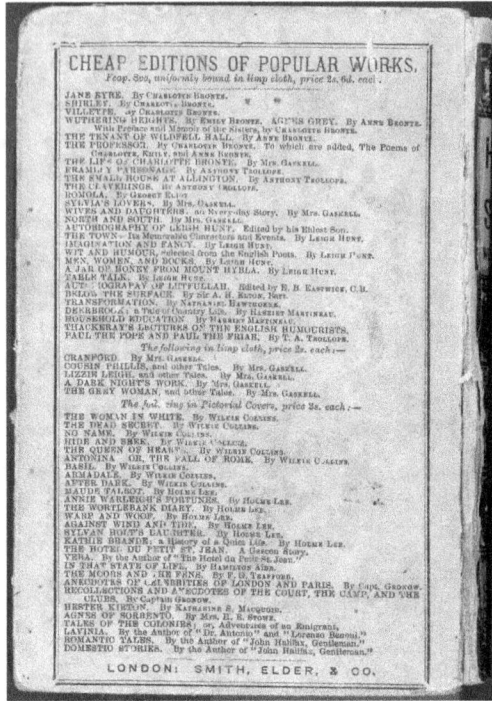

Figure 2.3 Backside of the yellow-back for Collins's *Hide and Seek*. Private collection.

that made colour printing and mass production possible did not necessarily result in a better-made book.

Not all book illustration outside of the Revival of Printing was cheap or terrible. Lorraine Janzen Kooistra makes an important argument for the mid-century Victorian gift book as a 'hybrid form' that shares characteristics with both the mass-produced periodical press and highbrow publications for subscribers willing to pay high prices.[22] While these works could be beautiful, there was no attempt on behalf of illustrators or periodical editors to change or complicate the author's literary expression.

While the Revival of Printing criticises industrial bookmaking, its practitioners shared industrialism's middle-class values. For example, the notion of the family as a heteronormative ideology of Victorian culture was not just a means of structuring relationships, such as that between the factory owner as paterfamilias and the working-class men he employs, but also served as a means of communicating relationships at the level of bibliographic design.

We see this ideology inform the aesthetics of the Revival of Printing. Elizabeth Helsinger, for instance, argues that Dante Gabriel Rossetti saw books as 'objects to be designed'.[23] His inspirations were his biological family and his aesthetic brotherhood. Rossetti's designs also responded, in part, to the market changes of the 1850s and 1860s. Amidst this period of economic stability in England, he, like many other designers and decorators, balanced creativity with economic prosperity.[24] Rossetti's designs for books served as emblematic of the family of authors with a material presentation that gives the collector and reader a sense of unity modelled on a heteronormative idealisation of the family (see Figs 2.4 and 2.5).[25] His book designs presented the Pre-Raphaelite Brotherhood, as well as the published family of Rossetti's books, and used the language of heteronormative culture to present themselves united in their commitment to crafting beautiful objects for

Figure 2.4 Dante Gabriel Rossetti's cover design for *Poems* (1870). Harry Ransom Center, The University of Texas at Austin.

Figure 2.5 Christina Rossetti's *Prince's Progress* (1866), with cover design by Dante Gabriel Rossetti. Harry Ransom Center, The University of Texas at Austin.

the home. His designs make the Pre-Raphaelite school a quality brand in the literary market for beautiful books, while simultaneously distinguishing the work of their coterie from mass culture. The Rossetti brand can be seen in his choice to repeat the design for *Poems* of 1870, on future editions and on other books he designed for the family.[26] These books make for what Helsinger refers to as a pull between individual and collective identity within Rossetti's *oeuvre*.[27] Rossetti designed his decorative texts as a collective, representing a harmonious union between likeminded writers and artists who sought to present a common discourse of aesthetics opposed to industrialism and Victorian social conventions.

Design was not used to give the book an individual unity, but to associate it with a family – a brand defined by Rossetti's bibliographic narrative of collective unity, a hetero-beautiful book in opposition to the commercial marketplace. Rossetti's book would not offer consumers an alternative to the cheap books that flooded the market. To be popular and successful as a business proposition, it would take an appeal to the fashionable Victorian middle classes – an ethical compromise to sell Arts and Crafts ideology to the modern Victorian consumer. To understand the business of Arts and Crafts, as well as the beautiful book's revival of medieval arts, we must turn to Morris.

Morris joined Rossetti, as well as Ford Maddox Brown (1821–93), Edward Burne-Jones (1833–98), architect Philip Webb (1831–1915), mathematician Charles Falkner (1832–92) and painter Peter Paul Marshall (1830–1900) to form Morris, Marshall, Faulkner & Co. (M.M.F. & Co) on 11 April 1861, 'a commercial venture whose ultimate purpose was to transform the British public's appreciation of the decorative arts'.[28] This business, however, was not a profitable venture until Morris took what was little more than a hobby for Rossetti and the others and turned it into Morris & Co. in 1875.[29] Morris's larger investment of time and money into the original venture meant that he was financially dependent on the firm, and profit had to take priority. Morris's work with the firm is significant, in part because he takes his ideals regarding material craftsmanship and the Pre-Raphaelite arts to create a brand, a commercial market, and by extension an audience, for beautifully handcrafted goods. Once he found his success and Morris & Co. was profitable, he then developed a project that privileged art over commercialism. Financial security was a necessity to make the beautiful books Morris wanted to make if he were to operate within late Victorian market capitalism. This compromise allowed him to turn from Rossetti's high-art branding towards the improvement of everyday workmanship that was to define his own art. His commercial business tied craftsmanship to the economic system. However, market demand is what defined his success in business and his output as an artisan, paving the way for Morris to establish the Kelmscott Press in 1889.

With the publication of his romance, *The Story of the Glittering Plain* in 1891 (see Fig. 2.6), Morris achieves his bibliographic ideal, later outlined in his essay 'The Ideal Book' (1893). Morris did not intend book design and illustration to outshine literary content. Quite the opposite; he insisted that 'ornament must form as much a part of the page as the type itself, or it will miss its mark, and in order to succeed, and to be ornament, it must submit to certain limitations, and become architectural'.[30] Architecturally, the book consists of its various parts: binding, covers, illustration, ink, text, ornament and type. These elements are intended to merge into a harmonious whole whereby 'a book ornamented with pictures that are suitable for that, and that only, may become a work of art second to none, save a fine building duly decorated, or a fine piece of literature'.[31] Kelmscott books reflected Morris's architectural ideals; his revision of the past became an opportunity to create a demand for beauty and quality workmanship in everyday life.

Morris made use of Kelmscott to publish his fantasy romances, and to republish editions of his earlier works, such as his fictional history of the 1381 Peasant's Revolt, *A Dream of John Ball* (1886) and an eight-volume edition of his narrative poem *The Earthly Paradise* (1868–70), a retelling of ancient Greek and medieval mythic tales. However, he was also interested in publishing literary masterpieces that demonstrated what he saw as English culture at its greatest, including *The Works of Chaucer* (1896) and John Ruskin's essay of art criticism, *The Nature of Gothic, a Chapter from the Stones of Venice* (1892). By reprinting these titles through Kelmscott, Morris placed his own romances in material companionship with Chaucer and Ruskin while also reflecting his intense desire to integrate medieval literature and art into everyday life for his Victorian audience. Instead of compromising his ideals for the market, he created a product whose quality would demand a compromise from the low-cost, high-profits mentality of the Victorian marketplace.

Morris's work consistently argues for the rights of artistic expression for working-class tradespeople and labourers. He called for a return to the gothic style of the middle-ages – a period Morris perceived as an ideal moment in English culture for the development of arts and crafts based on the creative traditions of Anglo-Germanic culture. He noted that books of the Middle Ages were 'thoroughly "Gothic" as to their ornament',[32] a style that emerges, Morris claimed, from a religious society where 'the force of tradition' birthed a 'unity of epical design and ornament'.[33] For Morris, the Gothic represents a united culture without class. He suggests a collective cultural unity in the imagery of the church's architecture and design among the Germanic and Northern peoples of Europe. This aesthetic 'supplied deficiencies of individual by collective

Pomegranate Stains on the Ideal Book

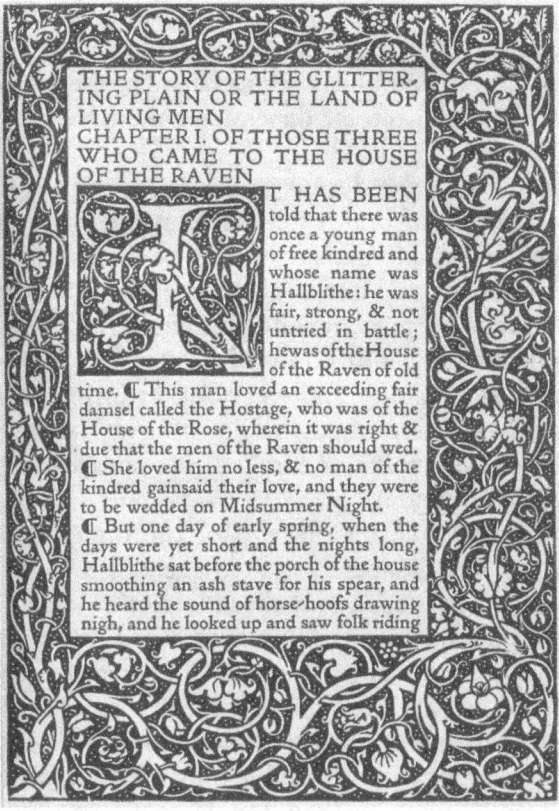

Figure 2.6 Title page with facing first page of chapter 1 from William Morris's Kelmscott edition of *The Story of the Glittering Plain* (1891). Harry Ransom Center, The University of Texas at Austin.

imagination', that according to Morris, 'ensured the inheritance of deft craftsmanship and instinct for beauty in the succession of the generations of workman [and] cultivated the appreciation of good work by the general public'.[34] English art before the Renaissance reflected a unified cultural practice, what he imagined as shared indigeneity or a cultural foundation for the peoples of the British Isles. Instead of changing his art to suit his culture, he uses his art to inspire cultural change for the sake of his Anglo-biased perception of everyday beauty.

Morris communicates these ideas, not just in his writing, but in the material designs of the Kelmscott book. Michelle Weinroth argues that the page in a Kelmscott book disables the purely intellectual eye and frustrates a literal utilitarian mode of reading. This ornamented text both 'agitates' the mind ... and breaks open new grounds for understanding the aesthetic frame as the element that induces three-dimensional thought.[35]

Like the queer book, the design of Kelmscott books informs and changes perceptions of literary content. While his business practices demanded that his artistic vision be necessarily revised to meet the demands of the marketplace, there would be no negotiation with the market in achieving the handcrafted beauty of his books. Significant is the autonomy with which Morris could realise his ideal fantasy of beauty and the book beautiful. Regardless of collaborating partners and regardless of who wrote the literary content, all these elements are rallied to appease the pleasure of Morris's textual imagination.

According to Morris, by the end of the fifteenth century, the influence of the Renaissance sees the degeneration of the work of English artisans. Morris laments that the Gothic art of the middle-ages 'was succeeded by a singularly stupid and brutal phase of that rhetorical and academical art, which, in all matters of ornament, has held Europe captive ever since'.[36] Formal rules set by artists of the Mediterranean and France superseded England's unique culture and limited art to a practice available only to the wealthy and politically connected. Morris sees the Renaissance as an interruption in the collective culture of Britain's Anglo-Germanic heritage.

The Gothic harks back to an idyll of 'collective art' where 'the men who build it up not only give their gift of free will, but give it joyfully day by day, and take as they give, to the extinction of moody pride, to the fostering of goodwill'.[37] In effect, everyone, every man at least, contributes to an artist-socialist collective of 'friends and good fellows'.[38] For Morris, art had to be an expression of social unity, whereas he associates the Renaissance with the values of a hierarchical European aristocracy: the ostentatious glamorisation of wealth held in the hands of the few at the cost of ignorance for the many. Such a system denigrated the artistic efforts of tradesmen and serfs, people Morris anachronistically equated with the nineteenth-century proletariat. Like Karl Marx and Friedrich Engels before him, Morris spoke for the masses without first consulting them.[39]

Not everyone finds beauty in the same ideals; where Morris sees elitism, queer designers like Ricketts and Shannon see niche audiences. We will also see how, even among heterosexual readers, Morris's ideals were only presumed to offer a consensus concept of beauty. This brings me to the second point, that his ideal of unity is in fact imposed through a beautiful, but autocratic practice. In addition, the ideology behind his vision is both nationalist in its rejection of other European cultures and paternal in its presumption of selecting an aesthetic ideal for everyone to embrace.

While the racial and male supremacy of these ideals is recognisable in hindsight, resistance to the singularity of Morris's ideal can also be seen in contemporary reviews of his works. *The Spectator*'s review of the 1893 Arts and Crafts Exhibition shortly after Ford Maddox Brown's death demonstrates mixed critical impressions. Of the Kelmscott books placed on display, the review says that while they demonstrate 'an intelligent experiment by a lover of beautiful books', there is a lack of 'lucidity' of the page 'as a thing to be read'.[40] While the books are declared 'very handsome', possessing 'solidity as a thing printed', the presentation of type and decoration on the page lacks 'the last refinements on which the excellence of type depends' resulting in a 'want of elegance'.[41] Medievalism, it seems, was not everyone's ideal for the improvement of books at the end of the nineteenth century.

Collective, unified culture is a form of heteronormativity that reflects Morris's cultural moment, as much as it informs his art. He did not seek to exclude but saw his work as bringing more people together in a classless homogeneity that erases the divisions of capitalism. Morris's message of an idealised collective culture of arts and crafts was consistent. R. Jayne Hildebrand notes how Morris's work privileges 'collective historical agency and change' over 'alienation and stagnation'.[42] Morris's work at Kelmscott reflected his ideals but also revealed the privileged autonomy required to achieve those ideals. The hands of his collaborators, printers, papermakers or binders were silenced by Morris's desire to realise his vision for collectivity.

Morris effectively presents himself through his books as the Revival of Printing's paterfamilias. Morris saw himself as re-creating Britain's artisan culture, suggesting that the modern artist had to be indoctrinated in his ideals and meet his standards before a real collaboration was possible. Until that day arrived, Morris would make all the decisions.

Morris lamented the loss of quality that came from industrialisation and insisted that the solution lay in the hands of 'handicraftsmen, who are not ignorant of these things like the public, and who have no call to be greedy and isolated like the manufacturers or middlemen'.[43] Without pride in artisanship, the worker was emasculated, silent and useless. Morris questions the servitude of the working classes to industrial institutions of the nineteenth century. He characterises it as a degeneration of masculinity for an entire class of Britons: the working-class tradespeople who make substandard products for their employers. In this sense, Morris's argument demonstrates the influence of sexology's pathological interpretation of femininity and suggests that he wants to empower labouring men to take his lead and claim mastery over their economic and aesthetic futures.[44] James Eli Adams points out that such a model of manhood

> gained wide currency because it attached to the economic power of the entrepreneur the status of a traditional martial ideal and thereby solidified the social authority of what had been at best a fragile norm of manhood under an aristocratic ethos contemptuous of trade.[45]

Morris asks when the artisans of the working class will 'see to this and help to make men of all of us by ... selling goods that we could be proud of both for fair price and fair workmanship'.[46] Although according to Morris, modern factory workers, if they want to recover their manhood and restore the masculinity of the British nation, must challenge the current labour system by changing the way in which they produce goods. However, during his lifetime, he retained control of fount and type design, page layouts, title page design and 'special lettering'.[47] The promise of reclaimed working-class manhood through artisan practices would have to wait until Morris first realised his own.

In his rejection of neoclassical influences, Morris seeks a mythic foundation that can narrate a reinvigoration of English art through a return to its Gothic roots. 'By going back to their true source', Morris argues that 'the arts could once again begin to develop normally and organically'.[48] This meant reinventing the bookmaking process from its beginnings in artisanship. Disappointed by earlier attempts to make *The Earthly Paradise* a beautifully decorated series of books in the 1860s with illustrations by Edward Burne-Jones, Morris saw only limitation in the mechanised bookmaking practices of his contemporaries. There was no economically sound means in the 1860s to reproduce all of the Burne-Jones illustrations that he wanted to include.[49] With Kelmscott Press, Morris could now reimagine the book's peritextual materials: binding, ink, paper and type.

For Morris to rescue the book from the damage done by industrial manufacture in the name of efficiency, he had to make changes at the level of the very cellulose fibres that hold the page together. Cellulose is 'found in nature as the cell walls of plants in the form of minute threads which have certain remarkable properties' and, according to McLean, these 'fibres vary greatly in size, strength and exact nature from plant to plant, and in ease of extraction'.[50] Wood chips, rag made of cotton or linen, straw, bamboo, mulberry bark, nettles and esparto grass have long cellulose fibres that hold the paper's ingredients together once formed into a sheet.[51] The longer the cellulose, the stronger the paper; most vegetable matter, for instance, has cellulose fibre, but much of it is not long enough to support a quality paper. For the Kelmscott book to be worthy of canonical works by Chaucer and Ruskin, the fibrous structure had to withstand the wear and tear of time.

Only newspapers, penny magazines, and other forms of print that had expected short life spans would use 100 per cent wood pulp.[52] Most papermakers dilute quality materials with chemically treated wood pulp to make better quality, low-cost paper for the book trade; however, few of these books survive. These machine-made papers were typically a difficult-to-read grey page for wide circulation at low cost.[53] Many nineteenth-century bookmakers turned to acidic papers made from either mechanical or chemical wood pulp mixed with esparto grass due to increasing demand for books and the rising cost of handmade papers.[54] The Royal Society of Arts complained that the paper used in these books was of poor quality and it was impossible to properly repair it.[55]

Earlier in the century, paper's dominant ingredient was rag, literally cotton and linen rags discarded by members of the public and collected by paper manufacturers from the dust heaps. By the late nineteenth century, only the most expensive papers were pure rag content. Since the financial crisis of the 1820s, paper costs (that is, rag costs) rose due to an increase in market demand that coincided with a decrease in supply.[56] In other words, there were more and more readers as the century progressed and not enough cheap cotton rag to keep up with the growing demand. As a result, experiments sought more efficient (that is, cheaper) sources of paper.

McLean indicates that these cheaper mechanical or chemical pulps were 'the result of grinding de-barked wood logs on a grindstone under a stream of water, which fragments the fibres'.[57] Manufacturers began to rely more frequently on wood pulp mixed in with their rags to make the more expensive rag material spread further over more products. Books became disposable.

Acidification of the low-quality paper has erased most books published for wider markets from the mid- to late nineteenth century in Britain from the surviving archive.[58] While a democratisation of reading occurred with books becoming available to an increasingly wider and economically diverse market, something was lost in quality as suppliers attempted to meet demand. Many could buy affordable reading matter, but few could purchase a beautiful book.

D. C. Coleman points out how, before mechanised papermaking, England, like other countries, saw a rise in paper-making associations which would train individuals for positions as skilled tradespeople, able to command wages as per their guild's rules. However, such organisations were on the wane as early as the 1820s and 1830s. Members with 'Cards of Freedom' numbered 3,000 in 1825 but only 700 by 1874, with only 420 workers at the remaining 19 vat mills in the UK.[59] Skilled vat men earned anywhere from 14s to 30s per week in 1820s Northumberland and Durham, while machine mill labourers as early as the 1840s in Scotland earned in the range of 10s to 18s per week, with children earning even less.[60] Subsistence wages, substandard work conditions and the repetitive efforts of menial labour resulted in an unmotivated and disinterested labour force. Morris understood this market glut of poor-quality cheap books to be the root cause of degraded quality of life for the labouring class.

Kelmscott operated in the wake of this papermaking revolution. Never had so many options existed before, even options without acidic wood pulp. Yet Morris was still unsatisfied. His solution for the Kelmscott book was to buy his supplies only from producers of handmade paper. He found his ideal supplier in Joseph Batchelor & Son in 1890 whom he contracted to make the paper for *The Story of the Glittering Plain*. Morris had the paper used in Kelmscott books made entirely of linen, based on a fifteenth-century pattern from northern Italy taken from Morris's sample of Bolognese paper dated to 1473 (see Fig. 2.7). Morris's insistence on linen suggests a return to old methods of bookmaking that stressed quality over efficiency. But his choice also dilutes his Anglo-Germanic vision of the book as an English art form, selecting materials and imbuing his nationalist vision with cosmopolitan craftsmanship. Pure rag was the only option for Morris who sought, anachronistically, to abide by the standards and practices of medieval artisan culture.[61] Batchelor & Son became the sole paper supplier for the Kelmscott Press;[62] they would later go on to design three watermarks exclusively for Kelmscott books: 'Primrose' or 'Flower', 'Perch' and 'Apple', marking the page as a Kelmscott creation and erasing any visible sign of their contribution to what was now positioned as *Morris's* handmade paper.[63] Morris is a paratextual presence: every part of the book is his vision, an artificial harmony that appears to be the natural product of his vision.

While Morris does not directly control the means of production, relying on secondary suppliers, he manages to narrate a story of quality and design with Kelmscott's material assembly. With his handmade paper secured, Morris arranged for Henry Baud of Brentford, Middlesex to produce his vellum editions and Jaenecke of Hanover to produce his ink. Once again, while Morris would have preferred to work with only English suppliers, the quality of his ink, and the use of linseed oil in its making, were more important to him than its national origin.[64] Again, it is the *appearance*

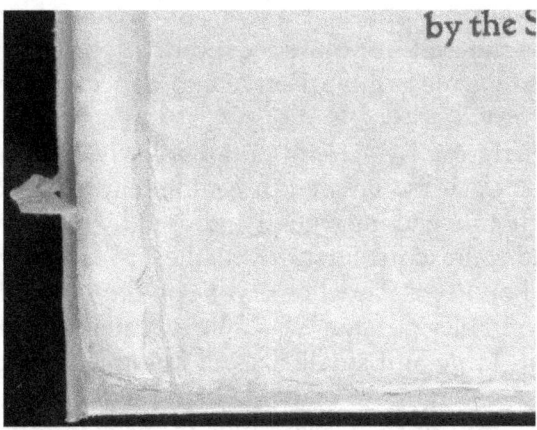

Figure 2.7 Example of the paper used in Kelmscott books. Note the edges where the density is visible. Kelmscott edition of *The Story of the Glittering Plain*. Harry Ransom Center, The University of Texas at Austin.

of Britain's natural supremacy in the arts of crafts that matters. Morris's compromise makes his ideal book a commemoration of medieval English books expressed in a material purity, and untainted by the degenerate practices of modern publishing. He does not allow, for example, chemical treatments for removing oils from inks. Instead, he insisted on the use of stale bread and raw onions to remove grease in the ink's production. The product then had to be 'matured' for 'six months, after which the organic animal lampblack was ground into the mixture'.[65]

The page, densely stamped with his golden type and designs that smothered the white page with dark black ink, leaves no space for the reader's marginalia. The page is so elaborate that one fears damaging its unified effect by scrawling in the margins. The margin, as I argue regarding *Silverpoints* in Chapter 1, plays an important role in reading; it allows room for pencilled notes so that readers can remember their interpretations of themes and metaphors. With chapter and book openings, Morris fills every crevice with a large typeface, surrounded by intricately designed foliage. Throughout the body of the story, he offers marginal paratext in red ink, and more foliage: Morris's hand fills the margins. White space, spaces where there is room for disagreement, are filled with the dark and strong voice of Kelmscott's black and red inks imposing an interpretation onto the reader. His decorative margins silence the reader's opportunity for lexical intervention, making the book a homily or spiritual speech from the self-appointed captain of bibliographic craft where the reader may only observe and concede to his vision of cultural identity.

The very lettering of a Kelmscott book visually interprets the literary content. Morris created three different founts of type, that is, type design punched into metal and used by his printers at both Chiswick and Kelmscott. First, it was the Troy and Chaucer types that he based on Peter Schoeffer's work on the Mainz Bible (1462) because its 'simpler' design was more readable.[66] Respectively these were his large and small sizes of a gothic 'black letter' type that Morris felt were more readable than the Roman types typical since the invention of the Caslon type in the eighteenth century.[67] He then improved on these types with his Golden type in 1891, which is what he used in most of the Kelmscott books.[68]

Chiswick Press was the initial choice for Kelmscott printing needs before Morris's purchase of an Albion hand press in

January 1891.[69] Chiswick was also the choice printer for Morris's trustees after his death. Chiswick's accounting ledgers provide evidence of Morris's hand and the costs incurred due to the quality of paper he required for his works. For example, Chiswick ledgers show that they charged Morris £16.2.6 in 1890 to print seventy-five paper and three vellum copies of *The Story of Gunnlaug*.[70] Such large costs for a limited print run suggest that Morris's ideas were potentially marketable. As a means of comparison, for Leonard Smithers anonymously published edition of Oscar Wilde's *Ballad of Reading Gaol*, Chiswick Press charged £12.8.3 for an initial run of 430 copies (thirty printed on Japanese vellum, the remainder on Chiswick's own handmade paper), and £11.8.6 for an additional reprint on 8 February, only days after the first print run. The third printing of *Reading Gaol* cost another £12.19.0.[71] These costs, considering the material differences and the nature of the work (popular ballad poetry versus academic lecture series), indicate that the investment in material production was worthwhile, due in part to high expectations for a return on investment from the collector's market for Morris's works, previously established with Morris & Co.

Covers and bindings were not a decorative priority for Morris because the reading experience is at the heart of his work. He emphasised the decorative interior: the page and the literary content as the focus of all beauty and artisanal skill. Paul Thompson notes Morris's complete lack of interest in binding, choosing either vellum or grey-papered millboard. Neither were practical with the first awkward to hold while reading and margins too wide for the millboard to be replaced with a fine leather binding.[72] That meant that the reader was supposed to retain the book as it is. The focus is on the beauty of the content, the book's inner beauty, with a humble exterior that reflects the working classes who, to be clear, could not afford to purchase a Kelmscott book. This was humility that appears natural, performed for the middle-class collector. Without decorative bindings, the Kelmscott book is best displayed on a book pedestal putting it in material competition with family Bibles and dictionaries for display space. Morris's use of limp vellum to bind Kelmscott books gives them a distinctive appearance but these books were not jewel boxes to appreciate on display on a shelf. His goal, according to Peterson at least, was physical comfort for the reader, not promotion in the shops.[73]

Archived copies of *The Earthly Paradise* republished by Kelmscott are good examples of Morris's vision where the material book and the literary text stand in harmonious unity. Today, these volumes are dirty and worn from usage; the ribbons that held the books closed have browned and become rough over time. The vellum, while stiff from time (less used copies are cleaner, softer and more flexible), is thin. The vellum is the substantive material of the binding without any card or wood boards to make the cover firm. The reader is directed by the design to forget about the covers once they open the book because the soft vellum curves to the shape of the pages being read, allowing the book to sit open. Conceivably, the reader could even curl back the pages and cover on either side as readers do with modern trade paperbacks (a supposition best left untested in the confines of the British Library or the Harry Ransom Center).

Where William Morris had to revise his ideals for Morris and Company to remain a successful business in the Victorian economy, the Kelmscott Press was one project where he would not bend to anyone else's needs. For Kelmscott, Morris asked that consumers revise their conception of beauty and pay for the quality craftsmanship he offered. Papermakers, ink manufacturers and printers would have to change their modern methods if they wanted to help Morris make his beautiful books. This model was the only way for Morris to achieve his aesthetic ideals. Charles Harvey and Jon Press stress that Morris's 'personality so dominated the enterprise that his executors decided that it should close on completion of the work in hand when he died'.[74] Morris's vision is not necessarily authoritarian, but it is paternal in its heteronormative and realist conceptions of truth and beauty in book history. In that sense, Morris's vision of the beautiful book is decidedly Victorian in its espousal of historical precedent in the medieval as a model for middle-class aesthetic virtue. As will be examined in the next section, it is the ideal book's demand for consensus regarding what is beautiful that the queer book rejects in favour of alternatives made possible by technological and cultural change.

Queer relationality in *A House of Pomegranates*

While the beauty of a Kelmscott book emerges from respect for traditional bookmaking practices, the beautiful queer book represents a compromised space where traditional artisanship and technological innovation collide to create or imagine something new. Compare the uniformity seen in Kelmscott books with the multiplicity of visual strategies found in Charles Ricketts's and Charles Shannon's designs for *A House of Pomegranates*. Nicholas Frankel argues that the book's design was connected to the literary narrative resulting in 'a merger of printed word and visual icon' that went far beyond the illustrated books noted earlier.[75] Decoration becomes a vibrant part of the book's aesthetic discourse. The material book, as a collaboratively created space juxtaposes the heteronormative space of a children's book with a queer space for dissident sexual discourse. These contesting presentations of the fairy story are interconnected because both children and queer readers are marginalised from the discourse of heteronormative adulthood. For children, the book is an imaginative collection of cautionary moral tales for impressionable young minds. For queer readers, it retains its childlike imagination, but also addresses the ugly consequences imposed upon expressions of queer sexual desire in heteronormative convention: misunderstanding, marginalisation, ostracisation and death. Just as the queer individual must adapt to the demands of a dual life balanced between visible conformity and coded dissidence for the sake of a Victorian moral ethos, so too must the queer book. *A House of Pomegranates* is a site of collective contestation where Wilde, Ricketts and Shannon queer the material space of Morris's ideal book by merging his ideas with the advantages and limits of modern bookmaking technology. Just as a queer reader was required to embody a dual life, so too was the queer book.

Published by James R. Osgood McIlvaine & Co., with a run of only one thousand copies and priced at a guinea, *House of Pomegranates* was not specifically aimed at a children's market. Wilde himself argued this point in a letter to the editor of the *Pall Mall Gazette* in response to the paper's negative review of the book on 30 November 1891, where he insists that he 'has about as much intention of pleasing the British child as I had of pleasing the British public'.[76] If anything, Wilde targeted adults, specifically the 'connoisseur collector', a consumer that emerged in the late nineteenth century, who paid high prices for material quality in literary production.[77] The opposite of a mass commodity, these books were, at best, modestly successful and marketed to maximise profit from small sales in the hundreds and occasionally in the thousands in the case of rare commercial successes like the aesthetic periodical, *The Yellow Book* (1894–7).[78] These books were the symbolic objects of a subcultural community of primarily Londoners, often male, and often queer, with a shared interest in unique aesthetic examples of beautiful bookmaking, literary prose and heterogeneous textual intercourse. While honouring Morris's art of constructing the beautiful page, Ricketts, who along with Shannon, was hired by the publisher to design *Pomegranates*, introduced designs, inspired by Wilde's tales, that destabilise the centrality of the book's literary content.

American photographer and entrepreneur Fred Holland Day (1864–1933), co-founder of Copeland and Day who would later publish Wilde's Symbolist drama *Salome* (1894) and the era-defining quarterly periodical *The Yellow Book* (1894–7) for distribution in the United States, gave the book a positive review that supports the book's queer cultural status. In Day's review of the book, this confirmed bachelor, and presumed homosexual, tells his readers that the book is a collectable work of bibliographic dissidence, 'a volume so unusual in appearance' that it was intended for a specialised audience who 'will doubtless comprehend the subtlety with which its name was chosen'.[79] Day speaks to the book's unspeakable eroticism and recognises its potentially subversive message, not just for its 'specimens of the most forcible and picturesque prose ever given by its author' but for its unique beauty as a 'square octavo ... printed throughout on heavy, rich toned, plate paper, by the Chiswick Press'. Ricketts and Shannon's ornamentation also contribute to 'making the volume a notable target for men who have stationed themselves outside the bastions of Materialism, to leave unmentioned the multitudes within'.[80] Day suggests a niche, or even cult audience, of men who see the world in the manner of Wilde. It positions the book's design quality as neither good nor bad, but different and suited to particular tastes outside the conventions of 'Materialism', used here as a reference to the commercial literary market. By extension, the book lays outside the realm of the heteronormative, middle-class reader, outside of the conventions of family entertainment, and enters a world of men who have 'stationed themselves outside'. *House of Pomegranates* exists in the margins of the literary marketplace, a queer space, transformed by the textual intercourse of Wilde, Ricketts and Shannon.

Michelle Ruggaber supports Day's assessment, arguing that *A House of Pomegranates* is written to engage adult readers with dark and complex stories beyond a child's full comprehension.[81] Because the stories end with death and a melancholic outlook on the world, the reader's pleasure is evoked by the tragic beauty of their symbolism, for both children and queer readers. *A House of Pomegranates* offers the queer reader what Donald E. Hall refers to in his study of sexual hermeneutics as a 'sense of critically and self-consciously imagined agency' and 'an alternative to the facile forms of agency' found in mainstream culture.[82] Hall, who references mainstream queer culture in the twenty-first century here, speaks to the sort of public space necessary for queer individuals to create and develop a sense of identity, a profound message for the queer reader of every age.

At the same time, it must be remembered that the late Victorian fairy tale was a site for social, cultural and political inquiry for many authors and artists. Lorraine Janzen Kooistra notes that fairy tales like *A House of Pomegranates* were adapted by innovative authors seeking to imagine alternatives to the reality of Victorian culture's inequities.[83] In the case of Wilde's tales, readers may experience a marginalised point of view as an othered figure challenges their tenuous relationships to the wider world.[84] Wilde's stories hold many meanings for many readers. Those interpretations depend upon the point of view that the reader brings to the intercourse, including queer concerns regarding transgression and homoerotic symbolism.

Looking to the past, Morris sought to rebirth the ideals and cultural values he associated with medieval culture. Morris's socialist ideals and appreciation of the beautiful inspire his monologic model of textual harmony – a chivalric code of cultural and bibliographical myth lacking in an industrialised society and in the bookmaking industry. Many aesthetes, including Pater, Wilde and Ricketts, appreciated his work and his ideals. Ricketts wrote about the 'great debt owed by book lovers to the late William Morris for motives in decoration (such as the half-borders) that to [Ricketts's] knowledge are not to be found in old printed books, and for which he was indebted (if at all) to the great periods of decoration and illumination'.[85] Ricketts's essay, published three years after Morris's death, interprets Morris in a manner that contradicts Morris's bibliographic self-portrait. Ricketts says that it has always seemed odd to me, that while the man of past ages provides the utmost conditions of beauty or elaboration for such books in his possession, ... today, with the accumulation of literature, no thought whatever should be spent upon the shaping of work inconceivably more stimulating and precious to us than those illuminated books of piety or admonition upon which so much beauty had nevertheless been bestowed.[86]

Books can improve in their beauty and quality and not just by returning to medieval practices, but by creating something *more stimulating*. For Ricketts, new artisans could create new forms, rather the preserve or restore old ones.

A *House of Pomegranates* is an assemblage of stories. Together, they reveal a complex and subversive approach to the fairy tale, what Anne Markey calls Wilde's 'unsettling, original approach to ostensibly familiar material'.[87] Two of the four stories had been previously published in the periodical press. 'The Young King' originally appeared in the Christmas 1888 edition of *The Lady's Pictorial*, suggesting a middle-class female audience for his work. 'The Birthday of the Infanta' was originally published in a French translation for *Paris Ilustré* in 1889, suggesting a cosmopolitan reading audience due to the periodical's incorporation of news, art criticism and society gossip.[88] These diverse publications suggest diverse audiences for Wilde's fairy tales. 'The Fisherman and his Soul' was written but, as yet, unpublished.[89] The only new story written for this publication was 'The Star Child'.[90] These tales were not envisioned as a single work, but are an assemblage, or selection of Wilde's efforts in the genre. The book, however, transforms them from tales into visual compelling aesthetic statements, existing as such for this edition alone.

Wilde dedicates the book to his wife, Constance Mary Wilde, and while that seems a natural choice for a children's book, the imagery of the book with erotic nudes of men and women scattered through the book, suggests she serves a material purpose as well: to balance the volume's queer sexuality and themes of difference and death with the genre expectations of mothers, family and heteronormativity. The book is almost square measuring 8.5" in length, and 7.5" in width, with a thickness of one inch, due to using a heavy super-calendared art paper that gives the volume weight and density atypical of children's books. The front board is decorated while the back is blank. The green-cloth spine contrasts with the cream and red cloth and gold impressing. It is a bright and colourful object, like many children's books, but the imagery on the front is that of peacocks and pomegranates – symbols of decadent mythologies and desires. The lettering makes it almost personal with the title and author name drawn to appear handwritten, offering the reader an intimate invitation to enter this garden of forbidden fruit.

Even more strange, interleaved between the stories are four faded and uncanny illustrations prepared by Charles Shannon. Markey tells us that Shannon had the drawings printed in Paris using a new process that damaged the images, leaving Shannon's work disfigured and 'barely visible' (see Fig. 2.9).[91] While accidental, the fading speaks to an important textual reality of the book. The images are shadows of an original where the reader can make out faint traces of scenes from the stories. Their faintness does not capture these moments in full detail. Details are left to the reader's imagination. The faintness of the illustrations suggests that Shannon's images are bibliographically out of context and that makes them compelling in *A House of Pomegranates* – images from another medium, imposed on children's book but refusing a clear interpretation within the context of that genre. His work has been adapted by Ricketts to a different medium, creating new, spectral images that haunt the stories with the presence of something, incomplete, unseen and perhaps unspoken to each story as they appear. While completely inadvertent on Shannon's part, the plates are unfinished and waiting for the reader to imagine their full meaning and creative potential.

Josephine Guy and Ian Small comment on the failure of the designs for this book.[92] This failure, they claim, is largely due to Shannon's contribution of plates at the beginning of each story. Critics at the time were also very hard on the bookmakers for this error. No one actually details what this error and new printing method are, but it was likely an issue with the level of resin and heat applied when the book was printed.[93] Despite their flaws, Shannon's drawings are still included in the book. Either Ricketts or the publisher must have decided that they would still enhance or speak to the text in some manner. While these faded images are unintended, they are beautiful symbols that heighten a sense of two stories emerging within the book, one image of childhood innocence, and a second queer image, spoken, yet visibly obscured from the normative reader.

Unlike Morris who demanded small runs to accommodate handmade products, aesthetic bookmakers like Ricketts and Shannon embraced the new technologies used by mass-produced books, changing perceptions of those industrial mechanics from the cheap vulgarity that Morris saw, into an employable medium improved upon by the interference of an artistic hand.

Industrialisation did not limit aestheticism's decorated books to what was handmade; instead, mechanised processes such as photomechanical illustration created possibilities to use the book's material construction for artistic invention. By allowing their medium to inform their methods, these innovative young designers allowed art and industry to collide to create material experiments in bibliographic design.

The book draws attention to an obscure code of queer sexual discourse, available to critics today, but not many members of the 1890s reading public. Queer readers, like other readers, seek themselves in books so only they would seek out the interpretations made available in this text. The desire to represent queer experience means that it is important to also consider the influence that the designers' and author's queer lives may have had on their approach to the interaction between visual and literary art. That dissent is found in the contradictory styles of illustration that Shannon and Ricketts bring to *House of Pomegranates*. For one thing, despite being partners – lovers who lived and worked together – they had very different visual styles, seemingly separating their artistic visions. I would argue that their preferred mediums and the innovations in each field explain the contrasts created in the book. Shannon was a painter of portraits and landscapes, and also a sketch artist, in addition to his book design work. In those works, his imagery focuses on the presentation of light. Take, for example, his sketch, 'The Wounded Amazon', as published in *The Pageant* (1897) (see Fig. 2.8). The image focuses on the sunlight falling on the figure's skin, white robes and leg armour. Her face is shadowed as is the greenery. These shadowed areas are out of focus, much like an impressionist's point of view, giving focus to the areas where the light falls. In addition, her body is painted in a realist fashion. She does not have stark lines defining her edges.

Of course, Shannon's contributions were not the only elements to come under fire. Critics were equally hard on Ricketts's binding designs, but these criticisms suggest an expectation of a book that

Figure 2.8 'The Wounded Amazon' by Charles Shannon from *The Pageant* (1897). Private collection.

would attract children. One critic went so far as to characterise the book as 'Swinburnian' – referencing the book's eroticism.[94] A book covered in pomegranates and written by Oscar Wilde potentially alerts the knowledgeable consumer of aesthetic literature that this was a book worth considering. Like Persephone, the aesthetic reader, particularly a queer aesthete, would be tempted to taste its fruit, a temptation symbolising the queer discourses of identity, beauty, desire and difference – the key elements of aestheticism's sexual discourse.

Ricketts read Morris's ideal book as a subjective reading of beauty, crediting Morris's 'ornamental tendency' for his own work, and suggesting that while the gothic beauty and artisanship of the fifteenth century may have inspired him, he also wanted to create something different.[95] Morris believed he was reviving an old, lost art whereas Ricketts saw that by subverting conventions of artisanship and queering the medieval tradition of the hand-crafted book, something new emerged. Through a textual and literary analysis of the volume's four fairy tales, it is possible to see how past practices allow for imagining new futures.

'The Young King'

The specific presentation of 'The Young King' from *House of Pomegranates* demonstrates how contesting visions of queerness can result in new textual meaning. *The Spectator*'s 1892 review of the volume makes no mention of the book's design or aesthetic, but declares that 'The Young King', the 'first of Mr. Oscar Wilde's allegories or parables, or whatever he may call them, is admirable'.[96] What is telling, however, is that the book is reviewed amidst a series of newly released books, aimed at adult readers such as *The Oxford Shakespeare* in six volumes and Arthur B. and Henry Farhquar's *Economic and Industrial Fallacies*. Certainly, a child would not be reading book reviews, but a mother might; the ad's placement in *The Spectator*, however, suggests that this review is aimed at an educated and primarily male reading audience, placing Wilde's work in the realm of intellectually challenging literature. This placement is emphasised by the reviewer's declaration that 'Mr. Wilde writes, as usual, in a highly ornate style, often beautiful, but somewhat fatiguing.'[97] The story involves a beautiful youth of sixteen who is recognised in his role as a monarch only by the beautiful raiment of the institution: his crown, sceptre and cloak. However, dreams haunt the beautiful boy king and reveal to him the origins of his material symbols of authority representing the ugliness of his tyrannical power: slavery, war, death and subjugation. The beautiful young monarch cannot bring himself to wear these symbols of power to his coronation. At the ceremony, he instead wears the robes of a peasant farmer, appearing as if he is not worthy of the crown he is to receive. The crowds and courtesans do not recognise God in the natural artifacts the king wears. Even the Bishop calls the king's humble Christ-like apparel an 'abasement'.[98] Everyone rebels.

Just as 'The Young King' attends to the concerns of childhood edification and queer sexuality, so it attends to the contradictory relationship between natural and artificial beauty. The book presents youth's sexuality as innocent and gender subversive in the figure of a beautiful bathing non-binary youth (see Fig. 2.9).

Figure 2.9 Image of Wilde's Young King as interpreted by Ricketts on the first page of the story. Courtesy of the Rufus Hawtin Hathaway Collection, Identification #991026002159705163, Archives and Special Collections, Western Libraries, Western University.

His beauty is further complicated by his disavowal of regulatory notions of sex as a function of the ideological apparatus of marriage, reproductive sex and power as masculine mastery over others through brute force. The young king's beauty is not the timeless beauty of inherited objects, but the peculiar, or queer, beauty of the boy, revealed to his kingdom only for a brief Paterean moment. Artificial beauty is born of his protection from influences of the outside world, allowing him to retain the innocence, simplicity, androgyny and finery of a child into his coming of age, despite the corruption that fills his court.

Part of the problem is a contested image of the king: that of the masses and that of the isolated boy king. Kings for the population are finely attired and surrounded by ostentatious rituals and ceremonies. The physical artifacts that a population conventionally associate with kingship are what strangely allow the privilege of a king to be perceived as natural. The story then draws self-conscious attention to the artificiality of his decorative gilt, emphasising that the political and monarchical institutions that take on a role within everyday society are themselves artificial structures, or so much gilt, mistaken by the masses for natural occurrence.

The young man associates his kingship with a religious epiphany that shocks and frightens the peasantry. Nature unnaturally appears to deem him worthy of kingship. When the young king turns around to face his people a ray of light shines through the stained glass of the church to reveal his superior beauty. His natural robes become beautiful, his 'dead staff blossomed', anointing the king with the materialisation of lilies, roses with stems of silver and leaves of beaten gold.[99] Even here, while anointed by God, the young king's transformation is unnatural, artificially decorated with precious metals and supernatural lighting. The beautiful young king's symbols of natural beauty are themselves transformed or improved upon by God so that his authority can be recognised by the peasantry. The image is a miraculous satire of the artificial ceremonial garb that the peasantry expected in the first place. Audiences acknowledge the artificial as a sign of an institution or authority figure's natural right to power. They know it is unreal and seek it anyway because ritual and ceremonial beauty suggest truth through familiarity even when truth is nowhere to be found.

The king's beauty is queer because of the ways that Ricketts and Wilde present his gender ambiguity as a desirable form. The book's aesthetic beauty is intertwined with the young king's body, defined by an *eros* associated with a beautiful innocent youth, whose body distorts 'regulatory schemas' of sex, gender, sensuality and beauty.[100] Ricketts's drawings and binding design only appear in this edition imbuing the young king's innocence with an expression of dissident desire. What was, on the surface, a children's book, was, since its release in 1891, criticised for the 'fleshly' style of Mr. Wilde's writing (a not-so-subtle reference to Robert Buchanan's criticism of the Pre-Raphaelite Brotherhood, and specifically the work of Dante Gabriel Rossetti, as the fleshly school of poetry) and 'the ultra-aestheticism of the pictures' seemed 'hardly suitable to children'.[101]

The king first appears to be within nature because of the rock formation under the waterfall filling his bath. However, the young king is indoors, enclosed within a building as depicted by the window he foregrounds. The flora and fauna are not nature, but an artistic arrangement, an improvement upon nature. Protected from the harsh realities of his kingdom by his beautiful walls, the king is not aware at this point of the harm that his beautiful life produces. The boy is also nude, asking the reader to sexualise and aestheticise the beauty of the youth's non-binary body. The violin in the background and the female sculptures where the water emerges suggest music and a chorus that sings and celebrates the beauty of the boy groomed as the symbol of leadership. His artificially cultivated innocence is celebrated in this scene as an ideal from which to rule. The eroticism of the image emphasises the king's innocence of the ways of the world will provide him with a means to resist the corrupt pleasures of his court.

Ricketts designed medallions that interact with Wilde's stories and appear in various places throughout in the side, top and bottom margins without any apparent pattern. This choice is an important example of the queer book's material narration of story and meaning. Their unpredictability makes them more startling, especially in 'The Young King' where the medallions depict strange faces alerting the reader to an unspoken secret: bug-eyed faces with their index fingers held to their mouth asking for the reader's silence regarding the contents of the book (see Fig. 2.10). The reader is asked to interact with the story and appreciate the aesthetics of Wilde's writing. The medallions extend the sense of unspoken desire – perhaps even a desire for which there are no words, only images – for the beautiful king throughout the story and they stop only when his beauty is revealed to the masses.

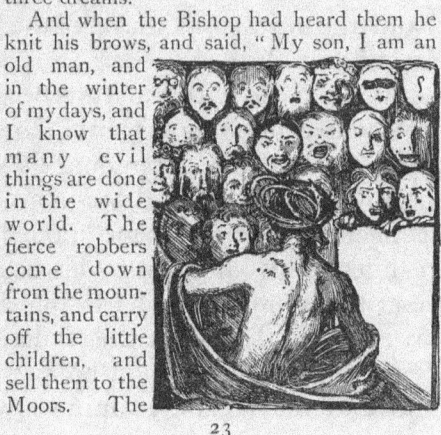

Figure 2.10 An example of the medallion's urging the reader to remain silent in the face of an open secret. Courtesy of the Rufus Hawtin Hathaway Collection, Identification #991026002159705163, Archives and Special Collections, Western Libraries, Western University.

The medallions also suggest that there is a secret to be exposed if the reader chooses to look. The queer beauty of the boy's secret is briefly exposed to the crowds, but they are too afraid to look. He becomes the beauty of God and 'the saints in their carven niches seemed to move. In their fair raiment of a king, he stood before them, and the organ pealed out its music, and the trumpeters blew upon their trumpets, and the singing boys sang.'[102] God's touch here is another artificial aesthetic, to make the youth's beauty queer beauty, rejected in its natural form, acceptable to a heteronormative world through Wilde's vision of 'roses redder than rubies' and lilies '[w]hiter than pearls'.[103] His beauty, however, remains dangerous because 'no man dared look upon his face, for it was like the face of an angel'.[104] The suggestion is that while the majority will look away or not see his desirability, a queer reader will understand and appreciate his beauty.

Ricketts never draws this moment of beauty's reveal. Instead, Wilde paints his portrait using his method of prose poetry. The repetitive refrain of the robe in a single sentence gives the impression that the speaker is caressing the king's raiment. The unnatural hues of white, red and gold reveal an unnatural amplification of nature's beauty. God, like the queer reader, sees the unacceptable beauty of the young king and creates an artificial revelation so that others respond to their fears with reverence, rather than violence. Ricketts's illustration draws our attention instead to the public who gaze upon the boy's queer beauty. Ricketts offers the reader an opportunity to view the boy's back and to see parts of the king hidden from the crowd.

Ricketts's designs arrest an erotic moment of queer beauty in the form of the beautiful and innocent young man who frightens those who expect convention and tradition in the depiction of beauty. What Ricketts draws instead is a society arrested by the young king's beautiful difference (see Fig. 2.11). His beauty is not fully appreciated by the heteronormative reader, so Ricketts mimics the act of Wilde's god and creates an artificial filter that both reveals and obscures the young king's queer beauty.

'The Birthday of the Infanta'

'The Birthday of the Infanta', in which the laughter of a precocious child and heiress to the Spanish Empire motivates the court clown – who now sees himself as others see him – to commit suicide, does not suggest a brightly coloured and vibrant image of conventional Victorian childhood. She is a symbol of Catholic decadence for a Protestant readership who may view both her and the Dwarf as alien to their vision of beauty. Outside of the girl's garden of artificial pleasures is a cruel natural world that rejects her Dwarf's appearance where even 'some of the violets themselves felt that the ugliness of the little dwarf was almost ostentatious and that he would have shown much better taste if he had looked sad, or at least pensive, instead of jumping about merrily, and throwing himself into such grotesque and silly attitudes'.[105] Nature and the Dwarf's privileging of what he perceives as natural

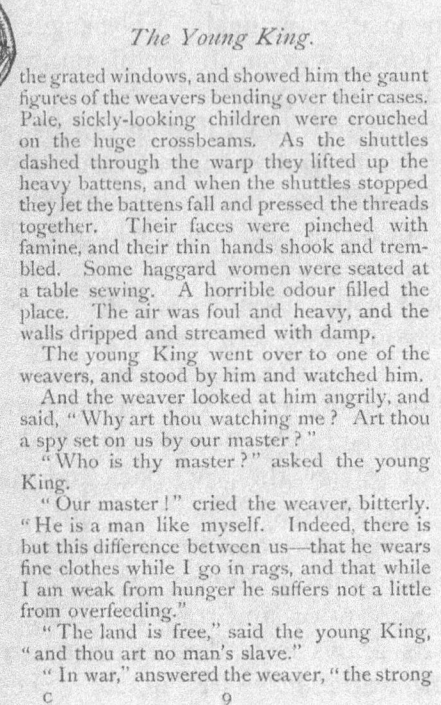

Figure 2.11 The reaction of the mass public to the King's beauty. Courtesy of the Rufus Hawtin Hathaway Collection, Identification #991026002159705163, Archives and Special Collections, Western Libraries, Western University.

beauty and ugliness destroys his colour and cheer, but Shannon's image complicates this vision, obscuring our ability to judge the appearance of either him or the Infanta. Just as the image requires the reader to pause, the portrayal of beauty in this edition of the story also requires a moment's consideration.

The key to understanding the story's decadent inversion of beauty is the imagery and theme of puppetry at the beginning of the tale. Ricketts's image presents the Infanta's experience of the court as a theatre. Those who are brought to entertain her are not people, but puppets, who exist only to bring her pleasure. For her, the dwarf is not different. She believes him to be artificial as anything else given to her. She has no reason to suspect anything different. Her court is about aesthetic pleasure. Even the ugliness of the dwarf is meant to amuse, so she does not see him as ugly in the same way that readers are taught the term. When she and her friends discover him in hysterics after realising that his appearance makes him something he does not want to be, an ugly amusement, she believes him to be 'acting'.[106] She does not understand his broken heart because puppets are meant to amuse her. Where he seeks to be desirable as an object of beauty the way he desires the Infanta, the Infanta seeks art in pursuit of pleasure. The Infanta cries at the end, grieving the loss of her beautiful object. Because she is only ever presented with artificial beings in artificial settings, she is incapable of understanding that her appreciation of his grotesque aesthetic would hurt the man. What society saw as horror, she saw as a delightful Art. The imaginary, for the Infanta, is preferable to the tragedy of natural deformity.

    The dwarf's sense of self, prior to the Infanta's impression suggests that he represents a form of decadent or queer beauty, a beauty that some can see, as the Infanta does when he dances, but a beauty that most others will not see, even if those others include ourselves. Justin T. Jones notes that the Dwarf existence in the Infanta's beautiful garden threatens the aesthetics of the space.[107] The Dwarf sees what others see in the mirror, losing the ability to conceive himself outside of aesthetic norms.[108] He does not appreciate his beauty, because he sees himself in comparison to the beautiful Infanta and he does not live up to that conventional form of beauty. His courtly self-image is made ridiculous to himself, and he cannot bear his reality. That reality is not pictured in Shannon's drawing (see Fig. 2.12). Instead, it is images of the Infanta and her birthday guests. The Infanta and her guests gaze upon a seemingly robed figure covered in peacock feathers. This may be the Dwarf, but his ugliness is hidden from view. Instead, we see the Infanta's gaze and that of her guests. Their faces are obscure, so it is difficult to determine if they are ugly or beautiful. Instead, they are representative iconography for the observation of normative desire and conventional beauty idealised by the Dwarf. He can only celebrate his own beauty when his body remains invisible. To that end, his beauty is retained by Shannon through a lack of portraying the ugliness that breaks the Dwarf's heart.

    While the children take pleasure in his ugliness, Wilde's conception of the Dwarf as beautiful speaks, not simply to the man's

Figure 2.12 Charles Shannon's drawing for 'The Birthday of the Infanta' by Oscar Wilde. Courtesy of the Rufus Hawtin Hathaway Collection, Identification #991026002159705163, Archives and Special Collections, Western Libraries, Western University.

spirit or outlook, but to the complex and diverse forms in which beauty can be revealed. Wilde sees its beauty because of his trained aesthetic eye, and he seeks to pass on the realisation of this beauty by stimulating the reader's sympathies and heightening the sense of the man's shame. Wilde's appreciation of the beautiful in the ugly is reflected in his portrayal of the Infanta who is devasted by the loss of her Dwarf. The Infanta has discovered that the world does not exist to amuse her. What she found amusing destroys the Dwarf's sense of self. Her pleasure was not

Figure 2.13 Rickett's interpretation of the Fisherman and his Soul in conversation after they separated. Courtesy of the Rufus Hawtin Hathaway Collection, Identification #991026002159705163, Archives and Special Collections, Western Libraries, Western University.

something that scared or insulted her. She took pleasure in his performances for her. He was ugly to her, but her decadent point of view allowed her to see a queer beauty in that ugliness. She appreciated it and wanted it in her collection of sensory pleasures. The Dwarf's appearance was not being cruelly ridiculed because she did not know he would be hurt by being ugly. She has no precedent to guide her to such a consideration.

Ricketts's illustrations give insight into the story's approach to beauty with his image of the puppets, but also with the medallions. Ricketts creates two different medallions for the story's margins, suggesting a before and after. Before, it is the beauty of the fountain, after, it is a heart broken by a rose's thorns. He positions the garden as a paradise, at first an Edenic garden that the Infanta enjoys represented by a repetition of the fountain from the book's cover. Its artificial innocence is lost because of the interference of nature, staining paradise with the heart's blood as both the Dwarf's and the Infanta's fantasies die. Ricketts also provides a sympathetic image of the dwarf on page 45, hidden in the shadows of the gardens, unaware of nature's ridicule of his appearance. We never actually see the Dwarf in full and that suggests that Ricketts and Shannon sought to alter our perception of his appearance. They support a more complex reading of the Infanta's appreciation of his ugliness as a form of grotesque beauty. Shannon's faded plate, while not matching the bright colour of Wilde's prose, certainly comments on the faded and inappropriate vision of beauty that the Infanta and her little friends represent, causing the death of the Dwarf. To picture him as ugly, when his spirit is so beautiful, is also inappropriate. Their physical appearances are all muted in the sun of the garden and hidden from the reader's judgement, lest we too misjudge either the Dwarf or the Infanta. Shannon erases from view the cruel words of the Infanta's world, distorting the reader's ability to confirm her beauty. There is room in Shannon's drawing for the Infanta to be as ugly as she perceives the Dwarf to be.

Exactly what is beauty's standard should remain unclear and undefined, creating a slippage between the binaries of beautiful and ugly that the Infanta establishes. The book's various ways in which to see and not see the Dwarf suggests a queer conception of aesthetic appreciation safe in an innocent garden where laughter is only unintentionally cruel but threatened by conceptions of natural beauty that dominate late Victorian society. Imagery by Shannon and Ricketts transforms the story into a broader allegorical condemnation of a society that destroys beauty it cannot easily recognise.

'The Fisherman and His Soul'

In his discussion of 'The Fisherman and His Soul', Frankel notes that Ricketts's 'decorative elements of the page violate all the usual conventions governing the placement of type and illustrations'. He goes so far as to call the bibliographic design an act of 'typographic violence' and 'graphic derangement' that mirrors the Fisherman's queer desire for the Mermaid, and perhaps, I suspect, the ungovernable desire of the Soul to reconnect to the beautiful body of the Fisherman.[109] Rather than having derangement and violence set the rhetorical tone, I would characterise the same bibliographic contributions as a textual dissidence that enacts an intercourse with the tale, giving it a queer character, one of sexuality and sensuality that defies heteronormative, Victorian convention.

Rather than enacting violence upon the reader, the visual presentation of the story enacts alienation, but specifically toward a heteronormative reader. While the male Fisherman's desire is for a female mermaid, she is not a woman, but a creature born in the imagination that resembles a woman, a cold-blooded, inhuman fish from the depths of the ocean. Her human appearance is artificial, heightened by a blazon of decadent proportions:

> Her hair was as a wet fleece of gold, and each separate hair as a thread of fine gold in a cup of glass. Her body was as white as ivory, and her tail was of silver and pearl. Silver and pearl was her tail, and the green weeds of the sea coiled round it; and like sea-shells were her ears, and lips were like sea-coral. The cold waves dashed over her cold breasts, and the salt glistened upon her eyelids.[110]

To be with this cold creature, that only appears to be like a woman, the Fisherman must abandon his Soul, personified as his doppelgänger (see Fig. 2.13). This Soul, once separated from his body, looks upon his lost body with the same desire that the Fisherman has for the Mermaid. Enacting a strange iteration of the homosocial triangle, the Soul conceives elaborate plans to seduce his body.[111]

The Fisherman consults a priest about his queer desire for a half human creature from the sea, and we discover that it is for 'her body' that he 'would give [his soul]'.[112] The priest is a vessel for Christian rhetoric, and thus the heteronormative ethos of late Victorian England, declaring that 'the love of the body is vile' and 'vile and evil are the pagan things God suffers to wander through His world'. The sea-folk that the Fisherman so desires to be with are largely hidden away from heteronormative society, marginalised to the dark depths of the sea. Their queer bodies and desirable lives are portrayed by the priest as a threat to social order.

Wilde's metaphorical exploration of queer desire continues with the figure of the Soul who narcissistically desires the Fisherman, literally his own beautiful body. When refused in favour of the Mermaid, he begs, 'send me from thee, send me not forth without a heart' but is refused because it belongs to the Mermaid.[113] It is at this point that something visual happens in the book with Ricketts's accompanying medallions: it empties. Before, the medallions contained an image of the Mermaid, tangled in seaweed, repeated as a visual refrain, reflecting Wilde's poetic repetitions in the text. After giving the Mermaid his heart, the creature is free for two repetitions, only to return at a point in the story when the Fisherman's love is corrupted by his Soul. He is captured again by his Soul several pages later and separated from his love. The Soul captures the Fisherman with a robbery and murder. Afterwards, 'he seized the nine purses of gold, and fled hastily through the garden of pomegranates', staining both his body and Soul with their shared crime and similarly dissident desires. Patches of pomegranates are represented on several pages between paragraphs of this story. Losing his Mermaid, the Fisherman never reunites with his Soul. He rejects his advances and mourns the loss of his love.

All love here is queer. To embrace one's bodily desires is represented in the Soul's desire to return to his body. The desire for dissident sexual experiences is represented in the Fisherman's desire for the Mermaid. The gendering creates a sense of aesthetic confusion, all of which rejects the authority of Christian rhetoric regarding the love of God. Desire, no matter the body, no matter how socially inappropriate, is worth the losses that the Fisherman must endure. When his infidelity with his Soul causes his love to die, the Fisherman chooses to die in the sea rather than return to the conventions of life he had abandoned for the creature. His Soul, an extension of the Christian ethos, embodied earlier in the priest, is the cause of his death and tragedy. By rejecting the Fisherman's un-Christian desire, it not only kills that desire through exile but damages the value of Christian thought on love and sex. The desires of the Fisherman and the Soul are stronger than the morals of an unforgiving church. Many queer readers would find the analogy apt to their experience of same-sex desire.

The final image of the dead bodies lying on the ground gives a tragic, but beautiful end to the fate of their bodies and the desires of those bodies. The Soul is not presented. The priest and others look on in horror, but the looks on the two dead faces are of peace. They made peace with their choices and their desires. It is society, that is now unmoored with the moral superiority of the church in disarray, and the very idea of the Soul itself as a deadly queer succubus, who'd rather kill his body than be without it. Pomegranates and blood stain their bodies, but it is the institutions held accountable.

'The Star Child'

What unites the four stories thematically and visually in this collection is the emphasis on difference. The characters are all very diverse. The children are atypical. Where the young king was Christ-like in his humility, despite his privileged surroundings, the Star Child is misery personified, a brat forced to find redemption. Wilde complicates that redemption by questioning the moral usage of beauty. Justin T. Jones says that 'Wilde's fairy tales use their subversive components and the motif of ugliness to denote the damaging effects of compulsory, imitative, spurious morality on the ideal realm of aesthetic beauty.'[114] The realm of beauty, a decadent realm in this story, sits outside of morality and challenges the conventions of what is moral or immoral behaviour as set out at the beginning of the tale.

The Star Child is found abandoned in the woods by a woodcutter and his wife, who take pity on the boy and raise him as their own. Despite their example, his aesthetic perception of fine people leads to his cruel treatment of his adoptive parents and their simple way of life.[115] As Rasmus Simonsen notes, his feminine beauty is not an outward projection of any inner gentility. Instead, his cruelty reflects his pubescent transition towards becoming an adult male.[116] His emerging masculinity is revealed through cruelty. However, rather than seeing it as a gendered position – women can be as cruel as men, after all – it also suggests that the Star Child is a failed aesthete. He thinks he appreciates beauty, but he lacks the discernment of beauty that comes from a decadent eye. He would reject the Young King without his godly raiment. He would take no pleasure in the Dwarf's ugliness as performance.

THE STAR-CHILD

TO
MISS MARGOT TENNANT.

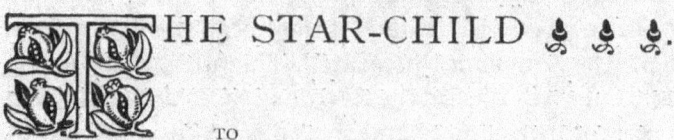

ONCE upon a time two poor Woodcutters were making their way home through a great pine-forest. It was winter, and a night of bitter cold. The snow lay thick upon the ground, and upon the branches of the trees: the frost kept snapping the little twigs on either side of them, as they passed: and when they came to the Mountain-Torrent she was hanging motionless in air, for the Ice-King had kissed her.

So cold was it that even the animals and the birds did not know what to make of it.

"Ugh!" snarled the

S   129

Figure 2.14 The Star Child rejecting his mother. Courtesy of the Rufus Hawtin Hathaway Collection, Identification #991026002159705163, Archives and Special Collections, Western Libraries, Western University.

He goes so far as to reject his own mother for her poverty and dishevelled appearance.[117] He cannot see beauty in unexpected places. He lacks the care of an aesthetic practice that comes from education and experience.

His path to redemption involves the loss of his physical beauty and moral trials that eventually reunite him with his parents, who are, in fact, royalty, confirming the Star Child's assumption of his rarity. With his physical beauty, he is restored to his former self, though, strangely, in the final paragraph we discover that this redeemed figure 'ruled . . . not long, so great had been his suffering, and so bitter the fire of his testing, for after the space of three years he died. And he who came after him ruled evilly.'[118] The discovery of empathy does not change the world. The boy's redemption is nothing more than a brief moment of beauty, limited by his brief experience of life.

The Star Child's life, however, like most aesthetic moments, is brief. It is not the moral journey that matters in this story so much as the aesthetic story in which he finds beauty that he could not see before. His beauty shines through after making the choice to give up his own life, so that a leprous beggar may live. It is not that the Star Child sees beauty in the beggar: he doesn't, he feels only pity. But it is the Star Child's beauty that is revealed after this final third test. All in the city see his rarity again; his inner beauty shines through and is reflected in his physical appearance. Like the Young King before him, it is the artificial symbol of accepted physical beauty that signifies power and rule.

Aestheticism is not just the beauty of objects in the material world, but their effect on our inner selves. 'Experience', Pater tells us,

> already reduced to a group of impressions, is ringed round for each one of us by that thick wall of personality through which no real voice has ever pierced on its way to us, or from us to that which we can only conjecture to be without. Every one of those impressions is the impression of the individual in his isolation, each mind keeping as a solitary prisoner in its own dream of a world.[119]

The Star Child's charity does not really tell us anything about those he pities. It reveals something in himself, allowing him to develop a new way of interacting as an individual to the stimulation around him. It changes him, and because he is a slave and a monstrous little creature, he develops the ability to see beauty where he once ignored it.

That point is emphasised with Ricketts's decisions for illustrating the story. There is only one medallion, and it features a bird of peace, standing in stark contrast to the cruelty of the boy at this stage in the story. There is one image of the boy with his back turned to the 'beggar woman', his disguised mother, demonstrating his rejection of her love. He literally gives her a cold shoulder (see Fig. 2.14). The image is faint and a secondary figure to that of his mother.

Subsequent images show the boy during his transformation into an ugly creature. But, unlike Wilde's toad-faced boy, we have a beautiful nature child amongst the thicket, and then later tied up and blindfolded in the magician's home. Ricketts finds the boy's beauty while under the curse of ugliness and models for the reader, an aesthetic discernment of the boy's inner beauty depicted in an aesthetic fashion. By not depicting Wilde's horrible Star Child, but a sympathetic elven creature, Ricketts softens the horror of Wilde's transformation, not with a physical description, but with a characterisation of his newfound inner life. As a child abandoned in the forest, his realisation in slavery as a creature like those he once tortured, he returns to his natural origins via aesthetic means. Aesthetics are emphasised in this presentation of the story and, as the only story written for this book, it is born of the diverse visions involved in the assemblage of this project.

Concerning hetero-beautiful and queer books

Where Morris altered bookmaking practices to serve the nature of the book, aesthetes did the inverse, altering their art to available means of production. Thinking queerly, Ricketts, Shannon and other bookmakers saw an opportunity to alter the art they created to take advantage of what the automated printing press could do. *A House of Pomegranates* demonstrates an attempt to create new visions of beauty, eroticism and sensuality that formed textual intercourse between modern printing practices and Morris's conception of the artisan book. This discourse meant that, inevitably, accidents would and did occur such as those that define *Pomegranates*: fading, raised print on glossy paper, garish colours and a heavy, uncomfortable book. However, these accidents were the result of experimental intercourse of textual discourses that recognise and subvert the confines of regulatory performance that defined social organisation for the Victorian middle classes. These accidents, while odd and queer, are also beautiful and worthy of critical appreciation.

Much like the grotesque Dwarf or the cursed Star Child, the book was beautiful, but not in the manner of a hetero-beautiful book. To appreciate its beauty, its grotesque flaws, is to appreciate it for being different from normatively beautiful books. It is a beauty that the Fisherman's Soul understands as it seeks union with a body that itself desires another inhuman creature. It is a beauty appreciated by the Young King, but one to which the masses are blind. Wilde, Ricketts and Shannon separately take advantage of that blindness, creating a complex text with an eye on the past and an origin in the myths of heteronormative culture, but in the process create a new conception of beauty only imaginable in the processes of modernity, where technology, an ambitious author, and a creative pair of artists with contesting visions and interpretations forge a queer space to imagine new forms of beauty yet to find a home within a society defined by heteronormative institutions and spaces. Such spaces are possible, however, because they were imagined and can be found in *A House of Pomegranates*.

As much as Morris would like to have returned to a medieval work ethic, such a return was not possible for most bookmakers and writers. In contrast, the queer book was the result of different creative perspectives on beauty and the demands of commodity culture – a queering of Morris's ideals that were unfamiliar and discomforting to conceptions of textual and sexual practices.

Morris's idea of beauty is heteronormative because it is singular and presumptuous – a reflection of his middle-class privilege as a non-queer Victorian man with a successful business. Queer books propose various forms of beauty. The publication of Wilde's *A House of Pomegranates* offers an important example of how diverse ideas of what is beautiful can co-exist, and even contest one another, in a single volume Queer books are not the first works to engage multiple senses, but they are the first where multiple mediums are deployed in a manner that enriches sensuous homoeroticism within the context of published fairy tales.

With a singular idealised vision, Morris is an example of a Victorian cultural ethos that did not make room for the possibility of alternative visions of beauty. He takes choice away from his reader in order to preserve his ideal in the consumer world of the nineteenth-century literary marketplace. *A House of Pomegranates'* imagined and as yet unrealised utopia is found, as Muñoz suggests, in the quotidian moments of everyday life, 'glimpsed in utopian bonds, affiliations, designs, and gestures that exist within the present'.[120] Rather than imagine a world that will be constructed after the current one no longer exists, queerness creates hope for the future via 'something that is extra to the everyday transaction of heteronormative capitalism'.[121] The queer does not have to tear down the here and now; instead, it subverts existing spaces such as the material books that queers write, design and read. Existing in the capitalist economy, the queer book gives the reader a glimpse into the future by creating moments in the space of the text for relational bonds between queer readers, authors and artists. The queer book emerges when aesthetes, who admired Morris's beautiful books, wanted to create equally beautiful works but, instead of being able to demand changes to the production process from printers or publishers, instead of demanding high prices from the consumer, they needed to conceptualise a subversive beauty. This queer conception of the beautiful book resulted in new and diverse ideas about modern bookmaking. Bibliography and lexical content both contribute to and contest what makes a book beautiful, through various coded systems of interaction between form and content to, in some instances, generate queer books.

The main differences between the hetero-beautiful and the queer book is the perception of nature's influence on art, and how that defines the role of the bookmaker in literary expression. For Morris, art reflects nature. He says in 'Some Thoughts on the Ornamented Manuscripts of the Middle Ages' that

> The mediæval workman not only lived amidst beautiful works of handicraft, and a nature unspoiled by the sordidness of commercialism; but also, he was deeply imbued with a sense of the epic of the World, as it was understood in his day.[122]

The epic implies a story for everyone, a story of culture and a story of consensus. Emphasised with a design that recalls nature and narrates humanity as the centre of the natural order, Morris positions the epic as an ideal form of literature and as an ideal perspective on culture. The influence of nature is something that those outside of the commercial culture of the nineteenth century could engage with and understand so it offered the best metaphors, inspiration and forms of beauty for art to imitate. Rather than surveying the various imitations of nature found in a Kelmscott book, *A House of Pomegranates* collects varying imagery and allows it to change based on the story in which it features. Art is superior to nature and the decadent focus on that concept in Wilde's stories inspires alternative concepts of art by both Ricketts and Shannon.

Notes

1. Judith Butler, *Bodies That Matter: On the Discursive Limits of Sex* (London: Routledge, 1993, 2011), p. 173.
2. Butler, *Bodies That Matter*, p. 173.
3. Butler, *Bodies That Matter*, p. 185.
4. William Morris, 'The Ideal Book: A Lecture Delivered in 1893', in *The Ideal Book: Essays and Lectures on the Art of the Book by William Morris* (Berkely and Los Angeles: University of California Press, 1982), p. 67.
5. William Morris and Emery Walker, *Printing: An Essay by William Morris and Emery Walker. From Arts and Crafts Essays by Members of the Arts and Crafts Society* (Park Ridge, IL: Village Press, 1903), pp. 6–7.
6. Ricketts, *A Defence*, p. 9.
7. Betsky, *Queer Space*, p. 12.
8. Michel Foucault, *The History of Sexuality an Introduction. Volume I*, trans. by Robert Hurley (New York: Vintage, 1980), p. 73.
9. Muñoz, *Cruising Utopia*, p. 7.
10. Muñoz, *Cruising Utopia*, p. 7.
11. Muñoz, *Cruising Utopia*, p. 9.
12. Frédéric Barbier, 'The Publishing Industry and Printed Output in Nineteenth-Century France', in *The History of the Book in the West: 1800–1914, Volume IV*, ed. by Stephen Colclough and Alexis Weedon (Burlington, VT: Ashgate, 2010), p. 13.
13. Elizabeth Carolyn Miller, *Slow Print: Literary Radicalism and Late Victorian Print Culture* (Stanford, CA: Stanford University Press, 2013), p.2.
14. Miller, *Slow Print*, p. 2.
15. Morris and Walker, *Printing*, pp. 11–12.
16. Mary Elizabeth Leighton and Lisa Surridge, 'The Plot Thickens: Toward a Narratological Analysis of Illustrated Serial Fiction in the 1860s', *Victorian Studies*, 51.1 (2008), p. 66.

17. Ruari McLean, *Victorian Book Design and Colour Printing* (London: Faber & Faber, 1963), p. 103.
18. McLean, *Victorian Book Design*, p. 104.
19. McLean, *Victorian Book Design*, pp. 104–5.
20. Kathleen Steeden, 'Evans, Edmund', in *The Oxford Companion to the Book*, volume 2 D–Z, ed. by Michael F. Suarez and H. R. Woudhuysen (New York: Oxford University Press, 2010), pp. 707–8.
21. McLean, *Victorian Book Design*, pp. 104–5.
22. Kooistra, *Poetry, Pictures, and Popular Publishing*, p. 7.
23. Elizabeth Helsinger, *Poetry and the Pre-Raphaelite Arts: Dante Gabriel Rossetti and William Morris* (New Haven, CT: Yale University Press, 2008), p. 175.
24. Helsinger, *Poetry and the Pre-Raphaelite Arts*, p. 177.
25. Helsinger, *Poetry and the Pre-Raphaelite Arts*, p. 189.
26. 'Binding Design: Poems (1870) [1], Dante Gabriel Rossetti, 1870', *The Rossetti Archive*. Retrieved from http://www.rossettiarchive.org/docs/sa122.1-1870.rap.html.
27. Helsinger, *Poetry and the Pre-Raphaelite Arts*, p. 189.
28. Charles Harvey and Jon Press, 'The Business Career of William Morris', in *William Morris: Art and Kelmscott*, ed. by Linda Parry, Occasional Papers of the Society of Antiquaries of London 18 (London: The Boydell Press, 1996), p. 6.
29. Harvey and Press, 'The Business Career of William Morris', p. 11.
30. Morris, 'The Ideal Book', p. 67.
31. Morris, 'The Ideal Book', pp. 72–3.
32. Morris, William. 'Some Notes on Early Woodcut Books with a Chapter on Illuminated Manuscripts', *The Ideal Book: Essays and Lectures on the Arts of the Book by William Morris* (Berkeley and Los Angeles: University of California Press, 1982), p. 10.
33. William Morris, 'The Woodcuts of Gothic Books', *Notes on Early Wood-Cut Books* (New York: Elston Press, 1902), p. 3.
34. Morris, 'The Woodcuts of Gothic Books', p. 3.
35. Michelle Weinroth, 'Redesigning the Language of Social Change: Rhetoric, Agency, and the Oneiric in William Morris's *A Dream of John Ball*', *Victorian Studies*, 53.1 (2010), p. 58.
36. Morris, 'Some Notes on Early Woodcuts', p. 10.
37. William Morris, 'Gothic Revival II', in *The Unpublished Lectures of William Morris*, ed. by Eugene D. Lemire (Detroit: Wayne State University Press, 1969), p. 91.
38. Morris, 'Gothic Revival II', p. 91.

39. See Karl Marx and Friedrich Engels, *The Communist Manifesto* (1848) (London: Penguin, 2002); Friedrich Engels *The Condition of the Working Class in England* (1845), ed. by Victor Kiernan (London: Penguin, 2009).
40. 'The Arts and Crafts Exhibition' (review), *The Spectator*, 28 Oct. 1893, p. 580. *Periodicals Archive Online*, proquest.com/pao.
41. 'The Arts and Crafts Exhibition', p. 580.
42. R. Jayne Hildebrand, 'News from Nowhere and William Morris's Aesthetics of Unreflectiveness: Pleasurable Habits', *English Literature in Transition, 1880–1920*, 54.1 (2011), p. 23.
43. William Morris, 'The Decorative Arts, Their Relation to Modern Life and Progress: An Address Delivered before the Trades' Guild of Learning', *The Decorative Arts, Their Relations to Modern Life, and Progress (Reprint of the Edition 1878): The Aims of Art (Reprint of the Edition 1887)*, ed. by Friedrich Adolf (Osnabrück, Germany: Schmidt-Künsemüller, Proff & Co. KG, Bad Honnef a. Rhein, 1975), p. 26.
44. See Thomas Carlyle's essay 'Captains of Industry', in *Past and Present* (1843), ed. by Richard D. Altick (New York: New York University Press, 1965).
45. James Eli Adams, *Dandies and Desert Saints: Styles of Victorian Manhood* (Ithaca, NY: Cornell University Press, 1995), p. 6.
46. Adams, *Dandies and Desert Saints*, p. 26.
47. Harvey and Press, 'The Business Career of William Morris', p. 17.
48. David S. Peterson, 'Introduction', in *The Ideal Book: Essays and Lectures on the Arts of the Book by William Morris* (Berkeley and Los Angeles: University of California Press, 1982), p. xxii.
49. Peterson, 'Introduction', p. xvi.
50. From Ruari McLean, *The Thames and Hudson Manual of Typography* (London: Thames and Hudson Ltd, 1980).
51. McLean, *The Thames and Hudson Manual of Typography*, p. 94.
52. David McKitterick, 'Changes in the Look of the Book', in *The Cambridge History of the Book in Britain. Volume VI: 1830–1914*, ed. by David McKitterick (New York: Cambridge University Press, 2009), p. 95.
53. Morris, 'The Decorative Arts', p. 26.
54. See Carlyle's essay 'Captains of Industry'.
55. Adams, *Dandies and Desert Saints: Styles of Victorian Manhood* (Ithaca, NY: Cornell University Press, 1995), p. 6.
56. McKitterick, 'Changes in the Look of the Book', p. 92.
57. McLean, *Thames & Hudson Manual of Typography*, p. 97.

58. David McKitterick, 'Introduction', in *The Cambridge History of the Book in Britain*, pp. 16–17.
59. D. C. Coleman, *The British Paper Industry, 1495–1860: A Study in Industrial Growth* (Oxford: Clarendon Press, 1958), p. 285.
60. Coleman, *The British Paper Industry*, p. 302.
61. McLean, *Thames & Hudson Manual of Typography*, p. 98.
62. Paul Thompson, *The Work of William Morris* (New York: Oxford University Press, 1991), p. 160.
63. *The Collected Letters of William Morris*, vol. III, 1889–1892 and vol. IV 1893–1896, ed. by Norman Kelvin (Princeton, NJ: Princeton University Press, 1996), 'Letter 1779', p. 223, n225.
64. Thompson, *The Work of William Morris*, p. 160.
65. Thompson, *The Work of William Morris*, p. 160.
66. Thompson, *The Work of William Morris*, p. 161.
67. Thompson, *The Work of William Morris*, p. 161.
68. Thompson, *The Work of William Morris*, p. 161.
69. *The Collected Letters of William Morris*, p. n247.
70. London, British Library, Add MS50913 Chiswick Press Papers Vol. CXV 1880–1890.
71. London, British Library, Add MS 50917 Chiswick Press Papers 1898 to 1899.
72. Thompson, *The Work of William Morris*, p. 155.
73. Peterson, 'Introduction', p. xxx.
74. Peterson, 'Introduction', p. 17.
75. Nicholas Frankel, *Masking the Text: Essays on Literature & Mediation in the 1890s* (High Wycombe: The Rivendale Press, 2009), p. 194.
76. Oscar Wilde, 'To the Editor of The Pall Mall Gazette', in *The Complete Letters of Oscar Wilde*, ed. by Merlin Holland and Rupert Hart-Davis (New York: Henry Holt and Company, 2000), p. 303.
77. Anne Markey, *Oscar Wilde's Fairy Tales: Origins and Contexts* (Portland, OR: Irish Academic Press, 2011), p. 141.
78. Nelson, *The Early Nineties*, p. 108.
79. Nelson, *The Early Nineties*, p. 29.
80. Nelson, *The Early Nineties*, p. 29.
81. Michelle Ruggaber, 'Wilde's *The Happy Prince* and *A House of Pomegranates*: Bedtime Stories for Grown-Ups', *English Literature in Transition (1880–1920)*, 46.2 (2003), p. 142.
82. Donald E. Hall, *Reading Sexualities: Hermeneutic Theory and the Future of Queer Studies* (New York: Routledge, 2009), pp. 46–7.

83. Lorraine Janzen Kooistra, 'Wilde's Legacy: Fairy Tales, Laurence Housman, and the Expression of "Beautiful Untrue Things"', in *Oscar Wilde and the Cultures of Childhood*, ed. by Joseph Bristow, Palgrave Studies in Nineteenth-Century Writing and Culture (Basingstoke: Palgrave Macmillan, 2017), p. 90.
84. Kooistra, 'Wilde's Legacy', p. 114.
85. Ricketts, *Defence*, p. 11.
86. Ricketts, *Defence*, p. 18.
87. Ricketts, *Defence*, p. 143.
88. Markey, *Oscar Wilde's Fairy Tales*, pp. 140–1.
89. Markey, *Oscar Wilde's Fairy Tales*, p. 141.
90. Markey, *Oscar Wilde's Fairy Tales*, p. 141.
91. Markey, *Oscar Wilde's Fairy Tales*, p. 141.
92. Josephine Guy and Ian Small, *Oscar Wilde's Profession: Writing and the Culture Industry in the Late Nineteenth Century* (New York: Oxford University Press, 2000), pp. 81–2.
93. Guy and Small, *Oscar Wilde's Profession*, p. 82.
94. Guy and Small, *Oscar Wilde's Profession*, p. 81.
95. Guy and Small, *Oscar Wilde's Profession*, p. 11.
96. 'A House of Pomegranates by Oscar Wilde' (review), *The Spectator* (19 Mar. 1892), p. 408. Periodicals Archive Online, proquest.com/pao.
97. 'A House of Pomegranates by Oscar Wilde' (review), p. 408.
98. 'A House of Pomegranates by Oscar Wilde' (review), p. 408.
99. Paraphrase of Wilde from *A House of Pomegranates*, pp. 25–6.
100. Butler, *Bodies That Matter*, pp. xxii, 9.
101. Markey, *Oscar Wilde's Fairy Tales*, p. 142.
102. Markey, *Oscar Wilde's Fairy Tales*, p. 24.
103. Wilde, *Pomegranates*, pp. 25–6.
104. Wilde, *Pomegranates*, p. 24.
105. Wilde *Pomegranates*, p. 45.
106. Wilde, *Pomegranates*, p. 60.
107. Justin T. Jones, 'Morality's Ugly Implications in Oscar Wilde's Fairy Tales', *Studies in English Literature 1500–1900*, 51.4 (2011), p. 889.
108. Jones, 'Morality's Ugly Implications', p. 890.
109. Frankel, *Making the Text*, p. 214.
110. Wilde, *Pomegranates*, p. 64.
111. See Sedgwick's *Between Men*.
112. Sedgwick, *Between Men*, p. 71.
113. Sedgwick, *Between Men*, p. 84.

114. Jones, 'Morality's Ugly Implications', p. 898.
115. Wilde, *Pomegranates*, p. 137.
116. Rasmus Simonsen, 'Dark Avunculate: Shame, Animality, and Queer Development in Oscar Wilde's "The Star-Child"', *Children's Literature*, 42.1 (2014), p. 25.
117. Wilde, *Pomegranates*, p. 140.
118. Wilde, *Pomegranates*, p. 158.
119. Pater, *The Renaissance*, p. 151.
120. Muñoz, *Cruising Utopia*, p. 22.
121. Muñoz, *Cruising Utopia*, p. 22.
122. Morris, 'Some Thoughts', p. 4.

3

Trans-Textuality in Michael Field's *Long Ago* and *Whym Chow*

> As to our work, let no man think he can put asunder what God has joined .... [T]he work is perfect mosaic: we cross and interlace like a company of dancing summer flies; if one begins a character, his companion seizes and possesses it; if one conceives a scene or situation, the other corrects, completes or murderously cuts away.
> – Letter to Havelock Ellis from Katharine Bradley and Edith Cooper, May 1886[1]

The textual intercourse of Michael Field's books is both complicated and enriched by the textuality of the author. Katharine Bradley (1846–1914) and Edith Cooper (1862–1913), niece and aunt, poets with intellectual pursuits in the classics and fine arts, as well as lesbian lovers, invented the persona of Michael Field to represent their collective work, first as a playwright, then as a poet. This figure exists on the page as the author and face of their poetry, but as the letter excerpted for this chapter's epigraph suggests, Bradley, Cooper and Field form a 'perfect mosaic' that can 'cross and interface like a company of dancing flies'. Bradley and Cooper are referring here to their own poetic practice as writers, but the metaphor applies to their aesthetic persona as well. They did not want the world to read their work as that of women, telling Robert Browning (1812–1899), who gave their identity away to *The Athenaeum* in 1884, 'We have many things to say the world will not tolerate from a woman's lips. We must be free as dramatists to work out in the open air ... we cannot be stifled in drawing-room conventions.'[2] Despite the exposure of their sex, and their lives as a lesbian couple, Bradley and Cooper continued to co-author works that defied conventions of literature written by women.

Edith's mother was Bradley's sister and their relationship as a couple began when Cooper was a teenager. They lived together their entire lives, literally since the day that Cooper was born until she died before her elder lover. Bradley had published poetry herself under the pseudonym Arran Leigh, and later took the shared pseudonym, Michael Field, with Cooper after they began writing plays and poetry together. Like many women authors before them, Bradley and Cooper were concerned that people take their work seriously as art, rather than as a lady's accomplishment. Hence their frustration at Robert Browning revealing their identity. However, the practice of taking male pseudonyms was common with George Egerton (Mary Chavelita Dunne Bright), John Oliver Hobbes (Pearl Craggie) and Vernon Lee (Violet Paget), only a few among many contemporaries sharing their practice. The result was that their personal and poetic identities were intertwined with their poetic work.

Long Ago (1889) and *Whym Chow: Flame of Love* (1914), the first and final collections of poetry published under the pseudonym Michael Field, both triangulate their intimate relationship with a third figure of poetic and textual significance. *Long Ago*, their first collective publication as poets, is a beautiful collection of poems inspired by the fragments of lyrics left behind by the ancient Greek poet Sappho. As women authors, this collection is significant as the first extended work by a woman to engage with Sappho in modern times. Their final collection of poems is *Whym Chow*, written mostly by Edith after the death of their beloved pet dog in 1906, and inspires a commemoration of a period of spiritual transition for both women and a queer companionship triangulated with their shared bond with their chow. These books incorporate cover and page design that situates Sappho and Whym Chow as contributing central voices in multisensory projects that transform two series of poems into tactile works of art. Just as speculation about the poets' gender was often intertwined with criticism of their poetry, their poetry often intertwined with the body of the material book. While the use of other voices and pseudonymous authorship suggests a distancing from the author, in the case of these works, 'Michael Field' is a textual presence that is always in intercourse with the books' creators and readers. The poetic voice of Michael Field reflects a conversation between authors and muses, frequently and intentionally blurring binary boundaries of gender and sexuality. In *Long Ago* and *Whym Chow*, the practice of ambiguity accessed through their nom de plume extends to the poetic engagement with history and spiritual practice found respectively in each volume. This chapter will argue that the resultant ambiguity that merges the poetic and the personal transforms these two volumes into works of queer introspection, personal to Bradley and Cooper, but accessible to a queer readership who, because of these works, can seek solace in the unconventional relationships that the textual intercourse of each volume embodies.

Jill Ehnenn notes the ways that Katharine Bradley and Edith Cooper's joint interest in bibliographic design complicates notions of literary collaboration as something aesthetic and visual, just as much as it is literary.[3] Ehnenn also characterises *Long Ago* as historical revision in which their poetic extensions of Sappho's fragments are writing a new history, a history that continues in their collection *Sight and Song* (1892).[4] Her forthcoming monograph, *Michael Field's Revisionary Poetics*, extends this scholarly look at how Bradley and Cooper as queer women and experimental writers reimagine the past in order to propose something new, aligning Michael Field with the concept of queer futurity outlined in this book.[5] Frankie Dytor establishes Michael Field's use of aesthetic masculinity as a means of differentiating their own identities from other aesthetic women.[6] Dytor argues that their non-binary attitude towards gender allowed them to align their work with that of male aesthetes, suggesting that their male persona, even after their identities were revealed, was an important part of their poetic experiments. LeeAnne M. Richardson's *The Forms of Michael Field* (2021) is an extended study of how their appropriation of aesthetic male identities reflects a similar appropriation of poetic form.[7] Both are structures defined for women by the male-dominated literary culture in which they worked and structural forms that they sought to intentionally bend and even break.

Richardson notes how they read works by Havelock Ellis on sexual inversion and were intellectually engaged in debates on same-sex desire and gender nonconformity.[8] Their non-binary engagement with these intimate topics extended to their complex relationship with the reading public. Carolyn Dever notes the tension between Bradley and Cooper's private relationship and their public persona, Michael Field. She pays particular attention to Cooper's struggles to find her own identity in the wake of her mother's (Bradley's sister's) death, while Bradley persists in their diaries that together, they are 'one living soul'.[9] While this caused personal issues among the women, this single identity was their means of access to aesthetic and intellectual cultures. Rather than subordinating themselves to a man, together, Dever argues that the women reimagined marriage, gender and creative expressions, suggesting that their poetic identity, as Katharine Bradley suggests, could not be severed from their intimate and private partnership.[10]

These two books embrace the twice-told tale of the queer book. Each depends upon textual intercourse between poetry and book design, each present themes that emerge from heteronormative culture, and each queers those themes. But there is an additional element of personal intimacy that the figure of Michael Field provides. Yes, the identity is positioned until 1884 as a means to protect the women's poetry from misogynistic dismissal, but it didn't work. Sarah Parker and Ana Parejo Vadillo note that the criticism of their work only intensifies as their career continued until the twentieth century when critics 'viewed them as stuffy, hopelessly *fin-de-siècle*, and a product of enervated decadence'.[11] If anything, the name Michael Field intensifies the presence of the women in these volumes because it gives their shared voice a body. Rather than disembodying the poets and separating them from their poetry, it gives them a presence that is further emphasised by the physical realisation of these two poetic projects.

The lesbian lives of Bradley and Cooper haunts our reading of Michael Field whom these women presented and treated as an embodiment of their creative union. And while much scholarship focuses on that haunting, following Terry Castle's lead in rediscovering hidden lesbian pasts, rather than seeking out an apparitional lesbian who has already been found, the role of lesbian haunting in trans* identity remains undiscovered.[12] Elizabeth Primamore notes that Bradley and Cooper's public appearances as female dandies, while maintaining their poetic persona already subverted the sexuality of the aesthete.[13] That twist, however, is a complex merging of trans-textuality with their discursive examination of queer desires. Michael Field embraces the queer sexualities of their fellow queer aesthetes, introducing a female perspective that complicates aestheticism's perspective on gender and desire. What results are books encoded with lesbian concepts of desire and trans* concepts of gender. These ideas merge here as Bradley and Cooper express queer same-sex desire, but do so as a queer male poet, while presenting their books as objects other than books. Michael Field is a trans-textual identity, born as noted in the chapter's epigraph, of the mosaic of their entwined creative expressions, alive in the pages of their books.

The women's public life suggests that they embraced their status as Michael Field. After their identities were known and the women made public appearances, they did so as the dandy, 'Michael Field'. They did not cross-dress; instead, they embraced the practices of aesthetic men like Wilde and 'adopted a dandiacal style in dress. Adorning themselves with specially made hats and dresses, the two women dressed to be seen.'[14] Michael Field was not a disguise, it was a public persona for Bradley (Michael) and Cooper (Field, or more frequently, her nickname, Henry). Together they are the man that they created, but that man is content to exist as a textual body, empowering the women to embrace the social and poetic practices of an aesthete.

A combination of gender fluidity and sensual spirituality defines *Long Ago* and *Whym Chow* as art objects. While the volumes are quite different in many ways, they both encapsulate Michael Field as a materialist aesthetic project. To understand this phenomenon, this chapter draws on recent developments in transgender theory because the published identity of 'Michael Field' and the women who created them, used here in both a non-binary and plural sense, offers contemporary readers an important historical intervention into feminist, queer and trans* conceptions of gender. Michael Field's relevance to feminist and queer thought has been explored in detail, but their choice to take on a male identity is also relevant to trans* critical practice. Specifically, it is the male identity imposed, not on the women, but on their books, that I want to consider. Bradley and Cooper found inspiration and community among the aesthetes and decadents, with queer authors like Walter Pater, Oscar Wilde and John Gray. These men and others in the movement of various sexual orientations, inverted gender conventions as much as sexual desire. By taking on a similarly aesthetic male persona in the publication of their works, they present themselves as another queer man within the dissident literary movement.

That queerness is complicated, however, by the textual body, one of poetry and design that transforms and changes with each project they produce, and by the queerness of Bradley and Cooper whose lives as lesbian women haunt their art and Michael Field's male identity.

After the publication of the second edition of their plays *Callirrhoë* and *Fair Rosamund* in a single volume in 1884, critics, for the most part, identified Michael Field with female pronouns (she/her). By 1889 when *Long Ago* was released, their genders were known, so hiding behind a male pseudonym doesn't make sense as a disguise. In addition, it is understood now that Bradley and Cooper saw Michael Field as a figure who was born of their poetic collaboration, an identity that emerges from their creative union. Like Wilde, they embraced a public life of theatres, clubs and music halls, while simultaneously living a second life of queer sexuality that was both intimate and intensely private. Unlike Wilde, they embraced an artificial public identity that allowed them to protect their intimate domestic relationship. They formed deep friendships with men in the aesthetic movement who lived similarly queer domestic lives, including couples like Charles Shannon and Charles Ricketts, and John Gray and Marc-André Raffalovich. Their queer male identity aligns them as one public persona created to engage with a coterie of queer and gender non-conformist male artists. At the same time, this persona's alignment with Bradley and Cooper's lives as women by critics and readers meant that their engagement with aestheticism is also a commentary on the gendering of poetic practice.

Aligning their work with Algernon Charles Swinburne, Walter Pater and Wilde, they ally themselves with aesthetic and decadent ideals that were part of a discourse of same-sex desire dominated by queer men. Their reverence and respect for Robert Browning emphasises this queer identity. Browning was only publicly celebrated after the death of his more revered wife, poet Elizabeth Barrett Browning (1806–51), and it was the aesthetes who first embraced his dramatic monologues and the complex sexual politics of his *oeuvre*. Browning's influence can be seen in Bradley and Cooper's interest in history and narrative practice, but it is Swinburne who influences their turn to the poetics of Sapphic love. Their passion for Swinburne's poetry is further influenced by their study of Pater and his collection of critical essays, *Studies in the History of the Renaissance* (1873). Both women benefitted from the chance to study at university. Bradley attended classes at the Collège de France, Newnham College, Cambridge, and later

University College, Bristol where she attended classes with Cooper from 1879 to 1884.[15] Their education meant that they could read and understand classical texts and ancient Greek culture in a more scholarly manner than their female peers with fewer educational opportunities. They understood the pursuit of sensation and the artist's ability to record a response to those sensations as deeply as any male aesthete.

Michael Field reflects the queer lives of their creators, Bradley and Cooper, but possesses their own trans-textual identity. By taking on a queer male identity, and giving him bibliographic life in their published works, they engage with and challenge their fellow queer male aesthetes with a perspective on sexuality that blurred the boundaries of the gender binary. Textually, Michael Field is a complex experience of lesbian desire, trans* identity and queer intellectualism that we have only begun to understand. One means towards better understanding is through the ways in which Michael Field, as well as Bradley and Cooper, come to life as multiplicities and discourses in the pages of their books. In *Long Ago*, we see not only Bradley and Cooper communing with Sapphic love and Sappho's poems, but the history of women expressing sexual and emotional desire. We also see Michael Field, a queer aesthete, engaging in a queer discourse with a male tradition in British poetry where Sappho is reimagined through new poetic works.

In relation to H. T. Wharton's *Sappho: A Memoir and Translation* (1885), a collection of Sappho's surviving fragments, with critical apparatus and translations, the intervention of mostly men in the volume is significant because Michael Field's *Long Ago* presents Sappho's fragments alongside their own poems, challenging the male-dominated tradition preserved by Wharton's book. Wharton gives readers not only Sappho but prose translations by John Addington Symonds (1840–93), along with a number of examples of poets who have written Sapphic poetry in conversation with the ancient past. Men, by the end of the nineteenth century, for the most part, facilitated English readers' engagement with Sappho. Bradley and Cooper were educated, and their diaries show an ability to write and understand ancient Greek.[16] However, they use the discourse of male scholarship to talk with Sappho, layering equally important dialogues with both editor, Wharton, and queer translator, Symonds.

Whym Chow presents a discourse of death among the dead and dying. Cooper was in deep grief for their lost and beloved dog when she drafted these poems. Years later when Bradley collected the poems together for publication, she was grieving Cooper who died in 1913 from cancer.

Publishing the book with the Eragny Press at her own expense was an act of commemorating her earthly bond with Cooper, and the family they created together with their pet chow. The presence of Michael Field is significant because, even though it was primarily Cooper who wrote these poems, their shared identity emphasises the book's focus on commemorating a queer familial relationship made spiritual through the symbolic and literal figure of Whym Chow. Unlike their experience on *Long Ago*, or the experiences of Charles Ricketts and Charles Shannon outlined in the last two chapters, Bradley had room and the money to create *Whym Chow*. While it may seem an eccentric and privileged expense to create a book around a pet, such an impression ignores both the emotional state of a dying woman and the textual relations that the material book brings to the poetry. I seek to redeem the materialist project for the commemorative act of queer love that it represents.

This book's exploration of dual tales, much like its author(s), is a tale told in trinity. The chapter tells the story of trinities in three sections. First, it will examine trans* theory in relation to the concepts of the book's larger concern with queer relationality. Trans* conceptions of gender and change will allow for an understanding of Michael Field's *trans-textuality*, that is, his material presence as a male figure who is further enriched and transformed by the creative focus of each book. Second, the chapter turns to *Long Ago* as a text that materially and poetically destabilises binaries between the classical past and late Victorian present, between history and myth, and between women and men as poets. The third section is a study of *Whym Chow: Flame of Love*, where the subject of commemoration is a space of transition between pagan and Catholic that is left beautifully unresolved, and not finishing with their Catholic conversion. The queer space of the journey and experience of change transform conceptions of binary opposition between Christian and pagan practices into an ambiguous and queer relationality achieved and realised in the wake of their dog's death.

Michael Field's trans* unknowability

Preparing this book involved several trips to the British Library and an examination of the Ricketts and Shannon Papers. Bradley and Cooper were regular correspondents with these two men, as friends and as collaborators. For example, their historical play *Equal Love*, a Symbolist reimagining of Byzantine Empress Theodora, appears in the first volume of *The Pageant* (1896), where Shannon was art director and Ricketts unofficially supported both Shannon and literary editor Gleeson White (1851–98).[17] Reading letters written by Ricketts and Shannon, it is striking that they consistently address Bradley and Cooper with the collective and singular noun, 'Poet'.[18] Addressing them together as one transformed the women into a singular entity in their personal correspondence, just as the name 'Michael Field' sought to achieve the same in public spaces. Its usage suggests a recognition, at least among their close queer friends, that as Poet, they were a unity, simultaneously plural and singular.

The use of 'Poet' highlights the careful consideration that goes into references to Michael Field. Bradley and Cooper were cis-gendered women so she/her seems appropriate since they are using a non de plume as did George Eliot (Mary-Ann Evans) and the aforementioned Vernon Lee (Violet Paget), both of whom identified as women. However, Bradley and Cooper created Michael Field to be a male intermediary between them and the public, so it seems dismissive to ignore their choice. At the same time, these two people, Bradley and Cooper as Michael Field, are also a 'they'. Today with advances in trans* discourses surrounding gender identity, they/them has since become a common singular to use and it makes increasing sense to apply it to Michael Field, both in recognition of the plurality of the two women who wrote under the name and in acknowledgement of the male poet, a trans* figure whose presence textually engages with issues of gender and sexual desire as found in their poems. Michael Field is male, Bradley and Cooper are female, but that binary is undermined within the poetry that these multiple identities, together, create.

The use of trans* theory in this chapter brings up an issue with presentism that should not be ignored. Bradley and Cooper certainly did not see themselves or Michael Field as trans* gendered. However, they also would not think of themselves as feminist or queer. Since the 1970s, the discourses of feminist, queer and other forms of critical theory applied to the study of historical literature and subject matter have helped scholars better understand the past. I argue that trans* theory presents a similar opportunity to discover something new about the past, by interrogating it from a contemporary perspective. That perspective is limited to reader response and does not offer insight into these women's lives. Rather, it offers insight into literary and, specifically, bibliographic analysis of their publications only possible today because of the work done by feminist and queer scholars responsible for the renewed interest in Michael Field since the late twentieth century. Trans* theory is rarely taken up by Victorian studies scholars, but it offers new critical insight while acknowledging both the historical differences between the *fin de siècle* and today, as well as the value that new theoretical perspectives bring to our understanding of historical literature.

Michael Field exists in tandem with Bradley and Cooper both on the page and in their lives, reinforcing the fact that their own writing and creation process is collaborative and disruptive. Kristin Mahoney argues that Bradley and Cooper understood their collaborative writing practice 'as a radical process that called into question conventional ways of conceiving of work, possession, and the boundary between the self and the other'.[19] Their radical process and practices deserve an equally radical means of interpretation for today's reader, which is why trans* theory, which emerges from, and simultaneously challenges queer theory, is a valuable analytical perspective.

To understand trans* theory as a means of understanding Michael Field's textual intercourse, consider how sj Miller aligns emerging trans* identities with 'a pedagogy of refusal' in which the student (for Miller, this would be primary school aged trans* children) does not need to take on the burden of self-definition. Such a practice, Miller argues, 'opens up spaces where their trans-sectional and ever-evolving indeterminate gender identities are understood and recognized to be asset-based, rich courses for learning'.[20] Miller doesn't want clarifying categories of identity to influence childhood development and learning. Instead, they imagine the possibilities of difference not previously communicated. Gender becomes something that is always in question and indeterminate.[21] While such an approach complicates matters for those who have normalised gender binaries, for the children Miller is focused on, it frees a generation from the limits those binaries

impose and imagines a future without gender norms. J. Bobby
Noble earlier took on this notion of incoherence arguing that
'Trans marks not only gender trouble but also category trouble
that has the potential to reconfigure not just gender but embodiment itself.'[22] Incoherence has two meanings: 'first, it means a lack
of organization, or a failure of organization so as to make that
thing difficult to comprehend; but it also means failing to cohere
as a mass or entity'.[23] Trans* gender, then, is a position in which
gender binaries as we know them do not cohere. How the individual identifies defies the binary and exists somewhere in between,
not sexual inversion as it was understood in the nineteenth century
where masculine women and feminine men introduced androgyny
into gender discourse, but something in between that rejects male-female juxtaposition. Michael Field then is both male and female,
and neither: a figure who asks the reader to read the poetry contained in these volumes as outside of the gender politics of late
Victorian society. This theory applies to Michael Field because
of how the book, his body if you will, mixes the work of Bradley
and Cooper with other voices. His body is very different when
influenced by the fragments of Sappho and changes again when
placed alongside their pet chow. Who Michael Field is, is unclear,
and made more so by how the book is presented to the reader. The
presence of Bradley and Cooper is also complicated; they are there
as poets, but the Poet's paratextuality, on bindings and title pages,
makes the book, an extension of Michael Field, someone more
than just Bradley and Cooper.

A 2018 issue of *Victorian Review* is dedicated to the concepts
of trans* Victorians, exploring what Ardel Haefele-Thomas
positions as gender non-conformity in the nineteenth century
through the language of trans* experience rather than more conventional approaches of gender inversion that has emerged from
cis-gendered-focused feminist and queer theory. While those
approaches are important developments in Victorian studies and
continue to shape our readings of the past, they are also fields
that, Haefele-Thomas says, argue for the importance of trans*
considerations.[24] Lisa Hager's article calls for a careful parsing of
gender from sexuality from one another in order to better access
an understanding of the complex identities and self-expressions
in the nineteenth century.[25] Simon Joyce's article parallels current
social controversies surrounding trans* women in public washrooms in a recounting of Fanny and Stella, two people arrested for

using a women's public washroom at the Strand Theatre in 1870 and stripped at the police station to 'verify' that they were biologically male. Joyce positions these events as a trans* narrative because of the ways in which issues of gender and sexuality were divided and complicated by both defence and prosecutors. It also considers what a transgendered experience may have been like before the idea of medical transition was even a consideration.[26] Joyce extends his project with *LGBT Victorians* (2022) where he gives equal consideration of separate and overlapping experiences of gender identity and sexual desires in order to expand our understanding of queerness beyond the figure of Oscar Wilde.[27] His turn to transgender theory will hopefully expand scholarly engagement in nineteenth-century gender studies going forward.

Patricia Elliot details the sometimes-conflicted discourse between trans*, queer and feminist discourses of gender and sexuality and how these concepts influence a questioning and breakdown of socially constructed gendered binaries, far too often discussed as if they were naturally realised.[28] Many trans* people have diverse outlooks on their own gender identities that do not fit with this politicisation of their bodies by what could be criticised as a queer gaze. To be in a position to challenge social norms is a privileged position that many trans* people do not have the luxury to perform as figures marginalised in both heteronormative and queer communities.[29] Additionally, the political positioning of trans* often forgets to recognise trans* individuals seeking to transition their biological sex to become male or female, for whom trans* is not in itself an identity, but a transitory period.[30] Similarly, Michael Field's gendered identity, while tied to Bradley and Cooper, does not change their gender identities or their queer sexuality. A human in the late Victorian age had only a limited and privileged access to gender inversion practices, and I do not wish to suggest that Bradley and Cooper were themselves trans*. The importance of trans* concepts of gender incongruence apply to the reception of poetry and art in the late Victorian age. Michael Field's presence, as both the union of Bradley and Cooper, and as the textual body of the queer male aesthete, offers an incoherence regarding gender differences that enriches the poetic exploration of sexual and gender conflicts in their work. The book then is where the Poet and poetry merge to become indistinguishable. Marion Thain notes regarding Bradley and Cooper's refusal to publish their work in the *Yellow Book*, that 'Lyric poetry, more than prose, is altered by the context in which it is placed, and Bradley and Cooper did not want the multiplicity of their lyrics resolved, and destroyed, by the strong narrative and character of the *Yellow Book*.'[31] Such a text would alter the figure of Michael Field to the textuality of that periodical. The effect of controlling Michael Field's presence meant that Bradley and Cooper could protect their persona and avoid having it influenced by a book whose body they had no control over. It is not surprising that they turned to Ricketts and Shannon's Vale Press to publish many of their works. They trusted these men to understand, and not abuse, Michael Field's identity.[32] That identity was one of ambiguity, subtle gender subversion, with a critical engagement with the aesthetic practices of their male counterparts.

Today, scholarly research into Bradley and Cooper's lives and the availability of their journals make the role of lesbian desire in their work biographically central to the study of Michael Field. As has been argued elsewhere in this project, however, the desire of the authors is not necessarily what the reader of their volumes read when engaging with *Long Ago* or *Whym Chow*. Other figures stand between the reader and the authors' lives. The books are certainly haunted by the apparition of Bradley's and Cooper's desires and personalities, but Michael Field also has a presence to appreciate. That presence resembles Alyosxa Tudor's theory of 'transing', as underlining a historical genealogy of gendering.[33] Tudor uses their own experience, as a trans* man who once identified as a lesbian to discuss the idea of 'lesbian haunting to be constitutive for trans feminism, to be a transing of gender that might have been forgotten or denied, but that nevertheless does its work for feminism and queer and trans knowledge production'.[34] As someone whose gender has changed, Tudor's own experience gives credit to a historical experience as a lesbian for informing and helping them understand the here and now of their trans* identity. Tudor argues for an integration of lesbian history into contemporary transgender male discourses. Changing one's identity over time as Tudor describes also means that the individual is haunted by past choices, and past selves. The lesbian past remains visible for some trans* men and *her* visibility in *his* or *their* body is not something that needs to be erased. Instead, the past informs the present, enriches experience and encodes history on the body. The difference between lesbian experience and trans* male experience is not neatly divisible and, in relation to the study of Michael Field, any binary division between these experiences is erased by their books, which remain thematically ambiguous.

The trans-textuality that is proposed here is about questioning gender's influence on poetry and its themes; Michael Field's trans* presence, I argue, facilitated lesbian haunting, queer history and queer community. The Poet, as persona, becomes part of that material engagement with aestheticism. We find this alignment extended into the material book's role as art object. *Long Ago* resembles a piece of marble, a fragment or ruin of the past with pieces written on it and in it. A tombstone for the past, but a book for an as yet unrealised future in which same-sex desire experienced by women can be celebrated by women and haunted by the history of male intervention. The presence of a male author, as we shall see, adds additional layers of ambiguity to the concepts of sex and gender presented in the book. *Whym Chow* looks like their dead dog and embodies the warmth of a queer domestic idyll, the warmth of the russet colour of book and dog ask the reader to reimagine family and its conventions to see love between women and between human and animal as a valuable reimagining of modern living beyond gender conventions. To acknowledge the transing of gender in the book is not to revise our understanding of these important lesbian poets.

Long Ago

> O Sappho, bitter was thy pain! Then did thy heavy steps retire,
> And leave, moon-bathed, the virgin quire.
> – Michael Field, *Long Ago*, XVII

The queer book offers the reader a multimedial narrative, and Donald E. Hall reminds us that narrative affects how we perceive sexuality.[35] The narrative found in *Long Ago* is a historical reflection on the poetics of desire, beauty and love. Its focus is on the desires of women and how those desires are interpreted by readers of all genders and sexualities. History and myth are central, asking readers to engage with the stories of the past to better understand who they are in the here and now, and to imagine future possibilities of queerness. Difference and change are important considerations here because the narratives of same-sex desire and gender non-conformity are not stationary. *Long Ago* presents the past and asks the reader to engage with both the present and future of queer desire.

Figure 3.1 Front cover of *Long Ago* (1889). Courtesy of the Thomas Fisher Rare Book Library, University of Toronto.

Long Ago is a queer space mediated by trans-textuality – a work of art that makes space for queer relationality with particular attention to the act of temporal transition: that is, the space between the past and present. As a work of art, it tells a story not just in its poems, but in the juxtaposition of historical context with intimate modern poetry. As their critics noted, Bradley and

Cooper lived outside of time and could be anachronistic; that is because the text was a space where they could contemplate the idea of history in relation to the present. In addition to seeing modernity as a chance to create something new, it was also a time when the past could inform or change the future.

Sappho, like her poetry, is known only in fragments and this lack of detail has inspired generations of mythmaking around her as a historical figure.[36] She lived on the island of Lesbos in a community of women and the fragmented remains of her poetry continue to inspire a long history of modern poetic tradition of translating, rewriting and responding to her poetry.

She was a public figure who performed her poetry as song and is depicted often with her lute (see Fig. 3.2). Her songs suggest that she desired and loved both women and men. In tackling Sappho and the poetic tradition surrounding her history and myth, Michael Field centralises an ambiguous reimagining of gender and

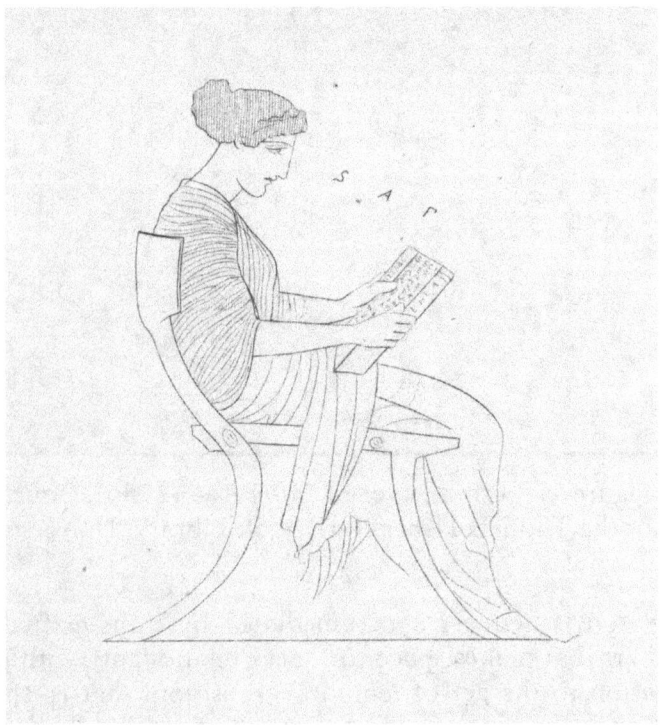

Figure 3.2 Frontispiece from *Long Ago*. Courtesy of the Thomas Fisher Rare Book Library, University of Toronto.

femininity that is influenced by both the ancient past and Bradley and Cooper's contemporary aesthetic community.

In a review of *Long Ago* from 1889 in *The Spectator*, the reviewer questions why a woman poet, as they identify Michael Field (Katharine Bradley and Edith Cooper), would place 'herself into apparent competition with a writer who stands by common consent in the front rank'.[37] And, while the reviewer claims to hold 'a profound respect' for Michael Field, they still argue that 'It is in dramatic verse that she has won her laurels, and she would do well to keep to it.'[38] As Parker and Parejo Vadillo note, this negative view of Michael Field's writing persisted throughout their lifetime, quoting their journal in 1893 where Edith Cooper laments that they are shunned and boycotted by both reviewers and by their fellow writers.[39] It is important to note that in reference to Sappho, the reviewer does not use gendered pronouns; it is only in criticism of Michael Field that gender is given any attention. Such was the atmosphere in which Bradley and Cooper published their work.

George Bell and Sons published 100 numbered copies of *Long Ago* on 23 May 1889.[40] Founded fifty years earlier, George Bell's son Edward was running operations at the firm and would oversee its continued expansion.[41] At this time, the firm had already purchased Chiswick Press, which would print *Long Ago* for the firm, and had a history of experimenting with the subject matter it published. For example, it acquired the Aldine Edition of British Poets series in 1854 and would go on to publish William Morris's *The Defence of Guenevere* (1858) as a part of that series.[42] Edward Bell, who attended Trinity College, brought with him an interest in classical literature and architecture. *Long Ago* would have appealed to his interests and served as a prestige publication to help to enhance the firm's reputation for publishing quality volumes of note.[43] The volume was bound in stiff white vellum over boards with creases on the surface of the skin that seem intentionally left. It features a gilt roundel with Sappho in profile similar to how faces are etched into coins and her name etched in Greek beneath.

Not only does Sappho impress the cover, but she is also pictured in profile on the frontispiece. This second image is from a vase dated 420 BC held at the time in an Athens museum, a reproduction of which was accessed by Bradley and Cooper via a Mr Murray at the British Museum.[44] She is pictured playing her lyre, singing the songs from which her fragments derive. In the text itself, Michael Field claims to have selected the images with a singular 'I' used in the paratextual note after the last poem, in addition to selecting the fragments from which their poetry emerges. While not the book designers, Bradley and Cooper were closely involved in its design and production selecting and approving its context and creating a physical exhibition for their poetry. That united creation is given the singular 'I', confusing identity and keeping the reader's attention on the material book's own voice through its prefatory and postscript text.

Dr Henry Thornton Wharton's *Sappho, A Memoir and Translation* not only inspired *Long Ago* poetically but it was also an important source of bibliographic influence.[45] The large-copy first edition of Wharton's book was bound in vellum with a gilt impression of Sappho's lyre in the centre of the front cover (see Fig. 3.3). Inside, Wharton's book follows a specific structure: a fragment all in Greek, followed by a prose translation in italics

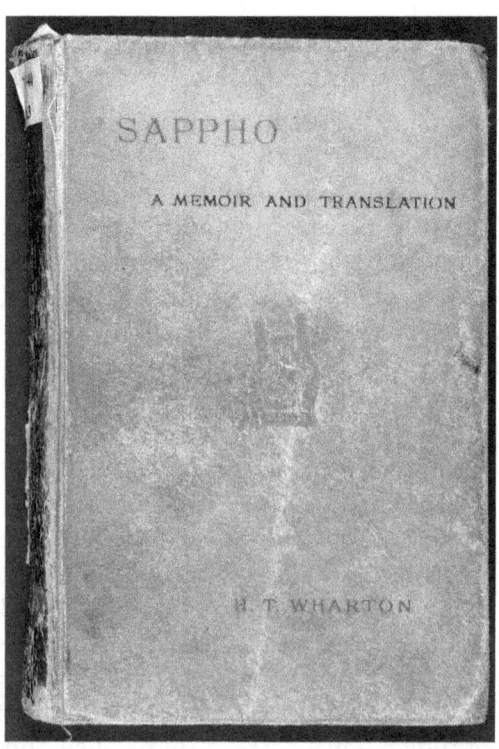

Figure 3.3 H. T. Wharton's *Sappho: A Memoir and Translation* (1885). By permission of the British Library.

by John Addington Symonds (1840–93), followed then by English poems written by a variety of mostly male authors inspired by and incorporating Sappho's words and metre. Many fragments have nothing but Symonds's prose translation accompanying them. All 170 fragments that were available in the 1880s are included. Wharton presents the collection as his work, but it is the work of numerous others who mediate access to Sappho for Wharton and his readers. Of all these authors, it is only Symonds, himself a queer aesthete and historian, who is in direct discourse with Sappho herself as someone who can read the original fragments. The result is a bibliographic story of reference where Sappho's influence on the history of western poetry is made abundantly clear.

Conversation in this book about her influence, however, is dominated by men. Wharton's own role is that of editorial authority over the subject matter. The book is Wharton's Sappho – his interpretation and archive of a possibly historic, but certainly mythic, figure of classical Greek literature.

The trans-male identity of Field in *Long Ago* serves to bring heightened attention to both the role of women in literary history and the role of men in mediating that discourse. Like Wharton in his book, Michael Field has editorial control, but their male dominance is ambiguous because it is undermined by the public knowledge that 'he' is the poetic voice of women. He becomes they; his effeminate pose allows the reader to then imagine a history of women talking with women about Sappho's role in literary history. While mediated by a man, the text's centralisation of Sappho's image with both the cover and the frontispiece places him second to Sappho herself (see Fig. 3.1). She dominates Michael Field's trans-textual body, and despite critics claiming the opposite, he gladly defers to her superior presence.

Sappho is further empowered through page placement. While not exact, Sappho's fragments are nearly in the centre of the page. The fragments are presented in a more costly red ink, typically used for titles or decorative marginalia as found in William Morris's Kelmscott books. The red draws the reader's focus to Sappho's fragments and simultaneously sets her apart from the text of Michael Field. This change is a bibliographic response to the more cluttered page of Wharton's book where italicised fragments are squeezed between modern poems and translated text. Wharton's book presented a tradition in which Sappho is a means to an end for male poets and historians. Michael Field's book returns Sappho to her central place in the tradition of western poetry. Like Wharton, Bradley and Cooper are preserving Sappho's work and celebrating it with the surviving fragments as the central thought and concept for everything that follows. To achieve this affect, the book makes creative use of white space leading down to the fragment. Before each fragment, the reader must pause on the empty page before moving to the next poem. It gives a grandeur to their introduction and physically positions the poems of Michael Field as responses and inspirations taken from the far more important originals.

Whatever conversation follows in the poems themselves, Bradley and Cooper want readers to know that it begins always with Sappho. Unlike Wharton, Michael Field offers no prose translation. Quite the contrary, they reimagine Symonds's translations poetically to suit the structure of their lyrics. Symonds and Field are both queer mediators of women's voices and female expressions of desire. They both conceive the value of female desire and same-sex desire as a significant aesthetic consideration. Remembering that the translations are actually Symonds's work and not Wharton's, the reader can understand Michael Field's engagement as a continuation of queer interest in Sappho's work and influence. The queerness of Symonds, Bradley and Cooper undermines the heteronormative dominance of Wharton and other Victorian men. Michael Field's queer manhood challenges and brings critical attention to that gendered tradition, with his mediation of Bradley and Cooper's work, serving as an ironic satire of heteronormativity and a complication of male homosocial engagement with female homosexuality. They introduce uncertainty and their presence haunts Michael Field's identity, directing the reader's gaze to the gendered demands of their work.

Unlike the various poetic examples in Wharton's book, Michael Field is not trying to master Sappho's style but responds to it with their own poetic voice. Most fragments selected are ones with little to no examples accompanying them in Wharton's text. The selected fragments are also out of order, defying not only Wharton's ordering but the ordering of the fragments in Sappho scholarship. In addition, their translation of the fragments in their poems does not match Symonds's translations in the Wharton. Michael Field trusted their own choices and their reading of the poems to alter what was presented to them to suit their poetry.

Take for example, XXXV., Ἀλλα, μή μεγαλύνεο δακτυλίῳ πέρι, which Symonds translates as 'Foolish woman, pride not thyself on a ring.'[46] Their poem does not chronologically follow the fragment but serves to prelude the line with a conversation between Sappho as speaker and a woman named Gorgo, who she reminds of the power that her beauty commands over other men. She asks, 'Art thou so glad the sardonyx / Becomes thy shapely hand?'[47] The sarcasm of the line mocks the privileging of men's love for women and the expectation of women's subservient appreciation. Sappho reminds her that the ring does not have power over her, but that Gorgo's 'fairest hands' possess the 'power to thrill and cling'.[48] The poem ends with their revision of Sappho's line: 'Oh foolish woman, does thou set / Thy pride upon a ring?'[49] The change is subtle but important. By ending the poem with their interpretation of the fragment, they emphasise Sappho's undermining of male power over women through marriage, allowing Gorgo's power as a sexual being to dominate their poem. They also change it from a chiding command to a question. The revision shows respect for the woman Sappho critiques. Here, she is a friend persuading her companion to see her own inner strength and to make the decision for herself. Wharton offers no example poems of this fragment, suggesting room for an interpretation that would honour the agency of the women Sappho loved so dearly. By challenging Sappho's poetry, Michael Field demonstrates respect for Sappho's female voice and that they imagine Sappho in a different context. It is context that the fragments are missing, and it is the agency of a woman's point of view that Michael Field recuperates from a fragment preserved from 160 AD by a grammarian named Herodian.[50] Again, men serve as mediators here, both the preserver and the figure of Michael Field. However, what those men preserve here is space for women to share textual intercourse regarding sexuality, gender and empowerment.

Sappho, as a woman, makes homosexuality in the nineteenth century safe because it is something of the past: pagan and relegated to history. Her bisexual/pansexual desires also allowed scholars to focus primarily on her desire for men. However, to talk of Sappho's desires is to also talk about men's desires for Sappho's sexual discourse. She allows men room to discuss sexually inverted desires through the bodies of women. In doing so, nineteenth-century discourses of sexual pathology can influence their choices. Take for example Swinburne's 'Anactoria'.[51] In the poem, written from the point of view of Sappho herself, we see her desire for Anactoria who herself loves a man and does not appreciate Sappho, who ties her beloved up and whips her bloody:

> Ah that my lips were tuneless lips, but pressed
> To the bruised blossom of thy scourged white breast!
> Ah that my mouth for Muses' milk were fed
> On the sweet blood they sweet small wounds had bled!
> That with my tongue I felt them, and could taste
> The faint flakes from thy bosom to the waist!
> That I could drink thy veins as wine, and eat
> Thy breast like honey! that from face to feet
> Thy body were abolished and consumed,
> And in my flesh thy very flesh entombed![52]

Swinburne's Sappho is angry and aroused by both the infliction of pain to Anactoria's body and the act of touching and tasting her wounds and blood. She is vampiric, but Swinburne's verse also suggests that Sappho believes Anactoria would want her to take such pleasure. However, Anactoria's voice is not here, nor anywhere, after these proclamations. The result is an objectification of a woman's beaten body. None of Sappho's fragments suggests either sadomasochism or physical abuse between Sappho and other women. The scene is of Swinburne's imagination and allows him to explore what he desires, the juxtaposition of pleasure and pain through the bodies of women. Sappho is all passion without compassion or thought of Anactoria as a companion, friend or lover. It is Swinburne's agency that dominates the poem and pieces together a sadistic male sexual fantasy of hysterical lesbianism from the fragments of a woman's history. It is not a discourse between women, Sappho and Anactoria; it is a discourse between men, Swinburne and his presumed male reader.

Bradley and Cooper spoke enthusiastically of Swinburne's *Poems and Ballads, First Series* (1866), celebrated by many and controversial to others because of Swinburne's exploration of same-sex desire between women, male homoerotic desire, hermaphroditism and explicit explorations of sadomasochism.[53] In their 1889 letter included with a copy of *Long Ago* that they sent to Swinburne, Michael Field sends admiration to the man who, with 'flaming sword ... kept guard over the Lesbian lyrics'.[54] While their approach to Sapphic love is very different, they appreciate and admire his interpretation. They saw their own work as contributing to a discourse found in both Wharton and Swinburne's books. Rather than speak directly to either man, however, they return to the woman at the centre of the tradition.

In doing so, they create a change of tone, trusting their own reading of the Greek fragments and their own poetic ability to create something worthy of Sappho's voice. For example, poem XXXIII. Ταῖς κάλαις ὔμμιν [τὸ] νόημα τὦμον οὐ διάμειπτον·, translated by Symonds in the Wharton text as 'To you, fair maids, my mind changes not.'[55] Michael Field changes the line to 'Maids, not to you my mind doth change.'[56] Symonds makes Sappho the subject of the line, while Michael Field makes Sappho's maids the subject. Sappho, the speaker, declares love for her maids, the female priestesses committed to Sappho on the island of Lesbos. Sappho's deferral in the Michael Field interpretation provides a sense of queer community among these women. Sappho sings, not to sexual objects, but to her companions who, as subjects of their own sentences, have agency outside of Sappho's desire for them. While a man's 'patience' may 'tire', Sappho offers women her 'love's refrain'– a song that never complains of 'inward want or woe'.[57] Men, from the perspective of the poem are the source of women's 'pain' and 'woe' while the sisterhood of Lesbos and Sappho offers a place were women can be mutual comforts to one another.

Sappho tells her maids that, while with men she may 'defy, allure, [and] estrange', between her and women there 'is no thought of pain, / Peril, satiety'.[58] Instead, women are a tonic for Sappho's frustrations with male lovers, filling her 'weary bosom' with their 'soft vitality'. She compares that vitality to 'nymph from stream or tree' making the love of women both magical and natural. Where Swinburne sees objects to flay and objectify and female desire as something hysterical and even threatening, Michael Field presents desire between women as something complicated, certainly natural, but also artful – a nymph – whose magic soothes in the face of heteronormativity's games. Heterosexual desire is manipulation, a game where genders are in opposition. Same-sex desire is presented as a consolation. Michael Field's complex gender identity, both male and female in its composition, complicates the presentation of same-sex desire. As a queer man, Michael Field presents love between women as a palatable presentation of same-sex desire that could also be a consolation for men reading between the lines. As women, Bradley and Cooper present their desire for one another as a curative for the burdens of love outside of their union. As a discourse between Field and Wharton, the poem questions male discourses of female desire as exotic displays of forbidden otherness, making love between women a natural and mythical reality in western literature and culture. As a discourse between history and the here and now, *Long Ago* centres Sappho's desire and responds with a poem that imagines both the history of love and desire, and a future where same-sex passion is a curative to the gender binaries of Victorian heteronormativity.

That imagined community of women is brought to life on the page of the book for queer readers of Michael Field. The poem suggests an eternal commitment similar to the one shared by Bradley and Cooper. It is a promise of safety, love and an exchange of women's 'soft vitality' that can fill one another with as much satisfaction as a relationship with a man, but without the misery and betrayal of such relations. The poems critique heteronormative relationships from a woman's point of view where they are the objects of men's fickle desires. It also suggests a way forward into queer forms of love within a same-sex community. The queer book makes these works accessible, translating not the ancient Greek, but the affective emotions of Bradley and Cooper in response to Sappho's fragments. She is honoured, not as an object of desire, but as a poetic mentor. Michael Field, haunted by the lesbianism of Bradley and Cooper, creates a bridge between the past and the present and imagines a queer relationality between Sappho and queer contemporary readers. In the pages of the book a queer past both historical and mythic has been revealed, and it inspires the poet's hope for a similar community in the future.

Michael Field as a trans-textual identity is not a mere tool to facilitate lesbian sexuality. Such a characterisation would diminish actual trans* readers who may similarly find a historical precedent for their experience of gender in the pages of *Long Ago*. Michael Field is a beloved creation and a living embodiment of creative energy that intentionally confuses gender binaries. The masculine and feminine find homes on the pages *Long Ago*. Take for example, their poem on Tiresias, LII. Ἔγων δ' ἐμαύτᾳ τοῦτο σύνοιδα.[59] Responding to Sappho's fragment 'And this I feel in myself',[60] we witness Tiresias's transformation from a woman into a man. After which, 'when love came, and, when loving back, / He learnt the pleasure men must lack, / It seemed that he has broken free / Almost from his mortality.'⁶¹ *The Spectator* review was particularly offended that Field translates the 'rude and coarse' Tiresias myth, and that 'his general judgement is unfavourable'.⁶² The repugnance shown for Tiresias is, in a manner, a repugnance for Bradley and Cooper's experiment with identity. By calling the poet 'she', the reviewer rejects their chosen gender as a poet. The reviewer also rejects the idea that poetry can transcend gender and social mores surrounding women and their lives. In the instance of *Long Ago*, by taking on the identity of a queer man, one who enjoys the pagan and the homoerotic, they are shamed as a vulgar mockery of Victorian gender norms. They are for this reviewer a new Tiresias, once women, corrupted by decadence and queer masculinity.

Tiresias's change of biological sex is revelatory; not only does he discover the female orgasm, but he also goes outside of the experience of gender, breaking almost from his 'mortality' or human perception of desire and life. Tiresias learns something about the limits of binary opposition. Hera summons him to Olympus and demands to know who, man or woman, takes more pleasure from the sex act. Tiresias does not really answer. Nor is the fragment of Sappho's uttered in the poem. Hera's words are in quotes, and nothing is quoted in reply. The poem's speaker is not Tiresias and speaks of the 'mystic raptures of the bride', in response to 'man's strong nature draweth nigh'. His desire is as important to the experience of pleasure as her pleasure. No clear answer is given, but Tiresias's is changed from the experience. It is the speaker, Michael Field who declares at the end of the first stanza that,

> When womanhood was round him thrown:
>   He trembled at the quickening change, He trembled at his vision's range,
> His finer sense for bliss and dole, His receptivity of soul;
>   But when love came, and, loving back, He learnt the pleasure men must lack, It seemed that he had broken free Almost from his mortality.⁶³

It is significant that Michael Field narrates this passage and that it is not in quotes. First, as the poem's speaker, Michael Field blurs the traditional boundary between poet and poem, tying his textual presence to the literary content on the page. As a male speaker, queer in his aesthetic point of view, and connected to the lesbian imagination that brought him into being, they are the one who suggests women experience greater sexual pleasure than men. Such a position is transgressive for the period when, as we will see in more detail in the next chapter, women's sexual desires were not even universally understood as possible. For this particular man to speak in the text in sympathy with the poem's Tiresias – a man whose transitions from man to woman and then back to a man – is an acknowledgement of the relationship between the experience of the male poet and their origins in the lesbian imagination of Bradley and Cooper, as well as the aesthetic poet's own queer alignment with other aesthetes studied in this book. As a queer man, he is telling other men what they will never know. Bradley and Cooper have a position here rare in aesthetic poetry – one where a woman's desire is known from a woman's point of view. They undermine the binary of man/woman and suggest that Sappho's pleasure as poet, her female desire, is the one that reigns supreme in the book. At the same time, Tiresias remains silent. The poem does not give him agency, so we do not discover either an answer to Hera's interrogation, or his perspective. We only know through the poem that it was during his time as a woman when he experienced the most pleasure. His return to being a man is potentially informed by the history of transformation that he has experienced meaning that his perception of gendered sexuality is changed by the memory of uncertainty and exploration. Pleasure comes not from a certain answer, but from the mystery of Tiresias's unique experience.

In terms of Michael Field's male agency, consider the many poems in which desire for men is expressed. Sappho's love for men like Phaon is mediated by a queer male aesthete's voice. These poems, remember, are inspired by Sappho; the poet speaking is Michael Field, so when Phaon is 'bent / Above his nets, magnificent',[64] it is both Sappho and Michael Field who express delight in his beauty. As we saw in the Tiresias poem, the poet and speaker are interconnected. Michael Field is as much a figure in the poems as Sappho, and his embrace of her point of view, once again, confuses conventional gender boundaries, comments on the male poetic tradition of taking from Sappho and inverts the male tradition of objectifying lesbian desire, by objectifying a woman's male lover. Female desire for men is given queer overtones by a male poet who shares Sappho's desires. That means when the speaker asks Atthis to not 'flutter from my side' when dawn awakens them in bed together, Michael Field imagines Sappho speaking to Atthis, as a queer aesthete, and takes pleasure in the desire for the male body. In balancing these diverse and complex imaginings of gender and sexual desire, Bradley and Cooper have created a poetic landscape where men and women express and experience desire and question gendered perceptions of sex. Binary differences of heterosexual vs homosexual, male/female vs cisgender/trans* are blurred with no clear division. Such a breakdown of gendered sexual order is possible because the queer space of the book, as we have seen in previous chapters, makes a space for the possibility, even if such a possibility was not possible in late Victorian everyday life. They perform queer manhood, and the result is a transing that embraces the unknown and incoherence that occurs when the gender boundary is dissolved.

This section began with a quote from poem XVII. because of the double entendre of 'quire' – referencing both the speaker's genitalia, but also the collection of paper in a book. Both are intimate spaces in *Long Ago*. The poem is a lament for lost virginity and its aesthetic beauty. Here we see the separation between speaker and subject. Michael Field is once more the speaker who is telling the story of Sappho's lament. Her lost virginity is both tragic and pleasurable for both her and the reader. She regrets her lost innocence and the beauty of its purity, but that page has been turned. She will never have it again, but in its place comes new pleasures not yet imagined. In poem XXXIII., Sappho finds solace, love and desire in her relations with the women of Lesbos. Mediated by Michael Field, it is their desire too but expressed amongst women as a male sexual desire from someone perceived as only posing as a male. His presence does not make Sappho's lesbianism less subversive; instead, he reminds the reader of Bradley and Cooper's desires and presence in the text as well. The reader is then aware of the Poet's own non-binary gendering as someone who exists in the liminal space between the male body and the lesbian imagination. In *Long Ago*, these binary oppositions of sex and gender are transformed into intertextual pleasures, and their reunion, a union once held in Grecian times, is restored in this book where the present finds community with 'a long, long time ago'.[65]

Michael Field is entrenched in the material book; he is an aesthetic persona who is given a body through decorative bookmaking. Typography, paper choice, binding design and ink all serve to create a material ideal of the Poet that is at once deeply entrenched in the minds of Bradley and Cooper, and imaginatively materialised in the body of the book. The Poet mediates a literary history between classical poet, Sappho and new poets Bradley and Cooper. Michael Field mediates history, offering readers an opportunity to touch the past. History becomes a living artifact that can influence future queer relations. Just as Michael Field can touch Sappho, Tiresias, Phaon and the Maids of Lesbos by blurring gender boundaries and disconnecting sex from gender convention, he can also inspire readers to create similar relations between the past and their own lives, creating an imaginative history to inspire a queer future that lies outside of the everyday life that Michael Field's anachronistic poetics rejects.

Whym Chow

Whym Chow: Flame of Love was privately published at Katharine Bradley's expense by the Eragny Press in 1914. Only 27 numbered copies were ever printed, and the British Library currently holds copy number 25, donated by Emily Fortex and Mary Sturgeon in July of 1915. It is telling that Sturgeon, in her 1922 book *Michael Field*, avoids discussing *Whym Chow* in her study of their lyric poetry, ending instead with their collection *Mystic Trees* (1913).[66] As their biographer and a recipient of their final privately printed work, she does not give the volume a prominent place in her remembrance of either Michael or Henry, other than as a private text with only 'bibliographical' significance.[67] However, considering that the poems were written in 1906, mostly by Edith Cooper and not both women, it makes sense that Sturgeon's interest in tracing their Catholic conversion would focus more on *Mystic Trees* (1913) since it was the last work that they wrote together. *Whym Chow* has been largely inaccessible other than from archives until recently when the open library at the University of British Columbia created a digital copy from number 21, held in the Hawkesyard Priory Library in the UK (see Fig. 3.4). The book consists of thirty poems over fifty-eight pages. In between the bastard title and the main title page, in the lower-right margin of the left page, Whym Chow's date of birth and date of death are inscribed (see Fig. 3.5): 29 October 1897–28 January 1906. Their beloved pet lived for a little more than eight years, and he is commemorated in expensive red ink and a humble marginal placement. The epigraph on the full title page is a quote from Robert Browning's poem 'Rabbi Ben Ezra', a meditation on death and aging.

Figure 3.4 Cover binding for Michael Field's *Whym Chow: Flame of Love* (1914). Courtesy of the Rare Books and Special Collections, University of British Columbia.

Figure 3.5 Front matter with Whym Chow's date of birth and date of death. Courtesy of the Rare Books and Special Collections, University of British Columbia.

Some poems are titled in all capital letters, others are only numbered and acknowledged on the table of contents with a quotation of the first line. Each poem is numbered (roman numerals) and preceded with a small, black three-leaf clover. Each poem begins with a decorative letter designed at the Eragny Press in red ink, and the poem is presented in a typeface approved by Bradley in advance. The typeface used has a gothic appearance and its formality suggests the ritualistic materialism of Catholic ceremony. The heart of the book is emphasised by the placement of the title on the cover in the upper-left corner. In addition to featuring a heart-shaped leaf in the title pasted to the suede cover, it gives the front board the appearance of a chest with its heart labelled by a reference in the title to their dog. At the end of the collection, a beautifully designed label for the Eragny Press follows a statement in all capital letters that reads, 'THESE POEMS WERE WRITTEN IN 1906 AND WERE PRINTED IN THE

EARLY SPRING OF 1914.' Even the publication is presented as a commemoration.

The book was printed by Esther Pissarro (1870–1951), making the venture another collaboration between women from composition to print. It was printed as an octavo because the small size meant less paper and a reduced cost. It also allowed for the use of small woodcuts, which again were economical, allowing the press to print beautiful books at an affordable price. The Eragny Press was founded by Esther and her husband, Lucien Pissarro (1863–1944), in 1894; *Whym Chow* would be the last book published by the Eragny Press, with the outbreak of the Great War making their business venture financially impossible to continue.[68] They were not going to do the book originally because of the expense, but with Cooper dead and Bradley recently diagnosed and terminally ill, 'it had become a sacred duty to [Esther Pissarro] that the little book be printed'.[69] Esther agreed to work, at Bradley's expense, to finish the book, though at the expense of Esther's time as well. It was finished in April 1914, and cost Bradley 60 guineas.[70] It was not intended for sale, but as a gift for Bradley and Cooper's closest friends, a commemoration, not just of their relationship but a final work by the figure of Michael Field, whose voice was dependent upon the collaboration of both women, also passing onto the next world with this final publication.[71]

The book becomes a sacred object, a piece of privately distributed pagan and Catholic iconography that makes their union as Michael Field something sacred and valuable. It is significant that the name Michael Field appears as the book's author since Cooper authored the poems, and because it serves a funerary purpose to acknowledge Cooper's death, it seems strange to credit their shared poetic identity. The reason for Michael Field's presence, however, can be found in the book's purpose of commemoration. Bradley is commemorating the life that she shared with Cooper, a union that produced Michael Field, whose presence was as familial to them as that of their pet chow. Michael Field is the embodiment of Bradley and Cooper's creative union being commemorated alongside Whym Chow. Bradley is mourning the loss of her family, a family tied to artistic creation and Michael Field is central to that legacy. She may have done little more than edit the poems, but that is a part of their process, to finish and correct each other's work. In addition, the book itself is the product of Bradley's imagination. Bound together in *Whym Chow* is the final creative union of Michael Field. Bradley herself was dying of cancer at this time, so for readers it becomes a commemoration of their entire queer family, lost to time, but preserved by the textual intercourse in the book.

Michael Field's commemoration is embodied in a discourse of memory that ties the dog, Cooper and Bradley together as a queer family. The family unit is queered by their absence of men, the lack of sexual reproduction to produce children and the non-traditional way in which they lived. Their lesbian union was also incestuous, as aunt and niece living as lovers or as a married couple; they lived a life that challenged many social conventions and that is reflected in this volume. Once again, as they did with *Long Ago*, their final work is an art object, something to be collected and appreciated for the textual intercourse between bibliography and literary context. The book prompts a soft and careful touch from the reader with its dark orange suede binding, giving it a warmth that reflects the intimate, warm relations between the figures who make up the book's pagan trinity.

Thain notes that the subtitle, 'Flame of Love', is a reference to St John's *The Living Flame of Love*, suggesting, as seen in Chapter 1's exploration of John Gray's poetry, a juxtaposition of sexual and spiritual ecstasy with the saint's most sensual poem.[72] The desire to be close to God is contrasted with an opening lament for remaining in a 'Hades of the living' where the speaker lives on without the company of their beloved 'little Chow'.[73] The poems are both laments and prayers to the lost animal as the speaker asks Whym Chow, 'Be our daemon, be / Guardian-angel near / To the cruel sphere / Of our destiny'.[74] The Poet wants to be haunted and connected to the afterlife with the dog as a medium to connect their hell on earth with the promise of eternal life that their dog's death represents.

From the collection, 'V. Trinity' receives the most critical attention, but its placement in the book is significant and deserves consideration. In poem 'IV.', just before it, they lay their 'Bacchic Cub' at the feet of Dionysus. They beg their pagan God, 'let us rove and rove with him' and ask that he 'bring him and thy wine-cup with thee only – / Our Chow, our Whym, / And thirst should end, and passion bind desire'.[75] The poem precedes 'Trinity' and stands beside it when opened to the poems (see Fig. 3.6). It is a contrast to their prayer to Bacchus, in that they are asking instead for understanding as the poem explains their relationship to a God, who, they worry, may misinterpret their love as 'blasphemy'.[76] Whym Chow serves as both the holy spirit of Cooper and Bradley's relationship, and 'Thy Dove', or messenger of peace. The poem suggests that they are leading a parallel life of pagan spirituality and Christian meditation. But the speaker warns that their love is 'Not white', with purity, but 'a thing of fire' and 'one desire.'[77] Their union is sexual, physical and earthly. That is why Whym Chow, 'An animal', serves as a 'symbol of our perfect union, strange / Unconscious Bearer of Love's interchange'.[78]

Where the Bacchic poem is a cry for Whym Chow to be received in death, 'Trinity' positions the dog as a peace offering, an innocent member of their queer family who can speak to the beauty of their relationship and begin to win God's empathy, despite their continued celebration of paganism and queer passion. The poems are a pagan cry for God's understanding

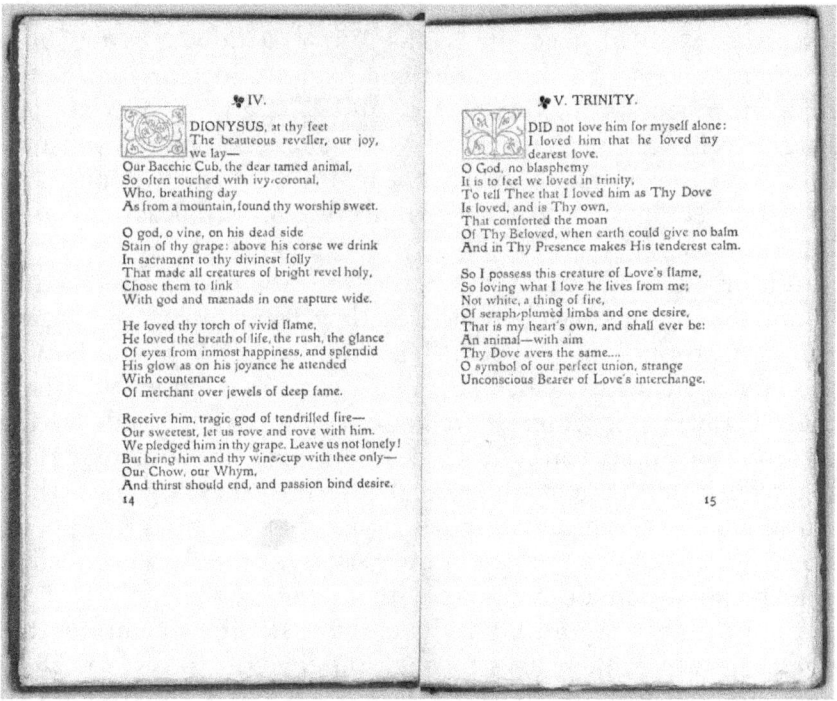

Figure 3.6 Poems IV. and V. Trinity from *Whym Chow*. Courtesy of the Rare Books and Special Collections, University of British Columbia.

of their queer life, and a love that included not just Bradley and Cooper, but also their chow:

> I DID not love him for myself alone:
> I loved him that he loved my dearest love. O God, no blasphemy
> It is to feel we loved in trinity.[79]

The poem acknowledges two trinities: that shared by Cooper as author, Bradley as her dearest love and the dog; and another trinity, between Michael Field, their Bacchanalian love and God. Dennis Denisoff notes how the poem complicates any notion of individuality, a pagan notion of connectivity that goes beyond human relations into the realms of nature and spiritual plains.[80] They merge paganism and Catholicism through the figures of both Whym Chow and Michael Field. In the process, they also parallel the Holy Trinity of the Catholic faith. Their poetic voice is who makes this appeal to God, and like Whym Chow, Michael Field is a product of their queer union. The physical intersects with abstract desire as Whym Chow/*Whym Chow* becomes a vessel to integrate their pagan and Christian spiritualism, a 'symbol of our perfect union, strange / Unconscious Bearer of Love's interchange'.[81] Michael Field connects spiritual love with the physical love between Bradley and Cooper, and the dog becomes a means of connecting spiritual ecstasy with human sensuality.

Within the context of the book, the poems narrate a story about the space between faiths as they transition from paganism to Catholicism. In Poem 'VI.', the loss of Whym Chow is the Poet's means by which to enter a metaphysical world where their beloved pet 'came / To his Creator's feet'.[82] Still feeling distant from their Catholic God, but deeply desirous that their pet transitions to a metaphysical afterlife, they visualise their chow by God's side, just as he sat by theirs. This sixth poem, however, continues the pagan imagery with the flame of Delphi and the positioning of worship with a dance at the end. The Poet does not simply beg for God's love, they ask Him to embrace the pagan beauty of their lives through the love of 'Chow, the glory and the gold-furred state / That smote beyond the strength of any verse'.[83] It is not enough that they convert to Catholicism, but they ask the Catholic God to likewise embrace their pagan spiritual practices.

The conversion, at this point, was incomplete and instead a balance between the two is proposed. The boundary between Catholicism and paganism is blurred as the poem records a period of transition.

The dog is a loved member of their family, and their trinity is not a sacrilegious equivocation of the women on earth and God in heaven, but a means of comparing families. Just as God has his son and Holy Spirit, Cooper and Bradley have each other and Whym Chow. They are certainly different, queer in their assemblage as family, but their bond is as powerful as the bonds God has displayed in His love for His son. The contrast of the two poems together gives 'Trinity' an added pagan point of view. Rather than being a conversion poem, it is an attempt to reconcile two contrasting belief systems.

Thain notes the significance of trinities in the work of Michael Field as 'not only a point of reconciliation between Bradley and Cooper's earthly desires and their religious passion but also a point of continuity between Michael Field's earlier pagan and later Catholic poetry'.[84] With *Whym Chow*, Thain praises their 'shameless' bathos in the use of their dog as a means by which to 'overcome significant anxieties about their erotic relationship in the context of their Catholic conversion'.[85] However, in the context of the book, the poetry is not made bathetic by their dog's presence. Their love for their dog is neither trivial nor ridiculous as the term implies. Instead, their pet plays a queer role in their lives.

To a reader with no personal connection to the women who wrote these poems, the continued appearance of Whym Chow is somewhat disconcerting. The collection reminds the reader repeatedly that they were writing about their dog. Someone who does not sympathise with the loss of a dear pet or understand the bond between a pet and their owner could misunderstand their metaphors. However, the queerness of the authors and the knowledge that Bradley and Cooper expected of their intended audience is significant. As Mahoney points out, by 'placing the dog in a series of spiritualized erotic and kinship positions [they] call into question the fixity of the distinction between species' and propose a queer theory of 'alliance and interrelation' that 'rethink[s] the distinction between human and non-human animals at the turn of the century'.[86] The book was intended only for close friends and relations. As was noted earlier, they were not famous poets, but poetic contributors to a small queer community. It was not meant for public consumption, but for circulation to intimate friends who knew the women and the role that the dog played in their lives. The pet was a family member who shared their bed, their food, their social space and intimate secrets. The book's mimicry of the pet's body means that it becomes a consolation for the loss of the bond they shared with Whym Chow.

Whym Chow also gives physicality to their bond without explicitly describing their sex life. In Poem 'XXII.', they speak of 'Sleeping together' and 'Eating together', 'Breathing together', and 'Loving together', and include the chow in their conception of their family as 'Thee and us'.[87] However, it is only in the morning when Whym Chow 'To our bed unwavering leapt'.[88] At night, they share their bed without the dog. He brought them joy, but the implication is that Bradley and Cooper's intimate relationship also brought joy. The book is careful in depicting their relationship but there is no apology for it, just as there is no apology for retaining their pagan beliefs and practices. Instead, they want the listener, and God, to accept their lives for what they were. More than consolation, the book as *Whym Chow* preserves a dying trinity: with the loss of Whym Chow and Henry prior to its publication, Katharine Bradley creates a material union of their shared love that can persevere in the face of death. Yes, they hope to be reunited in a metaphysical afterlife, but as long practitioners of pagan ritual, Bradley ensures that the trinity lives on materially in the warm body of the book. Just as Michael Field blurs the boundaries of gender and sexuality, *Whym Chow* blurs the boundary between life and death when half of the Poet had already passed, and the other was terminally ill. Michael Field is the one who, despite the death of the woman, can live on, their creative union embodied and commemorated in one final trans-textual book.

The book from its suede binding to the beautiful lettering of the typeface is an object that embodies the emotional experience of loss, grief, loneliness and consolation from faith. Whym Chow is grieved by Edith Cooper in the collection. At the same time, the book's preparation and publication is Katharine Bradley's commemoration of Cooper, who in her final years as she struggled with cancer consoled herself with the thought that she would be reunited with their beloved pet. Finally, it is Michael Field, left behind on the page by all three, who consoles the reader with their memory. The poetry, then, serves as a means of coping with unbearable loss and the publication allowed Bradley to do the same when she lost her beloved Henry to cancer the year before its publication. The idea that the book is their final work as Michael Field closes the complex relations that made the poetry published under that name intimate and aesthetic.

While sacrilegious on the surface, *Whym Chow*'s textuality shows the appeal of Catholicism to the women's pagan sensibilities. Take the use of metaphysical conceit in the seventeenth poem 'XVII. Created' where Whym Chow's soul is compared to flame captured in a 'brazier'. Fire is used as a source of power and light in pagan rituals with braziers featuring in ritual spaces for centuries. Just as it 'holds a flame / Close of rare incense in it sheathed', Whym chow held 'a soul' that 'was breathed' into his body.[89] The animal serves as a home for both a Christian soul and a pagan flame of magic power just as a flame can hold the sent of incense that it burns. The boundary between the religious and the aesthetic is blurred, and the trans-textual presentation of these poems narrates a breaking down of another binary: that of pagan spirituality and Catholic faith.

An aesthete's decadent pursuit of beauty and sensation in unlikely places was well established in the movement. By 1914, that movement was no longer as strong as it once was, but recipients of the book would likely have had a strong knowledge of the women's engagement with aestheticism and decadence. The dog may be a peculiar object of desire, but it is in keeping with the peculiarity of new sensations. To find spirituality in the body of one's pet is a desire that all may not relate to, but it is certainly a significant poetical experiment. The women's grief for their chow was intense and Cooper's choice to work through her grief by authoring these poems is an important part of their creation, hence the importance of the back endpapers acknowledging their date of composition. Whym Chow died at the end of January 1906 and the poems were written that very year. Years later, there was an urgency in 1913–14 when Bradley pursued private publication. It was not an urgency to remember the dog per se, but to record the beauty of Bradley and Cooper's spiritual path before her own death prevented such an act.

Michael Field becomes the messenger, as a blurring of the masculine and feminine in their trans* male identity, and they also suggest a queer amalgamation of the pagan with the Catholic.

It also complicates the object of grief in the book. For the reader, it is not simply the dog, but the women who loved him, the women who loved one another, and the readers who loved their poetry. Michael Field, if you will, is grieving the source of their creative life. Bradley and Cooper are ensuring the Poet's immortality. The tragedy of their final years is wrapped in the warmth of Whym Chow's unification of pagan and Catholic symbolism. In poem 'XIX.' he is a 'Wilde Bacchic Creature',[90] while in poem 'XX.' he is a 'Doomed little wanderer, doomed to move / As Lion or Bear in heaven above, O little star, our woe!'[91] He is both Bacchic and a star of heaven, depending on the poem being read. All the while his fiery coat of fur is a flexible metaphor. His 'ruby head!' and 'feet of gold' are pitied because he was held on earth by the speaker's love and kept from his 'destiny of Star' in heaven.[92]

The final poem of the collection, 'XXX.', returns to the collection's earlier image of thirst (see Fig. 3.7). The speaker addresses

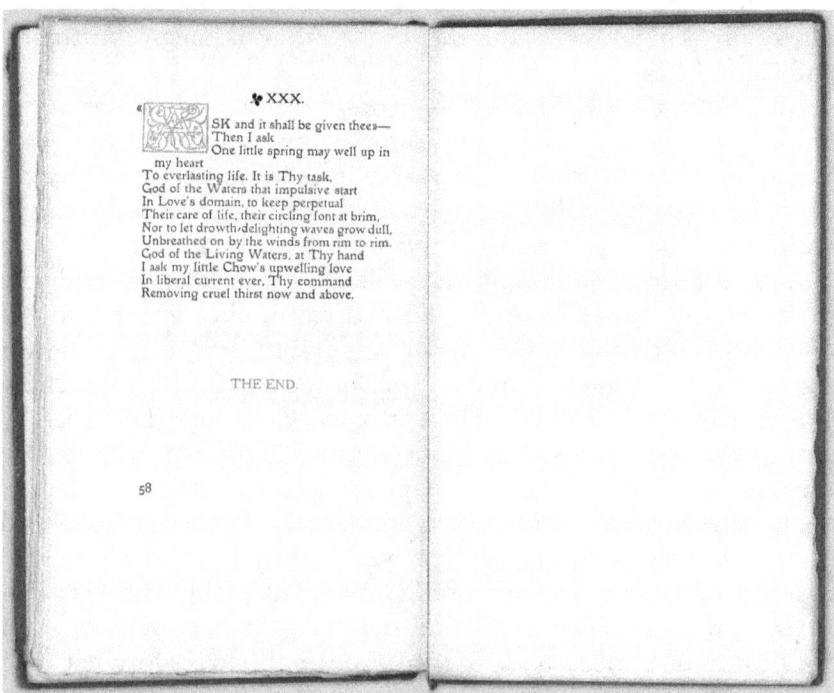

Figure 3.7 Poem XXX. from *Whym Chow*. Courtesy of the Rare Books and Special Collections, University of British Columbia.

the 'God of the Living Waters' by whom Whym Chow sits at 'Thy hand' and makes a request: 'I ask my little Chow's upwelling love / In liberal current ever, thy commend / Removing cruel thirst now and above'.[93] This poem shows a request. The women's conversion to Catholicism remains incomplete; instead, they ask for access to their Chow through God, who they want to grant the Chow's salvation. The dog's love is what will save the speaker. The lexical speaker is Cooper who wrote the poem and the bibliographic voice Bradley, who through her loss of both, thirsts for her beloved wife and love as well. It is also Michael Field conflating the pagan tradition of the women's poetry with their desire for Catholic salvation. Where others may see conflicts and disconnection, Michael Field sees bridges that connect differences together. It is a queer refiguring of faith and the spiritual through physical and material bonds between women, and between humans and animals.

Material Michael Field

Michael Field sought to 'reveal and acknowledge the past, while also rewriting its meaning'.[94] With *Long Ago*, the past explored was cultural, seeking a history of female desire and its discursive origins in the ancient lyrics of Sappho. By engaging with and responding to the fragments, Michael Field's work reimagines history through affective response and connection to a historical and poetic figure. The goal was not the discovery of historical facts, but an empathic relation between the past and the present through poetic exchange. With *Whym Chow*, the history is personal. It is an acknowledgement of the process of conversion and the pagan relationship that was shared by Bradley, Cooper and their pet. It revises the past by connecting paganism with the Catholicism that both women embraced in 1907, shortly after the poems were written.

In both books, binaries transition into ambiguities: male and female, present and past, pagan and Christian, family and queer relations all intersect and alter the reader's perception of their similarities and differences. History for Michael Field is alive, just as poetry is alive. Just as Sappho is preserved, they keep alive the value of Sappho through their own poetic experiments. Similarly, the space before conversion is encapsulated in the body of *Whym Chow*, brought to life, first in their pet, but preserved for posterity in a trans-textual collection of poems. Both books capture concepts of change and difference, and Michael Field, as a trans* gendered queer poet, became a vessel for the discourse of transformation. Like each book, the Poet is a material creation whose body comingles with the women who created them. They are best identified in the body of the material book because that is the space where they lived. Michael Field was a pagan creation and, like Uranus, he is born outside the norms of heteronormativity in a queer space designed to embrace the process, rather than the result. In a sense, Michael Field is unfinished, a trans* figuration of lesbian passion, queer aestheticism and of history's presence in the contemporary.

Notes

1. Quoted in Mary Sturgeon *Michael Field* (New York: The Macmillan Company, 1922), p. 47.
2. Katharine Bradley to Robert Browning, 23 November 1884, in *Michael Field: Decadent Moderns*, ed. by Sarah Parker and Ana Parejo Vadillo (Athens: Ohio University Press, 2019), p. 7.
3. Jill Ehnenn, *Women's Literary Collaboration, Queerness, and Late-Victorian Culture* (Farnham: Ashgate Publishing Ltd., 2008), p. 19.
4. Ehnenn, *Women's Literary Collaboration* p. 137.
5. Jill Ehnenn, *Michael Field's Revisionary Poetics* (Edinburgh: Edinburgh University Press, 2023).
6. Frankie Dytor, '"The Eyes of an Intellectual Vampire": Michael Field, Vernon Lee and Female Masculinities in Late-Victorian Aestheticism', *Journal of Victorian Culture*, 26.4 (2021), p. 583.
7. LeeAnne M. Richardson, *The Forms of Michael Field* (Basingstoke: Palgrave MacMillan, 2021), p. 2.
8. Richardson, *The Forms of Michael Field*, p. 3.
9. Quoted in Carolyn Dever, '"Modern" Love and the Proto-Post-Victorian', *PMLA*, 124. 2 (2009), p. 373.
10. Dever, '"Modern" Love and the Proto-Post-Victorian', p. 374.
11. Sarah Parker and Ana Parejo Vadillo, 'Introduction', in *Michael Field: Decadent Moderns*, ed. by Sarah Parker and Ana Parejo Vadillo (Athens: Ohio University Press), p. 3.
12. Terry Castle, *The Apparitional Lesbian* (New York: Columbia University Press, 1993).
13. Primamore, Elizabeth. 'Michael Field as Dandy Poet', in *Michael Field and Their World*, ed. by Margaret D. Stetz and Cheryl A. Wilson (High Wycombe: The Rivendale Press, 2007), p. 140.

14. Primamore, 'Michael Field as Dandy Poet', p. 140.
15. Marion Thain, 'Introduction', in *Michael Field, The Poet: Published and Manuscript Materials*, ed. by Marion Thain and Ana Parejo Vadillo (Peterborough: Broadview Press, 2009), pp. 24–5.
16. Katharine Bradley and Edith Cooper's diaries are now available as scanned documents as part of the digital humanities project, *The Diaries of Michael Field*, https://michaelfielddiary.dartmouth.edu/home.
17. Frederick D. King, 'The *Pageant* (1896–1897): An Overview', in *Pageant Digital Edition, Yellow Nineties 2.0*, ed. by Lorraine Janzen Kooistra, Ryerson University Centre for Digital Humanities, 2019, https://1890s.ca/pageant_overview/.
18. The British Library, London, Ricketts & Shannon Papers, Add MS 58085-58118, 61713-61724.
19. Kristin Mahoney, 'Michael Field and Queer Community at the Fin de Siècle', *Victorian Review*, 41.1 (2015), p. 37.
20. sj Miller, 'Gender Identity Complexities Turn', *GLQ: A Journal of Lesbian and Gay Studies*, 26.2 (2020), p. 241.
21. sj Miller, p. 240.
22. J. Bobby Noble, 'Refusing to Make Sense: Mapping the In-Coherences of "Trans"', *Journal of Lesbian Studies*, 11.1/2 (2007), p. 169.
23. J. Bobby Noble, 'Refusing to Make Sense', p. 171.
24. Ardel Haefele-Thomas, 'Introduction: Trans Victorians', *Victorian Review*, 44.1 (2018), pp. 31–6.
25. Lisa Hager, 'A Case for a Trans Studies Turn in Victorian Studies: "Female Husbands" of the Nineteenth Century', *Victorian Review*, 44.1 (2018), p. 40.
26. Simon Joyce, 'Two Women Walk into a Theatre Bathroom: The Fanny and Stella Trials as Trans Narrative', *Victorian Review*, 44.1 (2018), p. 91.
27. Simon Joyce, *LGBT Victorians: Sexuality and Gender in the Nineteenth-Century Archives* (Oxford: Oxford University Press, 2023).
28. Patricia Elliott, *Debates in Transgender, Queer, and Feminist Theory: Contested Sites* (Farnham: Ashgate Publishing, 2010), p. 34.
29. Elliott, *Debates in Transgender, Queer, and Feminist Theory*, p. 38.
30. Elliott, *Debates in Transgender, Queer, and Feminist Theory*, n39.
31. Marian Thain, *'Michael Field': Poetry, Aestheticism and the Fin de Siècle* (Cambridge: Cambridge University Press, 2007), p. 15.
32. For a bibliography of Michael Field's works published at the Vale Press, see *The Vale Press: Charles Ricketts, a Publisher in Ernest*,

ed. by Maureen Watry (London: Oak Knoll Press, The British Library, 2004).
33. Alyosxa Tudor, 'Im/possibilities of Refusing and Choosing Gender', *Feminist Theory*, 20.4 (2019), p. 371.
34. Alyosxa Tudor, 'Im/possibilities', p. 376.
35. Hall, *Reading Sexualities*, p. 3.
36. Marguerite Johnson, 'Sappho 600 B.C.E.–500 B.C.E.', *The Literary Encyclopedia. Volume 1.1.1: Greek Writing and Culture: Archaic, Classical, Hellenistic and Imperial, 800–100*, ed. by Vaios Liapis (Latsia: Open University of Cyprus, 2010).
37. 'Michael Field's "Long Ago"' (review), *The Spectator*, 27 July 1889, 63, 3187, p. 119; Periodicals Archive Online, proquest.com/pao.
38. Ibid., p. 119.
39. Parker and Vadillo, *Decadent Moderns*, p. 12.
40. Today, readers can download the entire volume through Armstrong Browning Library's Digital Collection at Baylor University, https://digitalcollections-baylor.quartexcollections.com/Documents/Detail/long-ago-by-michael-field/330619?item=330638.
41. '"George Bell and Sons": British Library Publishing Houses, 1820–1880', ed. Patricia Anderson and Jonathan Rose, *Dictionary of Literary Biography Complete Online*, 106 (1991), p. 22.
42. 'George Bell and Sons', p. 25.
43. 'George Bell and Sons', p. 28.
44. Michael Field, 'Note', *Long Ago* (London: George Bell and Sons, 1889), p. 130.
45. Henry Thornton Wharton, *Sappho: Memoir, Text, Selected Rendering and a Literal Translation*, 2nd edition (London: David Scott, 1887).
46. Wharton, *Sappho*, p. 90.
47. Field, *Long Ago*, p. 56, lines 7–8.
48. Field, *Long Ago*, p. 56, lines 13–14.
49. Field, *Long Ago*, p. 56, lines 15–16.
50. Wharton, *Sappho*, p. 90.
51. Algernon Charles Swinburne, 'Anactoria', *Poems and Ballads, First Series* (1866) (London: Chatto & Windus, 1910), pp. 64–74.
52. Swinburne, 'Anactoria', lines 105–114, pp. 67–8.
53. John A. Walsh, 'An Introduction to Algernon Charles Swinburne', *The Algernon Charles Swinburne Project* (14 May 2017), http://swinburnearchive.indiana.edu/swinburne/view#docId=swinburne/acs0000503-01.xml;outputAsDiv=true;anchor=dfo12d.

54. 'Letter from Michael Field to A. C. Swinburne, May 27, 1889', in *Uncollected Letters of Algernon Charles Swinburne*, 3 vols, ed. by Terry L. Meyers (London: Pickering and Chatto, 2005), vol. 2, p. 475.
55. Field, *Long Ago*, p. 52.
56. Field, *Long Ago*, p. 52, line 1
57. Field, *Long Ago*, p. 52, lines 8, 14.
58. Field, *Long Ago*, p. 56, lines 13–14.
59. Field, 'LII. Ἔγων δ' ἐμαύτᾳ τοῦτο σύνοιδα·', *Long Ago*, pp. 89–92.
60. Translation by Symonds for fragment 15 in Wharton, *Sappho*, p. 77.
61. Field, *Long Ago*, LII., pp. 52–3, lines 17–20.
62. Field, 'Long Ago', p. 119.
63. Field, '*Long Ago*, LII., lines 12–20.
64. Field, *Long Ago*, XI., lines 7–8.
65. Epigraph from *Long Ago*, unpaginated.
66. Sturgeon, *Michael Field*, pp. 101–13.
67. Sturgeon, *Michael Field*, p. 54.
68. Marcella D. Genz, *A History of the Eragny Press, 1894–1914* (London: Oak Knoll Press, 2003), p. 38.
69. Genz, *A History of the Eragny Press*, p. 112.
70. Genz, *A History of the Eragny Press*, p. 230.
71. Genz, *A History of the Eragny Press*, p. 112.
72. Thain, *Michael Field*, p. 193.
73. Michael Field, 'I. Requiescat', in *Whym Chow: Flame of Love* (London: Eragny Press, 1914), p. 9.
74. Field, 'III.', *Whym Chow*, p. 12, stanza 2, lines 4–7
75. Field 'IV.', *Whym Chow*, p. 14.
76. Field, 'V. Trinity', *Whym Chow*, p. 15, line 3.
77. Field, 'V. Trinity', *Whym Chow*, p. 15, lines 12–13.
78. Field, 'V. Trinity', *Whym Chow*, p. 15, lines 15, 17–18.
79. Field, 'V. Trinity', p. 15, lines 1–5.
80. Dennis Denisoff, *Decadent Ecology in British Literature and Art, 1860–1910* (Cambridge: Cambridge University Press, 2021), p. 93.
81. Field, 'V. Trinity', *Whym Chow*, p. 15, lines 17–18.
82. Field, 'VI.', *Whym Chow*, p. 16, lines 3–4.
83. Field, 'VI.', *Whym Chow*, p. 17, lines 42–3.
84. Thain, *Michael Field*, p. 186.
85. Thain, *Michael Field*, p. 188.
86. Mahoney, 'Michael Field and Queer Community', p. 38.
87. Field, 'XXII.', *Whym Chow*, p. 42, lines 1, 15, 25, 37, and 41.
88. Field, 'XXII.', *Whym Chow*, p. 42, line 48.

89. Field, 'XVII. Created', *Whym Chow*, p. 33, stanza 2, lines 12–15.
90. Field, 'XIX.', *Whym Chow*, p. 36, line 1.
91. Field, 'XX.', *Whym Chow*, p. 38, lines 1–3.
92. Field, 'XX.', *Whym Chow*, p. 33, lines 12–14, 24–5.
93. Field, 'XXX.', *Whym Chow*, p. 58, lines 10–13.
94. Thain, *Michael Field*, p. 199.

4

Collaboration and Conflict: Queer Space in *Salome*

THE VOICE OF SALOMÉ
Ah! I have kissed thy mouth, Iokanaan, I have kissed thy mouth.
There was a bitter taste on thy lips. Was it the taste of blood? . . .
But perchance it is the taste of love . . . They
say that love hath a bitter taste . . . But what
of that? what of that? I have kissed thy mouth, Iokanaan.
— Oscar Wilde, *Salome*[1]

Oscar Wilde originally wrote his play *Salome: A Tragedy in One Act* in French in 1891, in the wake of criticism surrounding his novel *The Picture of Dorian Gray* (1890). He was angry at what he saw as anti-intellectual philistinism in England and retreated to Paris where artistic expression was less censored. Wilde found inspiration in the work of Symbolist poets and painters whose anti-realist and iconographic decadence frequently turned to the study of this semi-biblical figure. Salomé is not named in the Bible but is the mythical step-daughter of the tyrannical ruler King Herod. She agrees to dance for Herod's pleasure in exchange for the head of John the Baptist. Wilde makes the story a decadent shocker with Salomé kissing the head of the dead Saint, prior to being executed herself by Herod's guards. The 1894 Bodley Head edition of Oscar Wilde's *Salome: A Tragedy in One Act*, with drawings by Aubrey Beardsley, was the first presentation of the play in English.[2] Wilde's depiction of biblical figures resulted in the Lord Chamberlain's Examiner of Plays denying a license for performance on the London stage. With no staged performance, the book became the sole means of transmitting Wilde's art to an English audience.

Figure 4.1 'The Stomach Dance' by Aubrey Beardsley from *Salome: A Tragedy in One Act* (1894). Private collection.

Similar to a staged production, Beardsley's illustrative dramatisation of female agency and queer desire creates meaning in juxtaposition with Wilde's written drama; the book's resultant queer space circulates unsanctioned desire previously unavailable within the publicly accessible British literary marketplace. Beardsley's illustrations inject the text with critical questions Wilde has already toyed with in the play: What is a woman who has an Adam's apple? What is a woman with sexual desire? Is she a woman? As a Symbolist figure, does she represent uncategorised sexual desires? Is she an allegory for of the sexual difference between men and women, unattached to a specific gender and made as androgynous as the hermaphrodite who greets the reader on the title page? This chapter argues that she is all these things. More importantly, she is a symbol of the book. Everything we associate with Salomé is something that the book is doing. The book is the object being held and read, and through the figure of Salomé, the book presents sexual dissent as a powerful act of subversion revealing dance as an act of deceptive wisdom. Where Herod is blind to her sexual desires, the book shows us her mocking face and masculine throat, the material site of her voice. We see she is up to something. The book's queer space lets readers in on her decadent manipulation of Herod's authoritarian power.

Aubrey Beardsley's 'The Stomach Dance' visualises this complex intersection of Salomé's agency with her affectation of 'object'. Oscar Wilde's play provides no stage directions other than '*Salome dances the dance of the seven veils*', so, in the book, Beardsley features Salomé posing with her peacock-feather adorned hair, staring eyes, bare breasts, exposed abdomen with a fine line of pubic hair running beneath, and a noticeable Adam's apple adorning her throat.

Chris Snodgrass argues that

> Beardsley obviously accentuates Salomé's female attributes, including a swollen abdomen and a naval and pantaloons that clearly encode genital characteristics; yet he also provides her with a male Adam's apple and a veil that juts rigidly upward from between her clenched thighs, like a stylized penis ejaculating the same rosegems that lie at her feet.[3]

A similar Adam's apple appears on the hermaphroditic figure on Beardsley's 'Title Page', supporting Snodgrass's interpretation. Beardsley's presentation of the dance, with a visual focus on her fleshy swollen belly, communicates her appetite instead of Herod's desire to exploit what he sees as her sexual innocence. She stares with intent at the reader pursing her lips as the musician at her feet points his phallic musical instrument directly toward her genitals. The fleshy sexuality that emerges from a simple contrast of black ink and white paper depicts a disruption of both male-female and subject-object binaries through the depiction of Salomé's queer agency.

Snodgrass notes that 'Beardsley often depicts hermaphrodites to be a combination of beauty and beast, a joining of the female with not merely the male, but the animal – satyr, snake, monster.'[4] Her ambiguous gender representation is not a critique of Salomé's femininity, but rather a critique of desire being associated exclusively with heteronormative men.

'The Stomach Dance' presents the moment when Salomé seemingly fulfils the desires of the male gaze. It is also where she inverts that gaze and challenges the assignment of gender to sexual power. This image is almost a parody of the dance of the seven veils. Brad Bucknell emphasises how Beardsley's drawings are not 'mere reflections of what is taking place in the play', but that images of Salomé conflate the story with its creators and that, as a book, it 'relies upon the interplay between written and verbal signs'.[5] Look in her eyes (see Fig. 4.1). Salomé stares directly at the reader. She smirks because she knowingly exploits the power of Herod's, and the reader's, gaze. Linda and Michael Hutcheon point out that Salomé 'is not objectified by the gaze but empowered by it', placing power in the hands of 'the one beheld and not in the beholder'.[6] She does not take her role as an object seriously and while her dance fulfils Herod's desires, Beardsley's image mocks that desire with a dance that reflects the vulgarity of Salomé's perverted stepfather. The image has her going through the motions. She is biding her time. Her desirous gaze is queer because her self-awareness disrupts the gratification of heteronormative desire. Bibliographically, Beardsley's image transforms *Salome* into an interactive multimedial experience where the book incorporates the reader's role in the execution of its material interpretation of the play.[7]

Salome/Salomé's sexual differences are hidden within the material expressions of Beardsley's art and available to a reader who seeks expressions of sexual difference. The book, unlike the stage for which it was originally intended, is a space of intimacy where the reader can fully engage with its queer sexual discourse without risking death at the hands of Herod's guards, or another consequence doled out by more modern policing practices.

Collaboration and Conflict: Queer Space in *Salome* 179

Salomé becomes a sacred figure of satire, dying for the reader's supposed sins of hysteria and homosexuality. Removed from the stage, *Salome* as a book becomes an intimate queering of religious experience, offerings a satirical and sacred revelation of sexual dissent realised in the textual intercourse of Wilde's poetic prose with Beardsley's iconography.

Salome's textual body reflects the diverse discourses of sexual desire and pleasure that are bound together in the book. A lack of agreement or even, at some times, the failure to conduct professional consultations during the book's creation influenced its final form. In *Before Queer Theory*, Dustin Friedman examines aestheticism as one of queer theory's 'unacknowledged ancestors' and proposes that the queer artists and authors of the aesthetic movement positioned art as a space where queers could redefine themselves and create identities with 'a limited yet powerful sense of independent self-direction, of partial freedom from pre-ordained metaphysical, social, and biological orders'.[8] As discussed in previous chapters, such spaces emerge by transforming existing heteronormative spaces for queer relations, both social and sexual. The queer book becomes a space for identity formation and sexual discourse between like-minded readers, mimicking the exchange of *Salome*'s artist and author. As a work of decadent aesthetic collaboration, *Salome* imagines a location for an as-yet-unrealised queer community, not possible outside of these aesthetic mediums of expression. A material analysis of the English version of *Salome* with its contradictory presentation of Beardsley's overtly sexual aesthetic with Wilde's use of innuendo reveals a discourse that disrupts heteronormative characterisations of sexual otherness as something foreign, or part of a distant uncivilised past.

Salome's anachronistic fantasy of the biblical past recognises the agency of the queer individual and challenges conceptions of queerness in the late nineteenth century through its positioning of female sexual desire as a form of queer desire. Salomé's desire for Iokanaan, as a woman, is as taboo an expression as the desire between men. When Salomé realises her desires, takes possession of Iokanaan's severed head and kisses his mouth, female objectification is inverted to sensational effect.

Salome serves as a queer version of what Michel Foucault called an *ars erotica*.[9] That term, however, is loaded with issues of biological racism and colonial settlement because it places so-called eastern texts like the *Karma Sutra*, as books of erotic instruction, into binary opposition with western works of sexology, like Dr Richard von Krafft-Ebing's *Psychopathia Sexualis*.

These examples were both translated into English in the late nineteenth century, the period when, as Foucault famously argues, the homosexual became a species.[10] Sexual discourse at the end of the nineteenth century, however, was far more complex than Foucault's binary sexual discourse suggests. What complicates this cross-cultural sexual discourse is the ways in which Victorian culture regulated sexual discourse. Erotic pleasure was something that existed and was even prevalent, but it was not officially sanctioned by society's institutions of power. Its vast bibliography was archived and collected by rich and influential men, like bookseller Harry Sidney Nichols (1865–1941) and explorer Sir Richard Burton (1821–90) but kept out of the hands of women and lower-class readers. *Salome* stands apart from this crowded archive of erotica because it breaks the rule of silence around pleasurable sexuality. It neither disguises its queerness as intellectual curiosity nor censors its readership by the use of private distribution. Instead, *Salome* gives public voice to queer desire and the eroticisation of the male body for the sexual gratification of both female and queer male subjects.

As seen in the play, when queer sexual discourse is witnessed or made into something public, it is condemned. *Salome* as a book is equally controversial because it speaks of desires that were usually only publicly alluded to in the subtlest of terms. Beardsley's drawings made visible what even Wilde's play kept opaque. The French edition published a year prior, after all, did not create such a furore. In fact, as a text written in French and therefore unreadable for many English citizens, particularly lower-class readers, it was not a threat. Its form of circulation limited access to its dissidence to the hands of a select elite within society trusted with such material.

This chapter tells two intersecting stories. First, we will look at *Salome*'s significance as a textual collaboration and how its publication defies conventions of erotic discourse in late Victorian print culture. Looking at the publishing practices of Leonard Smithers with his Erotika Biblion Society, it will explore how erotic works circulated without political or legal interference due to the practice of private distribution. This review of the erotic marketplace prefaces a deep dive into Beardsley's process as an illustrator because of how those illustrations changed Wilde's authorial intentions. That will be followed by a detailed history of *Salome*'s contrasting creation and distribution with a careful look at the many hands who contributed to its beauty and meaning. This history reveals a story of conflict, compromise and controversy that defines *Salome*'s queer space separate from the sexual lives of either its author or illustrator. That history informs the chapter's next section on the role of the *ars erotica* in Victorian sexual discourse and queer sexuality in late Victorian culture. Dominant sexual discourse at the time aligned queerness with degeneracy and foreign climates. *Salome*, I will argue, reveals the presence of queerness in western sexual practice with the presentation of female acts of desire that aligns them with same-sex desires between men. Drawing on Dustin Friedman's and Natasha Hurley's recent work regarding queer relationality and queer publishing history respectively, this section considers how iconographic content interacts with the aesthetic community's coded language of same-sex desire to both dramatically engage with Wilde's text and mocks heteronormative regulation of sexual discourse. Close readings of Beardsley's images as they are juxtaposed with Wilde's play are integrated into a bibliographic and lexical analysis of *Salome* in order to reveal the book's merging of the sacred and the profane – in other words, a queering of the late nineteenth-century sexual-moral mythos to make space for queer desire.

Circulation, creation, and collaboration in *Salome*

The figure of Oscar Wilde is an important part of the study of nineteenth-century queer history and culture who often overshadows his collaborators, publishers and influences. While this chapter's focus will be on those collaborations and conflicts, it is also important to note the influence of Wilde studies on queer theory more broadly. Greg Mackie's *Beautiful Untrue Things* (2019) explores the role that bibliographic relics play in the development of Wilde's mythos and its role in queer history. Mackie's focus on forgeries and the proposed presence of Wilde as a means of legitimising fakes and forgeries actually embraces Wilde's own play with plagiarisms, falsehoods and self-aggrandising myths, as forms of theatrical and aesthetic creation. Joseph Bristow's work on Wilde has focused on his legacy and his influence on queer and literary cultures in the twentieth and twenty-first centuries, as well as an incredibly detailed historical record of Wilde's life and times. His preface and introductory essay for his edited collection, *Oscar Wilde and Modern Culture: The Making of a Legend* (2009), focuses on the Wilde myth born from the long history of literary and cultural criticism of Wilde and his works. It shows the difficulty that we continue to have to separate Wilde the human from the aesthetic artist's literary creations. That conflation of Wilde's personal identity and professional output is due in part to his role as a performance artist who created a theatrical persona that he performed on stage, at dinner parties and in his writing.

Wilde made celebrity one of his artistic creations. Bristow points out how that mythmaking, not just by Wilde but by others on Wilde's behalf, began during his short lifetime surrounding even his sad and tragic death at the age of forty-six.[11] As a legend, author, aesthete and individual, Wilde is both widely known and misunderstood. What is not well established in Wildean scholarship are his collaborations and the role the other artists played in his mythos. That influence, particularly that of Aubrey Beardsley, will be addressed in this chapter, where illustration supersedes Wilde's overwhelming persona.

To understand the ideological threat that *Salome* posed to the late Victorian literary marketplace, it is necessary to consider the methods of circulation employed in the production and distribution of erotica and pornography in the late nineteenth century. Leonard Smithers (1861–1907), famed publisher of the Erotika Biblion Society, the periodical *The Savoy* (8 vols, 1896) and Oscar Wilde's post-prison publications of *The Ballad of Reading Gaol*, *Lady Windemere's Fan* and *The Importance of Being Earnest*, collaborated with famed explorer and ethnological scholar Sir Richard Burton (1821–90) on *Priapeia sive diversorum poetarum in Priapum Iusus, or Sportive Epigrams on Priapus by divers poets in English verse and prose* (1890). The works translated in this book by both Smithers and Burton in collaboration are phallic celebrations of male sexuality and the role of the penis in a variety of sexual practices. *Priapeia* presents a cornucopia of sexual practices, including agriculturally based colloquialisms for sex acts and genitalia, as well as poetic examinations of masturbation, infibulation and sodomy with both men and women. Gender inversion is also explored. For example, Burton and Smithers present Dr James Cranstoun's translation of an epigram by Martial in which a Catamite is ridiculed because he 'arranges his tresses in order: / Smelling for ever of balm, smelling of cinnamon spice: / Singing the songs of the Nile or a humming the ditties of Cadiz'. These feminine social practices are made more blatant in the prefatory notes where Burton and Smithers claim that the epigram 'derides catamites for depilating their privy parts and buttocks'. The practice is positioned as a curiosity by the editorial annotations and while Martial certainly calls the catamite 'a contemptible thing', Burton and Smithers seem to think differently, archiving the catamite's history as an important part of the history of male sexuality.[12] I say male sexuality because even when discussing sex with women, the book's emphasis is on the male body. The book tells male readers across the spectrum of sexual desire that their bodies are both a site of pleasure and a beautiful vessel – something to be admired and even desired.

The book, however, caused little sensation when published. *Priapeia* was privately printed by Smithers and sold to collectors and confidential subscribers of his Erotika Biblion Society under the table at his shop, Et in Arcadia Ego, on Piccadilly for a substantially high price.[13] Lisa Z. Sigel notes how obscenity laws emerged to curtail the sale of erotic texts to lower-class readers; this practice meant that to circulate pornography, publishers would charge extraordinarily high prices for their works to make it clear that their audience remained rich and powerful men whose proclivities were not regulated by the dominant sexual discourse.[14] Private distribution to a subscription list of financially independent men did not challenge the regulatory sexual discourses. The men who could afford this book and others like it were wealthy captains of industry, professionals, aristocrats and other elites. Their behaviour, so long as it was not openly discussed in public, for example appearing as gossip on a society page or being caught and charged by the police, was acceptable because it did not disrupt existing authority structures.

Wilde's own sexual practices with men were acceptable when he was seen associating with members of the aristocracy or other successful artists. It was only when Wilde began appearing in public sharing a table and conversation with young men who were members of the lower classes: soldiers, valets and shop boys, that he became a threat to social order.[15] The secrets demanded by regulated sexual discourse could endure. *Priapeia* and many other similar works would remain hidden in the libraries of gentlemen and out of reach of curious wives, daughters, servants and the poor masses.

The distribution of erotica in the nineteenth century challenges the idea that *scientia sexualis* was the only means by which sex was discussed in the Victorian age. Smithers's Erotika Biblion Society was also the publisher of the period's most famous work of homosexual pornography, *Teleny; or the Reverse of the Medal* (1893), a story told by a ruined man, Des Grieux, who tells of his social downfall in the wake of an affair with a talented pianist, the titular character. The novel features several sexually explicit depictions of sex between men and ends tragically with Teleny's suicide and death in Des Grieux's arms. Where *Priapeia* could be interpreted as the self-aggrandisement of the phallus by men who desired women, *Teleny* presents same-sex desire as an arousing experience and is itself a compositional mystery because of the round-robin approach to its writing. As noted by Richard Gray and Christopher Keep, as well as in my own research, multiple hands exchanged the text writing it in pieces and sharing it as a collective sexual fantasy.[16] Today, we would think that such a text would have caused a furore amongst conservative middle-class Victorian culture, but the reality is that it did not. It was exchanged secretly among Smithers's list of subscribers from under the table at his shop. As another overpriced collectable, it was out of the reach of working-class men, and all women and children, so it could not corrupt their presumed weaker minds. That meant that a celebration of same-sex desire was accessible, at least to those privileged enough to be able to afford it.

While pornographic depictions may not be any more positive than a medical pathology, they still existed and challenge the idea of east and west sexual discourses being in binary opposition.

Most important, they were discreet. *Priapeia* is materially constructed to obscure its sexuality. Bound in plain grey boards, the book when opened appears to resemble an academic edition. Opening with a critical introduction, the book categorises the poems by the type of sexuality they suggest. The texts are presented as perverse curiosities intended for scholarly study; extensive annotations in the footnotes on nearly every page, as well as the decision to print both the original Latin and English translations, give the book a formal format. If you were unaware of the content, it would appear as any other scholarly text in a rigorous collection for serious academics. This appearance allows the book's queerness to circulate without being seen by anyone without institutionally sanctioned power. The collection of pornographic, erotic and satirical texts in *Priapeia* alone shows a complex understanding of sexuality amongst book dealers, antiquarians and booksellers. They collected and translated texts from around the world from France to India and created an English distribution system that establishes an erotic discourse amongst a privileged male elite whose '[c]ollecting, organizing, categorizing, and then labelling sexuality' was 'a distancing mechanism that tried to separate scientific interest from mere prurience.'[17] As educated or wealthy men, they were in a position to claim that they were not collecting pornography but compiling a scientifically necessary study, embracing sexual discourse of medicine as a cover for their pleasures.

In contrast, *Salome* was available for sale at the Bodley Head to anyone who dared enter. With the ordinary edition priced at 15s, and the large edition at 30s, the book was not necessarily affordable to the masses, but it was available at a much more affordable price than anything sold privately and displayed to everyone in the window at the Bodley' Head's Vigo St shop in London.[18] *Salome* gave voice to the desire, pleasure and fulfilment of dissident sexualities of both women and homosexual men. The secret was out, in so far as these covert sexual discourses were hidden. As we shall see, however, that open secret required a collaboration between literary content and bibliographic design to be achieved.

Textual studies tell us that books are multisensory experiences. Sonya Petersson (2018), for example, notes that illustrations possess 'medial' properties,[19] that is, illustrations mediate meaning in the literary text. However, illustration does not just reflect meaning, it can create and even change meaning. Petersson calls such works 'deviant illustration' because it changes the meaning of the lexical text.[20] Using the specific example of *Salome*, Petersson argues that Beardsley reimagines what Wilde wrote in the play.[21] Beardsley, then found meaning not apparent in the play's lexical form. Linda Dowling calls this presence of something absent in the lexical text an 'unutterability topos', or language's limited ability to convey meaning.[22] What meaning that is, may not be the meaning that Wilde intended, but an interpretation inspired by suggestion. Hence, the illustrations are an interpretation of Wilde's text that imagines sexuality left vague in his prose. Alongside that text, illustration, similar to a performance in a theatre, opens the play to further meaning-making for those who purchase access. The linguistic limits of lexical content are confronted by Beardsley's iconographic content, allowing the reader to consider the intercourse of lexical with bibliographical materials as a multimedial language unique to its material iteration that challenges or threatens bibliographic and cultural norms.[23] In other words, the sexual discourse of *Salome*'s material body, the body of the book, is a threat to existing socio-cultural conventions of sex and gender in the 1890s, imagining a queer world long condemned, but still available in bibliographic performance and accessible in a book that has uttered the unutterable.

Natasha Hurley defines the making of historical queer communities through literature as a 'circuit'.[24] Hurley argues that 'queer texts entextualize their own history, framing and reframing other queer texts in their circulation, curation, and consumption by reading publics'.[25] She conceives of a history of the queer novel based on a study of these circuits. Taking this theory beyond the study of fiction, *Salome* allows us to consider circuits of queer relations within the text in the various art forms that come together in the book's creation. With its imaginative, non-realist setting, *Salome* offers readers an aesthetic experience free of real-world consequences.

The reader is not crushed by shields at the order of Herod, only the fictional Salomé. The play offers a community experience of oppressed desire between Salomé in her imagined biblical past, and the reader in the 1890s, whose desires are stifled in similar, but different ways.

Aestheticism's non-realist literature, according to Friedman, created spaces that, by the very act of reading about dissident desires, could provide 'a sense of personal independence while still enmeshed within structures of oppression'.[26] That space owes as much to Beardsley as it does to Wilde. The play changes when publisher John Lane integrates Beardsley's images of leering hermaphrodites and other drawings that blur the gender binary between Salomé from Iokanaan, and caricatures of Wilde in images depicting moments of utmost seriousness, and anachronisms that interrupt the historical setting with symbols of 1890s decadence. The dark tragedy of the play becomes ironic, even ridiculous as the monstrous and unhealthy are perceived as both familiar and beautiful.

The textual intercourse of imagery and poetic theatre transforms *Salome*, the book, into an art installation, or what Joseph Grigley describes as textualterity. Grigley explains how the term installation refers to the public exhibition of artworks and accounts for how the exhibition space affects the meaning of the art on display. 'The installation of an artwork', according to Grigley, 'like the installation of a literary text, is in all of these apparitions essentially a *pose*, at least in the sense that it constitutes a certain visual alignment of the work vis-à-vis its surroundings.'[27] *Salome* as a single iteration or installation of the play is no longer the central work of art. The play is in conversation with its material publication, with its cultural context at the historical time of its publication, and is open to interpretations. The textual intercourse aligns Wilde's work with the work of Beardsley on the figure of Salomé, a cultural, even sacred, symbol of decadent beauty and dissident erotics.

The Bodley Head edition was a translation of Wilde's original French play published in 1893. Inspired while reading Flaubert's 'Herodias' from *Trois Contes* (1877), Wilde was still a student of the French language relying on Pierre Louÿs and Stuart Merrill, friends who 'aided him' with his writing of the play.[28] Richard Ellmann notes that Wilde also consulted, at different stages, with Adolphe Retté and Marcel Schwob, multiplying the number of hands involved in its composition.[29] Since Wilde wrote his other plays without such help, I think it is important to point out the potential influence that these consultants likely had on the final written play. Even though Wilde retained control of the story and had final say over his translation, it is unlikely that he chose not to include ideas that emerged from these various consultations. The further one investigates the creation of *Salome*, the more decentred Wilde is as a singular author and the more the book becomes a space of cross-cultural intercourse between some of the period's most influential aesthetes, Symbolists and decadents on both sides of the English Channel. That intercourse is further complicated upon publication.

Before detailing the conflicts between creators, it is valuable to pause and consider Aubrey Beardsley and his drawing techniques because very little is said in criticism about the process of printing his drawings. Much is made of his line and Japanese-inspired linear style, but Beardsley's work varies from the strange medievalism of his *Morte Darthur* (Dent, 1892) to the black-and-white curvilinear contrasts in *Salome* (1894), to his later experiments in shading for Leonard Smithers on Alexander Pope's *Rape of the Lock* and *The Savoy* (1896). I do not think Beardsley's career was long enough to see these as different periods; however, Matthew Sturgis notes that Beardsley had mastered at least several different styles, allowing him to take on a variety of work in book illustration, theatre posters, book bindings and caricature work.[30] Robbie Ross noted Beardsley's experiments in styles as opposed to the more typical experimentation in medium: '[u]nperplexed by painting or etching or lithography, he was satisfied with the simplest of all materials, attaining therewith unapproachable executive power'.[31] Ross claims that Beardsley's work demonstrates how the 'grammar of art exists only to be violated'.[32] Beardsley's diverse artistry and his willingness to 'violate' art's grammar are important to *Salome* because the drawings are not 'typical' of Beardsley. Every project was a new challenge, both creatively and technically. Instead of being representative of Beardsley, the drawings considered in this chapter interconnect with the iconotextual *Salome*, as a book.

Beardsley's work is also dependent upon compromises with the capitalist system that pay for his art and labour. Compromise with what others desire and the limits of technology are acceptable because they are a means to his aesthetic ends. There were '[m]any artists trained in the era of engraving' who 'had trouble adapting to the new technology'; however, 'Beardsley was one of a new generation of artists who experimented enthusiastically with the properties of this new "line block" printing.'[33] He sees the limits of technology as a creative opportunity.

Layla Bloom notes that '[p]hoto-engraving enabled printers to chemically transfer and cut images into printing blocks, resulting in an exact reproduction of the artist's original work'.[34] Line-block printing involved, at least for Beardsley, the use of 'zincographs', a non-photographic method and form pioneered by Firmin Gillot in 1850s Paris.[35] According to Philip Gaskell, zincography was more cost-efficient than photographic reproduction and involved transferring 'a line drawing in a greasy and acid-resistant ink on to a zinc plate and then etching it'.[36] The greasy ink 'protected the lines of the design from the acid and left them standing in relief, while the whites were etched, and subsequently routed, away so that the plate could be mounted and printed like a wood-cut'.[37] Gaskell notes that zincographs largely replaced woodcuts in illustration and was modernised by 1872, creating 'a line (or process) block as we know it today, by projecting a reversed photographic negative directly on to a sensitized zinc plate and then etching out the whites. Again, the plate was routed mechanically and mounted for printing.'[38] While Morris was adamant that these new methods were detrimental to a book's beauty, Beardsley had significantly fewer resources and less choice over the commissions he received so he had to adapt his style to his employer's demands. As Ross states, he diversified the sort of art he could produce, while familiarising himself with modern methods of reproduction that were both cost-efficient, and, when designed well, could compete with the beauty of a woodblock illustration.

Printing was a collaboration for Beardsley. A 'C.H.sc.' appears on some of Beardsley's drawings. These initials stand for Carl Hentschel, sculpsit, the artisan who prepared the zinc blocks for Beardsley's illustration, a man Frankel credits with perfecting line-block technology in England.[39] Hentschel's presence via signature (see the bottom-right corner of 'Enter Herodias' for a good example) suggests that the industrial process was worthy of artistic recognition.

Hentschel's etchings and his work preparing photoengraved zinc plates for the printers is an important contribution to *Salome* as Beardsley's art. Print depends on collaboration between the technical crafts and the artists who made use of their skill. Beardsley was an innovator, but part of his innovation was his ability to utilise bibliographical collaboration in order to make the most of work produced using modern printing technologies.

Another celebrated illustrator and book designer, Walter Crane, was certainly aware of the innovations in printing that occurred during the early Renaissance when the later Gothic encountered classical design.[40] However, Crane defers to Morris's claim that eventually the 'youthful spirit of the early Renaissance became clouded and oppressed, and finally crushed with a weight of pompous pedantry and affectation. The natural development of a living style in art became arrested, and authority, and an endeavour to imitate the antique, took its place.'[41] The classical became a school by the nineteenth century against which the arts-and-crafts movement's return to the Gothic rebelled. Crane associated changes in printing during the Italian Renaissance with changes in the nineteenth century to industrialised bookmaking, both of which allegedly degraded and possibly degenerated the book's beauty.

Crane admitted that Beardsley was a 'very remarkable designer in black and white', whose 'work shows a delicate sense of line, and a bold decorative use of solid blacks, as well as an extraordinarily weird fancy and grotesque imagination, which seems occasionally inclined to run in a morbid direction'.[42] This backhanded compliment is the best Beardsley could hope for from the establishment of the arts-and-crafts movement as a young upstart in his early twenties. Crane admits that 'photographic-automatic reproduction' allows a designer the opportunity 'to write out his own text in the character that pleases him', making 'his page a consistent whole from a decorative point of view'.[43] Crane sees the benefit as a 'unity of effect';[44] however, his idea of the page's unity does not apply to the queer book. While these methods can ensure unity of design, Beardsley uses them in different ways. Beardsley's work shows the limits of the arts-and-crafts rebellion and the danger of idealising printing conventions in their focus on a particular style. Instead, Beardsley's innovations recall the experiments of the early Renaissance, in that he fuses *japonisme*, neo-classicism, decadence, the limits of line-block printing and the revival of printing, transforming individual ideas into something new, original, unique and dangerous in its refusal to conform to, or to placate, the moral hypocrisies of what he saw as the new establishment. With his cosmopolitan approach, looking at historical and international influences to reimagine art and beauty, Beardsley took the limits of the line-block printing process and expanded them. Rather than seeing modern print as a limitation on his work, it defined his work and his choices, creating something new. By paying attention to this innovation, we can see how queer visions of desire influenced the history of bookmaking and changed perceptions of technology's role in the creation of illustrative art and decorative bookmaking.

Creating the illustrations alone reveals multiple hands in intercourse with one another. Collaboration and conciliation do not end with the drawings but extend through all elements of the book. One of the first conciliations is price: how to produce a beautiful, and affordable, *belle lettres*. Lane figured cost into most of the decisions made about *Salome* from the very beginning. Beardsley's is one of these low-cost contributions because his technique of line-block drawings was affordable. One of the benefits of working in black ink is the price. A review of A. B. Fleming & Co., Ltd.'s price list for Litho and Letterpress inks reveals a significant price differential. Letterpress black ink ranges in price from 1s to 10s for supplies, while red letterpress ink (as an example of the cost of colour ink) from the same company sells for between 4s 6d and 15s (5, 17). These price lists do not indicate quantities, suggesting that these are prices for a typical print run order. At the same time, the differential even between the lowest-quality inks suggests that by printing in black the publishers saved money, as did the printers, for the work. It was therefore in everyone's interest that Beardsley created black-ink drawings for his contracts. This decision did not lessen Beardsley's art; instead, it defined his art and provided an opportunity for Beardsley to create something unique that he may not have considered if production costs had not been taken into account.

Beardsley, much like Charles Ricketts and Charles Shannon, had to concede to the limits of printing technologies at hand and the budgets of his publishers. Frankel notes Beardsley's choices to work with 'Whatman paper, Chinese ink (also known as India ink), and a fine Gillot nib' came from Beardsley's experience and understanding of the photomechanical process.[45] Consider too Beardsley's style of drawing: non-realist linearity with a stark contrast between swathes of black ink against huge white spaces. Instead of detailed shading, he creates sweeping curvilinear lines. Line-block processes were not useful when working with detailed shading and tiny particular details, as demonstrated in Chapter 2 with the work of Charles Shannon. The process requires a more simplistic form to be effective and beautiful. As a result, Beardsley's interests naturally brought him to the increasingly popular style of *japonisme*.

The influence of Whistler and Toulouse-Lautrec's use of 'Japanese stylistic elements' influenced Beardsley to take illustration in a new direction, incorporating techniques of Japanese printmaking, resulting in the presentation of 'varied formal structures and techniques' that form a distinctly western vision of Japanese art.[46] Linda Gertner Zaitlin draws significant attention to an important element of otherness or difference represented in Beardsley's art as multicultural and outside of Victorian visual tropes of realism. Zaitlin's book *Aubrey Beardsley, Japonisme, and the Perversion of the Victorian Ideal* (1997) remains one of the best scholarly examinations of Beardsley's work, particularly because of its focus on cosmopolitanism and extra-cultural influence on his drawing technique. Not only do the French symbolists influence him, but he also takes influence from other parts of the world. Beardsley is part of an avant-garde movement that conjoined occidental traditions with traditions discovered by the peoples of the colonised orient. In terms of printing and book illustration, Beardsley is the most significant advocate for *japonisme* as a means of interpreting western culture. For Beardsley, that which is different is not a threat to English art but an opportunity to learn new and different means of creation. While *japonisme* and the other influences on Beardsley's work can be read as cultural appropriation, Beardsley's work does not objectify or display Japanese culture for the pleasure of an English audience. Rather, Victorian England's empiricist ethos is subverted because Beardsley's drawing translates English and European culture through a non-western lens, subverting imperial supremacy and queering the power structure of artistic expression with a decadent beauty created and defined outside of British culture. The influence of these various internationally derived practices changed book illustration and Beardsley's success is significantly dependent on his innovative study of art from different cultures during his short career.

Lane, in his desire for sales, selected Beardsley's images after admiring his illustration 'J'ai Baisé Ta Bouche Iokanaan' in the April 1893 issue of the *Studio*. The illustration helped to make Beardsley's reputation and it is likely that Lane sought to capitalise on his controversial reputation as an artist.[47] Beardsley's cosmopolitan reimagining of beauty is heavily influenced by Japanese art as well as biblical myth, transforming *Salome* into a space where readers may consider queerness, and for our purposes, female desire itself is a form of queerness in late Victorian England, not as a crime or a pathology, but as beautiful. The ugliness typically associated with hysterics and homosexuals is placed on institutions of power and authority. *Salome*'s biblical setting makes the book's ideas mythological and lends an ancient, ingrained reality for many people, including English readers. *Salome* is also a book that dramatises and instructs the reader on the art of influence – that is, the history of art that goes into the construction of the book beautiful. That influence is queer in this instance because *Salome* flaunts the silent and unseen regulation of queer sexual discourse, forcing the public to see and invite them to speak the unspeakable.

Beardsley's art helps queer the book because his bibliographical methods are informed by the distorted perceptions of sexuality and gender that define the decadent aesthetic. This methodology leaves a space for interpretive possibilities that Wilde's play alone did not offer. Beardsley was not naïve about bookmaking practices. His work shows a self-reflexive awareness of his position within a wider collaboration on preparing a book for publication. Beardsley stands in contrast to William Morris who, as explained in Chapter 2, insisted on a completely artisan process without any automation or modern technology. His illustrations were hand-carved into wood blocks in a reverse image in order to print every different design that Kelmscott used. Beardsley, while he could work with woodblocks, used photoengraving within the line-block printing process to capture the spirit of the woodblock method, while saving effort and money in terms of printing his work. Beardsley's work was dependent upon intercourse between artisan ideals and modern technology. These choices do not make his work less than Morris's but a queer development of Morris's model in textual intercourse with the modern publishing practices of his employers.

Beardsley's conflict with the Revival of Printing's ideals finds representation in *Salome*. The play is set in both the biblical past and the decadent 1890s. However, like Symbolism, there is a transformation of the symbol in the play; it is not the symbol of Salomé generally accepted but personal interpretations of her symbolism. With at least two different perspectives on what Salomé as a symbol could mean the resulting book, *Salome* is the consequence of creative intercourse. Beardsley's art takes a place at the forefront of the material text, and unlike Ricketts's designs, offers characters and interpretations, performing a reading of Wilde that is not what the author intended, but that reflects the theme of social discord instigated by Salomé in the play. Like Beardsley, Wilde was taking influence from a foreign art movement: for Beardsley, it was Japanese illustration, for Wilde, it was French Symbolism, and Beardsley used that influence to shift focus from realist storytelling to aesthetic emphasis on the printed word as visual art. Frankel says that 'Wilde aspires to a language that is incantatory, evocative and poetic rather than naturalistic and conversational', taking inspiration from his source material, the Bible, as much as he does from Symbolist authors like Maeterlinck and Mallarmé who praised *Salome*'s literary value.[48] Beardsley's book design is a complex interpretation that Wilde was certainly capable of understanding once his emotional connection to the book's creation was in the past.

Wilde did not choose Beardsley for this project. In fact, he rebelled against the decision. G. A. Cevasco writes that, '[a]gainst his better judgment, Wilde was finally persuaded by his close friend Robbie Ross to allow Beardsley to complete the illustrations for

Salome'.⁴⁹ Wilde's assessment of Beardsley's talent is ambivalent. Wilde wrote to Mrs Patrick Campbell in March of 1894, telling her that Beardsley was 'a very brilliant and wonderful young artist' and that his drawings for *Salome* 'are quite wonderful'.⁵⁰ However, we know from a letter written by Ellen Beardsley (Aubrey's mother) that the conflict between the two artists arose because of *Salome* and lasted until Beardsley's death, despite Wilde's kind words to Mrs Campbell. Mrs Beardsley wrote to John Lane, criticising him for sending her a review of Beardsley's work, countering the article's claims, and saying, 'he was most decidedly not in pictorial art what Wilde was in literature. One has only to look at the illustrations to *Salome* to see that. At any rate Wilde resented them very much and they were enemies in consequence.'⁵¹

In *Recollections of Oscar Wilde* (1929), Charles Ricketts writes in the 'Postscript' letter to his fictional correspondent Jean Paul Raymond that Wilde, who was inspired by Gustave Flaubert's *Temptation of St. Anthony* and *Trois Contes*, was offended by 'Beardsley's entire disregard for Flaubert's spirit of remoteness, ritual and romance'.⁵² This specific issue was the basis of Wilde's criticism of Beardsley's *Salome* illustrations. Ricketts attributes the following differentiation to Wilde:

> My Herod is like the Herod of Gustave Moreau – wrapped in his jewels and sorrows. My Salomé is a mystic, the sister of Salammbô, a Sainte Thérèse who worships the moon; dear Aubrey's designs are like the naughty scribbles a precocious schoolboy makes on the margins of his copybooks.⁵³

Wilde's comments certainly offended Beardsley who Ellmann tells us stayed clear of Wilde during this period, primarily because of other conflicts brewing with the creation of *Salome*. Regarding the play, and the book's artifice, the strange imagery of Beardsley's pictures has left critics in continual disagreement over their relevance to the play. Karl Beckson insists that the images are 'irrelevant to the play'.⁵⁴ Ellmann suggests that Beardsley's 'jocular impression of Wilde's face, as in the moon or in the face of Herod', has 'sinister, sensual overtones', as if the counter-poetics of his imagery were intended as a vulgar insult from an artist Ellmann dismisses as 'strange, cruel, [and] disobedient'.⁵⁵ Other critics, such as Elliot L. Gilbert, see Beardsley's drawings as intrinsically tied to Wilde's play. The drawings are not illustrations of moments in the play – the sort of imagery to which a Victorian reader would be accustomed. Rather, they are Symbolist interpretations of the moods, ideas, moments and feelings made aesthetic, 'creat[ing] an imaginative world without reference to any objective reality'.[56] By extension, where Wilde reflexively engages with the biblical myth of the death of John the Baptist, Beardsley plays with Wilde's reimagining of Salomé within the literary discourse of 1890s European decadence.

With both the green cloth *de luxe* edition and the coarsely woven blue binding for the regular edition, an aestheticised flower on the front cover immediately characterises the book as exotic (see Fig. 4.2). This startling flower begs for closer inspection. However, that inspection reveals little about the flower's nature. The reader is introduced to Wilde's work as a strange artificial flower, something that looks natural but is improved upon by art.

Figure 4.2 Gilt impressing from cover of *Salome*. Harry Ransom Center, The University of Texas at Austin.

The cover also invites us to touch, to feel the coarse denim-like material giving *Salome* a body. Like its eponymous character, the book demands that readers notice, desire and touch, suggesting a multisensory reading experience. The cover calls the reader into its aestheticised world where its decadent unreality demands that the reader reconsider what is natural and what is unnatural.

Beardsley's disconcerting imagery gives voice to things left obscured in Wilde's elaborate prose and has a particularly important influence on the book. However, like other queer books, it is the result of influences conjoining and creating something new and unexpected – a queer space.

Zaitlin notes how Beardsley's 'sinuous line with its serpentine whiplash', along with his work's other main characteristics, serve to dissolve 'borders between picture and frame, flatness, and two-dimensional bodies'.[57] Beardsley's works display their influences of not only 'his adaptation of Japanese art' but of 'William Blake', 'the signer Arthur Mackmurdo, the furniture designer Thomas Jekyll, and the architect E.W. Godwin', resulting in a modern visual that 'crossed aesthetic frontiers and decisively shaped art nouveau'.[58] Beardsley's various styles and influences contribute to the character of the queer book, with or without Wilde's consent. Beardsley's approach is one of incorporated influences, imitation and compromise. As a result, *Salome* is a powerful textual intercourse that decentres the author and the illustrator, with a decadent materiality characteristic of the conflicting intercourse between Wilde and Beardsley.

Take for example, Beardsley's illustration, 'The Black Cape', a satirical image of *fin de siècle* fashion that appears as the Page, Soldier and Cappadocian are watching Salomé after she leaves the banquet table and walks into the night air where she gazes at the moon. She is an object of desire, but for Beardsley, she is also a fashion model, a figure obscured by the dress she is wearing. The curvilinearity of the dress is contrasted by the sharp edges of her wrap and her elaborate coiffure. The Salomé these men gaze at is not authentic. She is a product of an artificial culture of cosmetics and fashion that transforms women into something unnatural, what Max Beerbohm refers to in his 'A Defence of Cosmetics' as an example of how 'surface will finally be severed from soul'.[59] Salomé's desires, her agency and her character are not visible to the men who watch her. She is obscured by the artifice that has been placed on her by Victorian culture and male-dominated sexual discourse. Her soul is hidden, much like the souls of readers who, like her, are silenced and unseen in a world made artificial by the pose of heteronormativity.

Male egos certainly dominated the creation of the *Salome* translation to English. Wilde had asked his tempestuous lover, Lord Alfred 'Bosie' Douglas, to translate his French play into English, seemingly in order to give the idle young man something to do after having done almost nothing creative during the past year.[60] Unfortunately, Douglas did not return this act of kindness. The translation was not up to par and when Wilde pointed out the problems and edits that were necessary, Douglas was furious. Douglas began to send Wilde a series of angry letters that turned the older artist's legitimate criticism into an ugly and mean-spirited war of insult. It was not until the very real possibility that Wilde would walk away from their 'fatal friendship' that Douglas calmed down.[61] Robbie Ross intervened in the conflict, pointing out to Wilde his unrealistic expectation of translation skills from Douglas when the young man had little experience with French.[62] Douglas was able to walk away from the commission with his pride intact, and Wilde could repair, and even redo the translation himself.[63]

Beardsley wrote to Ross about how Lane and Wilde pulled him into the middle of the '*Salome* row . . . between Lane and Oscar and Co. For one week', and teases that 'the numbers of telegraph and messenger boys who came to the door was simply scandalous'.[64] Beardsley then offered to provide his own translation.[65] Wilde, however, was not interested in hiring Beardsley as a translator and the flurry of telegraphs broke down into an 'acrimonious fourway controversy between Lane, Wilde, Douglas, and Beardsley'.[66] The result was that, instead of receiving a translation credit, something Richard Ellmann claims Douglas now equated with a tradesman's receipt, Wilde honoured him with a dedication that he decided to read as 'a tribute of admiration'.[67] The ugliness of this conflict, and the effect it had on Beardsley and publisher Lane at the Bodley Head, was typical of Douglas's lack of professionalism regarding his public association with Wilde. However, it was also an extension of the collaboration that Wilde found necessary to write and publish the play.

Wilde's frustrations are understandable when we consider his efforts to create something aesthetically new in the English language. While written originally in French, Wilde wanted *Salome* to be seen in England and he wanted his translation to reflect the work he put into the French original. Nicholas Frankel notes how Wilde considered moving to France after the Examiner of Plays refused the performance of *Salome* on an English stage. Frankel even supposes that Wilde, after a series of successful comedies, intended to refashion himself as 'a French Symbolist writer'.[68] Wilde's inability to control his access to the English stage, rewriting work completed poorly by his lover, Douglas, and now being told his book would be staged on the page by Beardsley, emphasises the decentred position of Wilde's authorial intention in the circulation of his text. Wilde had no control over the book's final design and vehemently disapproved of choices made by John Lane at the Bodley Head regarding the book's design.

With Ricketts, he would have gotten stylised arabesques sitting in the background of his book, highlighting his words for the reader and possibly creating an author-centric harmonious whole. With Beardsley, he knew that he would get provocative intercourse, drawings that spoke to and challenged Wilde's authorial supremacy.

Beardsley wrote to William Rothenstein in September 1893 before the book's release to say, 'The *Salomé* drawings have created a veritable *fronde*.'[69] Before its release, he knew he was generating controversy, and with controversy comes fame and, with any luck, more work for Beardsley. The delay in publication, however, was causing Beardsley considerable stress. He was even more distressed when he found out that Lane was not publishing all of his drawings, leaving out three submissions.[70] Lane took creative control – control he had seemingly handed to Beardsley by favouring the artist over Wilde's preferences. Lane now held the reigns on just *how Beardsley* the book would become.

The two images that John Lane removed from the edition feature two of the most feminine representations of Salomé in the entire collection with 'John and Salome' and 'Salome's Toilette'. Both images feature bare-breasted, extremely feminine portrayals of women. While the excision of 'John and Salome' makes sense due to Iokanaan's appearance as an effeminised object of a bare-breasted Salomé's less than subtle open-mouthed desire, the image of the toilette, even with her nudity, is traditionally female and recaptures Salomé's role as an object of desire. She bows her head, submitting to the control of her servants and the desires of men in the image, a submission that actually robs her of her androgynous power. The remaining toilette image has her fully dressed and shooting a look of frustration as she turns her head away from her harlequin hairdresser.

Beardsley relented to Lane's judgement. He writes,

> considering the matter of Salomé and I think the only feasible plan is to let the drawings remain in your hands. I quite recognize that they are legally your property as long as you consent to make them public, and that their transference to another publisher would only lead to trouble. I hope you may settle satisfactorily with Wilde.[71]

Beardsley is referring here to the more complicated negotiations that Lane was having with Wilde who was frustrated with the delays and his lack of payment from the Bodley Head. The British Library holds a facsimile of a letter dated February 1893 in which Wilde urges his publisher to pay him and Ricketts monies owed for previous works while also negotiating Lane's British distribution of the original French-language publication of the play: '*Salome* will be ready in a fortnight.' He is printing '50 on large paper' and tells his publisher 'they will be 10 / – each – sale price. Of course you will have them at a proper reduction. But kindly let me have as you promised a formal note about the whole thing – so as to have no misunderstanding about the agreement.'[72] Wilde also expresses concern in this letter for 'a large number of my poems still unpaid for – will you kindly close the account and let me live and cheque on them', as well as giving 'Ricketts his honorarium'.[73] Lane, despite his desire to print some of the most innovative literature of the 1890s, also had a terrible reputation for not paying his authors their rightful commissions. At every level, the interactions between *Salome*'s collaborators were tense and unpleasant.

This conflict is the basis of how queer spaces form. Heteronormativity sets the rules and creates the structures that queer people must first adapt to and eventually adapt for their needs. Sites of community both in the book and in the city are hidden because queer artists do not have the same freedom and authority as someone like William Morris, who in Chapter 2 we saw could reinvent the bookmaking industry to suit his ideals because, as a heterosexual man with money and influence, he can create an ideology that idealises middle-class aspirations of beauty and culture. Beardsley's work is not aspirational. But rather than a scribbling schoolboy, he is the creator of a vision that exposes the heteronormative world's hypocrisies. Where Morris saw beauty, Beardsley sees grotesques – he parodies heteronormativity and it is that parody that restructures the book so that in conversation with Wilde's suggestive play, he transforms bibliographic unity into a site of queer desire, decadent parody and even anger at the ideologies that condemn queers to the shadows.

It is likely that neither Wilde's nor Beardsley's suggestions were considered when arranging the ten illustrations included in the 1894 edition. After the difficulties with the translation process and Wilde's reactions to Beardsley's drawings, it is likely that Lane even avoided contact with these men when he went to print. We know that he ignored Wilde's critique of the binding for *Salome*. Wilde called the blue canvas 'coarse and common', suggesting that the 'horrid Irish stuff' be used on other books and fearing that it would do the book, as well as Lane, 'a great deal of harm', insisting that Beardsley also 'loathe[s]' the material.[74] Since the canvas remains, Lane clearly went with his own choice. Additionally, there are no accounts of the decision process indicating that the typesetters and form makers on the floor of T&A Constable's printing press in Scotland made these final decisions. Jerome McGann gives credit to Mathews and Lane for the placement of images, but I think this underestimates the influence of the printers. McGann argues that Lane along with Elkin Mathews privileged decorative value in their placement of Beardsley's illustrations and, with 'one exception, the designs are either inserted between (or before) the signature gatherings or they appear on pages with printed text'.[75] The bibliographical motive for positioning the pictures indicates that the actual typesetters and printers, in consultation with Lane, chose how to space images throughout the book. Typesetters and designers at the printers typically set up a 'layout' or presentation of their typographical design for the client prior to printing the book.[76] There is no indication that either the printers or publishers consulted Beardsley or Wilde during this process, so the art of assembly fell to the business interests of Lane and the skill of the printers at T&A Constable. The printer's use of a letterpress intaglio to print both images and type offers the advantage of cost efficiency and time management associated with the line-block and photomechanical use of etched zinc plates. The basis for the order of the images seems to be where they would fit into the printed text most easily for the printers. This compromise heightens the lack of harmony between image and play already formed out of its conflicted and even angry creation. By the time T&A Constable received the book for printing, there was no controlling hand.

At the same time, despite a lack of control, the influence of both artists is readily apparent. Beardsley, through his illustrative signature (see Fig. 4.3), merges artist with art. He objectifies himself with a symbol instead of using a signature. Beardsley is present, but he merges into the book's aesthetic, whereas Wilde receives little credit on the binding beyond the spine. The drawings demand intercourse with the play's material presentation. The book is not a harmonious whole because it contests Wilde's authorial intentions. Instead, *Salome* is a queer book because it is a unique agent of aesthetic and sexual discourse born out of discord, disorder and compromise. *Salome*'s queer sexual discourse passes that culture of fructuous intercourse onto the reader.

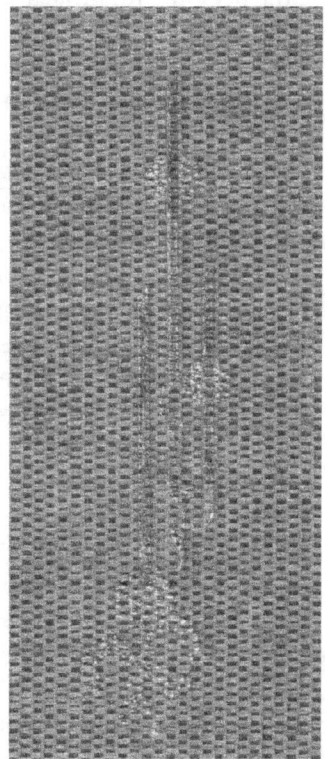

Figure 4.3 Gilt impressing of Beardsley's Colophon from back cover of *Salome*. Harry Ransom Center, The University of Texas at Austin.

Ars erotica and *Salome's* queer sexual discourse

Foucault presents the *ars erotica* as an alternative to *scientia sexualis* – the medicalisation of same-sex desire by sexologists like Dr Richard von Krafft-Ebing and critics like Max Nordau.[77] These writers, presuming same-sex desire to be abnormal, pathologised its practice and made patients out of men and women based solely on their sexual preferences and consensual practices. For women, the very experience of desire was pathologised as unnatural. Krafft-Ebing, for example, argues that for

> the hysterical the sexual sphere is often abnormally excited. This excitement may be intermittent (menstrual?). Shameless prostitution, even in married women, may result. In a milder form the sexual impulse expresses itself in onanism [masturbation], going about in a room naked, smearing the person with urine and other filthy things, or wearing male attire, etc.[78]

As the quote suggests, hysteria was seen as a female malady and the limits of sexual desire are deemed abnormal with acts like masturbation and alternative clothing choices put on par with urolagnia and scatology. It was when such acts were done by wives and daughters, women in respectable homes, when such behaviour was treated as mental illness. In such cases, instead of gratifying the Victorian gentleman's desires, she was acting on her own against his wishes, an act of dissent that the medical profession happily enforced with diagnosis, drugs and even institutionalisation. In this sense, Victorian women who expressed their desires or acted on them were, in our contemporary sense of the word, *queer*, because they did not align with the heteronormative demand to be an object of male desire and an obedient servant to his preferences. A woman with desire was seen as unnatural, to the point that sex workers were not seen as victims of economic inequality but as mad women, driven to the brothel by an unnatural desire to fuck. For the heteronormative reader, Salomé is such a hysteric brought to the stage in horrific excess. However, for the queer reader, and for women subjected to this misogynistic medicalisation, she is a rebuttal – a queer martyr enacting vengeance, ruining the male gaze and the heterosexual male's privilege over sanctioned desire.

The figure of Salomé represents a subversive revision of a biblical story, originally about King Herod but transformed by

European artists in the nineteenth century into a myth of the femme fatale. Pierre Puvis de Chavannes (1824–98) was the first to foreground Salomé in one of his paintings in 1856.[79] However, it was Joris-Karl Huysmans who, in *A rebours* (1884), has his decadent protagonist, Des Esseintes, after purchasing Gustave Moreau's two portraits of Salomé, declare her

> the symbolic deity of indestructible Lechery, the goddess of immortal Hysteria, the accursed Beauty, chosen amongst all others by the cataleptic paroxysm that stiffens her flesh and hardens her muscles; the monstrous, the indiscriminate, irresponsible, unfeeling Beast who, like Helen of Antiquity, poisons everything that comes near her, everything that sees her, everything that she touches.[80]

In spite of her destructive power over others, Des Esseintes's characterisation of Salomé is beautiful. Her beauty emerges from her dissident challenge of conventional portrayals of gender and sexuality. When Huysmans celebrates Salomé for her hysteria, her violence, and her self-destruction, it is a celebration of the decadent pose.

While not all Victorians saw women as strictly enduring sex for reproduction and marital responsibility for their husbands, many physicians, like gynaecologist William Acton (1813–75), actively promoted the idea that women did not desire sexual intercourse in the same fashion as men, suggesting that sex for women was an unpleasant duty instead of a pleasurable pursuit.[81] These views became fears when looking at other cultures and members of Britain's lower classes. In her historical study of prostitution, Nickie Roberts notes how the middle classes nurtured a fantasy of the poor and, by extension, the migrant population among this group as a threat to social order and its laws. Fantasies of immorality forming a part of the sex workers immorality narrate a justification of both the persecution of these women as well as an excuse for the privileged choices of men who pay for their services. Any consequences that befell such women was of their own making.[82] Because women were treated as such and offered little to no sex education, it is not surprising institutions that regulated sexual discourse propagated this narrative. Suffragette, playwright and novelist Cecily Hamilton (1872–1952) would later point out that marriage itself, for many women, was by necessity another trade. Hamilton argues that the 'housekeeping trade is the only one open to us – so we enter the housekeeping trade in order to live. This is not always quite the same as entering the housekeeping trade in order to love.'[83] Institutions policed female desire in the nineteenth century as something unnatural – her body is controlled by laws that sanction the exchange of women's bodies through the capitalist markets for sex work and wives. Women, like the fictional Salomé, who transgressed this discourse of sexual commodification were then subject to a medical discourse that pathologised their desires as hysteria, what Richard von Krafft-Ebing (1840–1902) defined as an 'an abnormal change and inversion of the sexual feeling' and its subsequent negative effect on 'the patient's disposition'.[84] As a woman presented as openly desirous of a man's body, Salomé subverts that narrative of commodified sex and challenges the notion of hysteria by queering the legal and medical sexual discourses that consider her desire unnatural.

Sarah E. Maier considers Salomé as a 'sexually subversive' *femme fatale*',[85] challenging the use of the character throughout nineteenth-century art as a 'ritualistic indictment of woman for her criminal demand for independent sexuality and desire'.[86] Like homosexual men, women who desired anyone at all were seen as unnatural and dangerous. Wilde's sympathy to her audacity in the face of judgement is up for debate, but not in the illustrated *Salome*. Beardsley portrays her as a sacred figure, gently carried by a Harlequin and a Faun to an oversized powder case for burial; she becomes a martyr for a readership, celebrating the decadence and artificiality of the play as well as giving value to the sexual subversive desires she symbolises. Consequently, the queer book serves as an interpretive space where discourses of diverse sexuality can be explored both metaphorically and even literally through a contradictory engagement with the play's meaning via bibliographic performance.

The symbol of Salomé envisioned by decadent French artists inspired both Wilde and Beardsley.[87] It is this symbol that appears in the pages of the Bodley Head book. In a historical and politically appropriate setting, the play is not a work of historical romance or realism. Both Wilde and Beardsley colour their respective words and drawings with contemporary references to aestheticism, decadence, symbolism and sexual inversion. The desire of Herodias's Page for his friend the soldier Narraboth; Salomé's gift of a green carnation to the same soldier; both express forbidden desires in late Victorian culture, male desire for the male body and female desire for the male body. In addition, Salomé's toilette filled with recognisable decadent novels, and the avant-garde women's fashions in some of Beardsley's drawings are features that subvert the play's temporality, disrupting the reader's sense of realism and mocking critical attempts at a moralistic interpretation.

Salome asks the reader to engage with his or her desires and the concept of pleasure in the face of moral judgement. *Salome* silences the prophet Iokanaan's voice of condemnation symbolically punishing the denial of desire's pleasure. Iokanaan has condemned Salomé's mother Herodias because she 'saw the images of men painted on the walls [and] gave herself up to the lust of her eyes'.[88] Men, as we have seen, have collected such images of both men and women and when they claim such acts are done for scientific research, they are believed. Herodias has no authority within accepted sexual discourse to hide. The details Iokanaan provides of Herodias's sinful gaze suggest that he spent a great deal of time gazing at her, while hypocritically demanding that she 'repent . . . of her iniquities'.[89] Recognising Iokanaan's gaze, which he now denies, Salomé expresses a desire for his eyes which she calls 'black holes! And 'black lakes' that are 'burned' and 'troubled' by 'torches' and 'fantastic moons'.[90] He is blinded and disturbed by what he saw of Herodias's agency and now devotes his gaze exclusively to a God who, ironically, is unseen.

Salomé attempts to seduce the prophet's gaze with a blazon of his dark beauty that diminishes his moralistic vision to an aesthetic, silencing his condemnation into an object of her desire. Salomé becomes a figure of queer sexuality because she invites the reader to enact a similar objectification of heteronormative sexual discourse. Salomé is not a moral figure like the Christ she parodies, but a symbolic fusion of the sexual and the spiritual in her seduction of Iokanaan. Her desire becomes sacred and transforms Iokanaan's words into an empty aesthetic, shifting social power to her gaze through the objectification of his body. She describes his body as white 'like the lilies of a field', and the snow that lies on the mountains of Judea.[91] Despite her appeal to his purity, he still only has eyes for his God. He will not look at her. Jealous of his unseen God, she declares his white body 'hideous' and 'like a plastered wall, where vipers have crawled'.[92] He is beautiful as a silent object, yet repulsive when he expresses his own desires. This disgust with his agency foreshadows the disgust Herod and others show when Salomé expresses her own. Salomé returns to her seduction reading Iokanaan's black hair as imitating the shadows of 'long black nights, when the moon hides her face', attracting her gaze by hiding the beauty of his phallic body. She completes her seduction describing his mouth as 'a band of scarlet on a tower of ivory' and like 'a pomegranate cut in twain with a knife of ivory' resembling a cut red fruit spilling seed and justice from the top of a phallic blade.[93] Her seduction is sacred: she repeats her desire to touch him three times, using multiple similes to make her point. Despite Wilde's emphasis on Iokanaan's refusal, Beardsley illustrates neither his denials nor his desire for God. The book visually silences Iokanaan's voice, insisting that the reader engages with Salomé as the subject of desire, diminishing his authoritative voice into sexually desirable red lips to be kissed and possessed.

Contrast Salomé's confession of desire for Iokanaan to Herod's appeals to Salomé. With the accompanying drawing 'The Eyes of Herod', the face of the Wildean moon in Beardsley's earlier drawings now moves to the face of Herod with a Wildean appearance gazing at the body of Salomé with an exposed breast, peacock-feathered hair and another peacock in the foreground. Wilde's play makes her an object and Beardsley's decision to show Wilde's gaze serves to acknowledge her objectification and to mock the heteronormative culture that mocks aestheticism and Wilde: critics may see themselves as better than Wilde, but his sexual desires are no more unnatural than their own. Herod does not attempt to physically touch Salomé, but he begs her to touch or taste intermediate objects that he can, in turn, touch in place of her body.

The reader mimics this substitution by touching the book of *Salome*, vicariously experiencing the desires that Wilde and Beardsley explore. Such secondary touches are portrayed as a means of quenching the subject's appetite. Herod's requests mimic Salomé's blazon for Iokanaan with the same triptych pattern of seduction. It turns out her desires are no more obscene than those in authority. First he asks her to drink from his wine and 'Dip into it thy little red lips, that I may drain the cup' in order to taste Salomé vicariously.[94] Herod then asks Salomé to 'Bite a little of this fruit, that I may eat what is left'.[95] Herod's appetite is based on his desire to taste, or to devour, things that her 'little red lips' have been dipped into or that bear the marks of her teeth.

He wants to control her appetite – mirroring Salomé's desire to kiss and possess Iokanaan's lips – as a means of validating his subjectivity by narrating her desires to suit his own needs.

Herod desires her body, not seeing her queer desires. She appears like any other object because he does not consider that she may have desires of her own. What Herod desires then is what he presumes a young woman to be, someone who trades sex for financial gain, much like a sex worker or someone in the marriage trade. Women bargain their bodies for capital. That is why his promises to her are based on wealth, even up to half of his kingdom. What he does not see is her queerness, because her desires would repulse him once spoken. Salomé, however, decides to compromise and use the capitalist trade in women to her own advantage. She secures a contract to grant her whatever she desires up to half of Herod's kingdom. Her acceptance and decision to dance and display her body are a means to an end.

It is this history of female sexual suppression that aligns Salomé's sexuality with queer sexual discourse. Queer readers whose same-sex desires are similarly criminalised by sodomy laws and pathologised as degenerate homosexuals find a figure of dissent, a martyr for the cause of an openly queer sexual discourse. The free circulation of this short, sensuous and shocking book by John Lane at the Bodley Head meant that readers could freely access queer sexual discourse.

Certainly, attempts to silence Salomé's desire were made; in the book, Herod has her crushed under his men's shields; but Wilde gives historical precedent for queer desires in western culture, challenging sexual discourses that place queerness on the periphery of Victorian life as either a degenerate practice of foreigners or a disease caught by a vulnerable poor who lack the supposed character of gentlemen readers to rise above its temptations. *Salome* as a material book makes available an open secret – that such a gentleman's sexual desires are neither more nor less perverse than the women and homosexuals his discourse condemns. *Salome* makes the ever-present queerness of nineteenth-century sexuality visible in an unsanctioned fashion – taking control of sexual discourse out of the hands of powerful men and placing it in the hands of the decadent figure of Salomé: a martyr to a beautifully unhealthy hysteria and homosexuality.

S. I. Salamensky complicates Wilde's portrayal of sexuality, presenting *Salome* as an intertextual homage to his 'many masters', from a range of aesthetic mediums including literature and painting.[96] Salamensky distances the play from Wilde's performance of 'Oscar Wilde' and suggests *Salome*'s place within the context of the aesthetic avant-garde of the late nineteenth century. The sexuality presented in *Salome* is cosmopolitan: informed by curiosity and study of eastern sexual discourse, but equally in debt to western texts of *eros*, and the Holy Bible. While Salomé is unnamed and silent in the King James Bible, in *Salome* she serves as a decadent parody of the Christ figure, a queer saviour who blurs the racialised boundary between eastern and western ideologies with a juxtaposition of sexual and cultural extremes. European authors, like Wilde, Burton and Foucault, created a queer space of largely western invention but located in an imagined 'east': a cosmopolitan reordering of sexual mores through the translation of international texts, as well as the creation of an erotic archive, influenced by eastern examples, but filled with western works that explore diverse sexual pleasures.

Salome, like Foucault's *ars erotica*, promotes sexual pleasure, a foundation for much queer theory today. To that end, queer theory is itself born from the study of book history, but that connection is typically unspoken. That erasure is in part due to Foucault's oversimplification of western and eastern erotic art. Taken from Ovid's concept of *ars amatoria*,[97] *ars erotica* is a book that serves as a means of initiating men and women into the sacred traditions of sexual practice within a culture.[98] Deriving from Ovid, the concept has its origins in classical Rome. *Salome*, as queer book, takes on the characteristics of an *ars erotica*, an 'erotic art' that Foucault says, conceives of 'truth [being] drawn from pleasure itself, understood as a practice and accumulated as experience'.[99] As a work that speaks to the concept of sexual dissidence in late Victorian culture, *Salome* speaks a decadent and often self-destructive truth – truth, that is, as it is conceived and constructed by the aesthetic community.

Such acts of defiance are a reflection of the racialised discourse of sexuality that also dominated nineteenth-century culture and influenced homosexual culture among the more privileged classes. So, it becomes necessary to understand the racialisation within nineteenth-century queer culture in order to realise how *Salome* subverts it. Leon Antonio Rocha notes the issue with our concept of *ars erotica* in queer literary studies:

> Since sexuality in the 'Orient' is 'degenerate', 'androgynous', and so forth, the Eastern Others had to be colonised and civilised. As such, the appropriation of Eastern erotica is at once transgressive and

conservative – it aims to expose and mock the hypocrisy and prudishness of the Europeans, yet simultaneously maintains the political status quo by exhibiting the 'primitive' rituals and practices of the 'barbarians' who were to be dominated and enlightened.[100]

To declare something eastern as other makes difference safe: queer desires exist but as a distant external threat, or as a sign of degeneracy, a social infection of the race when found in British communities. For queer writers and artists, the imagined east was presented as a magic land where their desires would not be condemned. It was not a real place, but a queer space, created by writers who, with their colonial perspective, did not see non-white peoples as equally human, but a remnant of an uncivilised past. No other author better exemplifies this simultaneous celebration and condemnation of eastern sexual discourse than Sir Richard Burton. In the terminal essay for his *The Book of the Thousand Nights and One Night* (1885), Burton defines 'pederasty' as sex between men. Typically, pederasty refers to a youth in his teens or early twenties in an erotic relationship with an older man, but Burton's essay doesn't refer to the ages of men, focusing rather on their sexual positions in the act of penetration.[101] He declares what he calls a 'Sotadic Zone, bounded westwards by the northern shores of the Mediterranean (N. Lat. 43°) and by the southern (N. Lat. 30°). Thus the depth would be 780 to 800 miles including meridional France, the Iberian Peninsula, Italy and Greece, with the coast-regions of Africa from Morocco to Egypt.'[102] He goes on to include Asia Minor, Japan, China and Afghanistan among other places. Burton claims that the so-called vice of sex between men is caused by 'climatic, not racial' conditions, and then defends its 'noble side' by drawing on Greek history and pederastic relationships of the ancient world. He presents modern same-sex practices as degenerate and degraded forms of that once great and noble tradition, suggesting that the people who practise it are simply lesser imitators of pederasts, clinging to outdated, pagan practices that belong in an ancient past. Burton's work shows the influence of Social Darwinism and beliefs in the superiority of Anglo-Saxon and Germanic-Teutonic races over even their nearest neighbours in Italy and Spain. Parts of France are as equally condemned as parts of Africa and China. The suggestion is that the English have outgrown homosexuality and by travelling into the Sotadic zone, individuals may find themselves degenerating.

Burton's scientific racism, however, has deeply influenced queer culture in its romanticisation of the east as a place where men can love other men without judgement. Joseph A. Boone brought significant attention to the western trade of boys for sex by colonial western gay men who travelled to places like North Africa to explore same-sex desire in a manner that would result in legal consequences in a country like Britain. But while these vacation cruises were the consequence of the persecution of gay men in Britain, America and parts of Europe, the 'intersection of this "sanctuary" for gay men with certain historical and economic factors of western colonialism allowed a level of exploitation potentially as objectionable as the experience of marginalization and harassment that sent these western voyagers abroad in the first place'.[103] The romantic objectifies the east and robs its peoples, including its queer peoples, of an agency in the sex trade that these men exploited. At the same time, Christopher Chitty challenges the dismissal of Burton's work as racist and points to the ways in which his study of a sotadic zone has actually been reiterated in more recent research on non-western conceptions of same-sex desire as a third gender being a traditional part of many cultural traditions misunderstood by Victorians.[104] While the framing of a sotadic zone is certainly outdated and reflects the colonial biases of Burton and his readers, at the same time, Burton's work is an early attempt by a western writer to engage with and understand non-western sexuality, rejecting hierarchical racial theories of sexuality that dominated the study of non-western cultures during his time. Chitty argues that Burton rejected these small-minded points of view and suggests that Burton's geographic conception of sexuality paves the way for the cultural studies of sexual difference of today. It is this complexity that Beardsley's visual art brings to Wilde's Symbolist play to complicate the reader's conception of sexual otherness that we find in *Salome*.

Salome opens with a discourse of desire between a young Syrian soldier and the Page of Herodias. The Syrian's amorous appreciation of Salomé's beauty contrasts with the Page's description of the moon as 'strange', and like 'a dead woman' that dances in a 'yellow veil'.[105] The moon is symbolic of Salomé's beauty as a reflective surface described to be 'like the shadow of a white rose in a mirror of silver'.[106] The Page notes that Syrian's obsession with Salomé is dangerous and warns him 'not to look at her' for fear of the consequences.[107] This sequence, as well as Beardsley's

Figure 4.4 'Woman in the Moon' by Beardsley for *Salome*. Private collection.

illustration of it (see Fig. 4.4), established the moon's relationship to Salomé and an atmosphere of fear surrounding her as an object whose beauty veils unknown sexual desires.

The eyes of this Wildean moon peer to the right at the two men, the young Syrian and the Page, who in turn, gaze at the moon as their object of desire. Their gazes do not meet in in the illustration, capturing the failure of the one gazing to recognise his object's gaze and, thereby, failing to recognise the object's individual agency. Conflated with both Salomé and Oscar Wilde, the moon's agency inverts the male gaze by expressing a desire for the nude male form represented by the lythe nude figure of the young Syrian instead of Salomé's female body. By placing the figure of Wilde onto the page in illustrated form, Beardsley calls on the reader to interpret Wilde as a reader seeking expressions of queer sexuality, transforming the moon, a symbolic femme fatale, into an androgynous, queer-reading, subject. The moon as subject engages with the reader's position performing the act of the cruising *flâneur*. The queer space shared by the reader and Beardsley as illustrator who mediates the meaning of Wilde's play, reveals the power of the gaze by empowering the reader with a self-reflexive awareness of their own gaze at the book. The power to define desire individually, rather than culturally, is generated within the queer space of the book for Salomé, for the moon, for Wilde and for the reader.[108]

Just as 'The Woman in the Moon' unites Wilde, Salomé, *Salome* and the reader, *Salome* unites Beardsley and Wilde's art into component pieces of the book's queer sexual discourse. It is how illustration and play *come together* to make *Salome* as well as the reputations of Wilde and Beardsley. Lorraine Janzen Kooistra notes that this 'unifying connection is ... social', resulting from both men being 'caught up in the period's cultural politics' such as the arts-and-crafts movement from which the queer book emerges and taking on roles as 'transgressive outsider[s]'.[109] The aesthetics of individual artists such as Wilde, Beardsley and the fictional dancer Salomé are set apart from the illustration and book designs in Morris's medieval artisanship and from realist narratives that dominate the press and most fictional novels of the 1890s. The book enacts an erotic penetration of Wilde's art with the art of Beardsley.

Beardsley's symbolic insult of the author actually distances Wilde from the play. It makes Wilde another character, a performer of the play instead of its maker. Ian Fletcher notes that just because Beardsley turns the moon into a caricature of Wilde, he does not necessarily do so in order to attack Wilde.[110] Beardsley is not seeking to insult Wilde; instead, he is having fun with Wilde, giving materiality to Wilde's ambiguous imagery and using this imagery to influence a book that becomes a reflexive commentary on its own creation. Wilde's cultural persona is tied to the queer book. Just as Salomé the character and *Salome* the book are symbols, Beardsley makes Wilde into a parallel symbol of decadent sexual pleasure.

The artificiality of the play, its symbolic movement, poetic language and illustrations, transform a shared myth into a celebration of the unhealthy, an exploration of the morbid, death and violence as acts of beautiful creation, and self-destructiveness as a satirical comment on late Victorian culture. Beardsley's imagery heightens this destructive aesthetic of the play for the reader – so much so that his work at times dwarfs the play. It is as if the images do what Salomé does to Iokanaan – impose an unwanted intimacy. Beardsley's vision was not Wilde's vision; as a result, the book is changed into something even more subversive, emphasising the fantastic elements of Wilde's Symbolist play further with a visual presentation that matches the violence of the play but presents it ironically to emphasise the symbolic tenor of the work. The material book, by its very materiality, makes the play even more unrealistic, and unbelievable, and suggests a reading of Wilde's play as an amoral, decadent and multisensory art project, unique to the 1894 edition.

It is significant that Beardsley never provides an image of the kiss. He shows the moment of 'The Climax' where Salomé floats in a state of ecstasy as she anticipates the realisation of her decadent desires. It is a teasing image that matches Wilde's stage directions where he calls for the theatre lights to be put out during the kiss. Salomé's act of sexual dissent is symbolic. The reader is not supposed to see her act of necrophilia as a specific desire fulfilled. Instead, her desire is symbolic, making the kiss symbolic of revealing the unspoken desires of institutionalised authority (Herod), resulting in Salomé's death, and suggesting potential for cultural chaos. There are consequences for decadence and its cultural dissent, but the consequences are desired, at least in the queer book, because the ensuing chaos that breaks down existing social authority provides an opportunity for decadent discourses of the avant-garde to create new conceptions of beauty and desire that are not marginalised within existing Victorian institutions of social organisation and control. Salomé dies at the end of the play and yet, she does not give the impression that she cares much about her death (let alone the fact that Iokanaan has himself been decapitated for her pleasure), gasping to herself in her final monologue, 'What matter? I have kissed thy mouth Iokanaan. I have kissed thy mouth.'[111] She does not glory in her death but her response to Herod's order of executive is, at best, apathetic. Just as she said of Iokanaan earlier, she does not beg for her life. She never screams from either fear or pain which is significant, considering that Herod has his soldiers crush her body with their shields If we are to read her death literally, as with a work of realism, then her death is a tragic moral warning about the consequences of sexual excess. However, by reading it symbolically, her death becomes a philosophical moment, not only for Salomé, but also for the moon and for Wilde, with whom Beardsley equated Salomé, and the moon at the beginning of the play.

Herod insists that his men extinguish all light: 'Put out the torches! Hide the moon! Hide the stars! Let us hide ourselves.'[112] To see Salomé realise her desires is to reveal the object of his desire to be an illusion. Her innocence was not real and the idea that his desire for her, man's desire for woman, and the sun's light shining on the moon, are all representative of a social order that imbues objects with beauty and meaning comes into question. Herod has the light extinguished because her acts (as well as his) are unsanctioned. Her desires are unhealthy and a morbid mockery of his authority. He cannot witness her actions because to do so would validate her choices and diminish his authority.

The play was designed so that Salomé's final sin would be committed in complete darkness. Beardsley, however, shines light on it for the reader in his second depiction of this scene in 'The Climax', a dream vision of a floating and smirking Salomé still gazing at the head she holds. Lifeless blood drips in a white ribbon down a black background reinforcing the phallic image of Iokanaan's head atop an ivory tower. Her floating implies the ecstasy of desire in the moments before the fruit of orgasm and she is blind to all but her object. Beardsley's vision is representative of Salomé's monologue, heightening the intensity of the coming experience not yet fulfilled: 'I will kiss it now. I will bite it with my teeth as one bites a ripe fruit', co-opting Herod's language of appetite. Salomé mocks Iokanaan's moral authority, noting how his 'eyes that were so terrible, so full of rage and scorn are shut now'. Iokanaan's voice, represented by his 'tongue, that was like a red snake darting poison ... moves no more'. She silences his 'evil words' and relishes this moment, this queer space: 'thou art dead, and thy head belongs to me'.[113] Salomé inverts moral judgement to judge those who desire her body while condemning her appetite. Iokanaan's moral authority is groundless within queer space where Salomé's agency decapitates his power over the queer subject. He cannot speak his words anymore because the book makes no room for the marginalisation of the queer subject.

Hidden from a heteronormative authority, the book becomes the space where queer agency is realised:

Collaboration and Conflict: Queer Space in *Salome* 215

Ah! I have kissed they mouth, Iokanaan, I have kissed thy mouth. They say that love hath a bitter taste. But what matter? what matter? I have kissed thy mouth Iokanaan, I have kissed thy mouth.[114]

At this moment after the kiss, Wilde's stage directions indicate that a ray of moonlight falls on Salomé, as a symbol for the reader within queer space now imbued with an appetite like the young Syrian and Page before her. The darkness provides the reader with safety from anyone's gaze where they may interpret the orgasm of his or her queer agency independent of a visual model. Salomé becomes a sacred distraction.

The queer book mocks even the orders for her death. Beardsley goes so far as to picture her being placed inside a cosmetic powder box, as if burial means a return to the toilette from which she came (see Fig. 4.5). Her death becomes a symbolic aesthetic without any real consequence other than a return to the materials from which

Figure 4.5 'The Death of Salome' by Beardsley from *Salome*. Private collection.

the symbolic Salomé was born. With her connection to the moon, Beardsley's choice to equate these images with Wilde's face is even more important. Is Beardsley suggesting the death of Wilde? While that may seem like a cruel joke of which Beardsley was capable, a better explanation is rooted in the book's material interaction with the play. Just as the symbolic femme fatale dies, so does the author. Beardsley extinguishes Wilde's singular vision of Salomé with bibliographical intervention. The author, and even the illustrator, are subsumed by the intercourse between text and illustration. The play was collaborative, and it could be said that Wilde as the author is just as symbolic as Salomé is symbolic of desire. It is not Beardsley's vision that extinguishes Wilde's influence either; rather, it is the queer book, born of this conflicting creative interference and a decadent, gleefully morbid, sense of humour.

Salomé's death becomes a moment of suppressed sexual decadence – a violent and bloody end but also an end that laughs at cultural authority. Salomé's death comes too late to stop her from realising her decadent desires. The play represents those desires in a manner that makes them symbolic of sexual dissent more broadly. Salomé's death in this edition is a symbolic failure to silence sexual dissent in 1890s avant-garde culture. While she dies, she fulfils her desires. Death is not a relevant consequence in the Symbolist context of the play because it does not stop her from enacting her sexual dissidence. Her decadence results in her death but it also results in the weakening of Herod's power. Similarly, the publication of *Salome*, the book, challenges the authority of the Lord Chamberlain who banned the play, offering the reading public a play more heretical than anything Wilde would have staged, and adding a new level of sexual dissent that could potentially end up in the hands of many readers. *Salome* also exposes the illusion of creative control within the mechanics of the publishing industry. The book becomes a cultural object of sexual indoctrination, a queer book that kills all forms of authority: author, tetrarch and the dominant sexual discourse. At the climax, her silence is broken and her queer sexuality, her desire for the male body, is given agency in Herod and Iokanaan's world. While Herod may turn out the light and the stage becomes dark, her queerness is now represented in the *fin de siècle* literary marketplace. The reader may not be able to see it, but they know now it exists and can be found through the discerning reading of aesthetic editions.

Notes

1. Oscar Wilde, *Salome: A Tragedy in One Act* (London: John Lane and Elkin Mathew, 1894), p. 68.
2. Please note that, as per the 1894 edition of *Salome*, I will not use an accent when referring to the book. However, Wilde and many others use the accent in reference to Salomé as a character and I will follow the same practice. The difference is also intended to emphasise when I am discussing the book and when I am discussing the characters visual referent so that it is clear if I am speaking about the book or the character.
3. Chris Snodgrass, 'Decadent Mythmaking: Arthur Symons, Aubrey Beardsley and *Salome*', *Victorian Poetry*, 28.3–4 (1990), pp. 61–109.
4. Snodgrass, 'Decadent Mythmaking', p. 79.
5. Brad Bucknell, 'On "Seeing" Salome', *ELH: English Literary History*, 60.2 (1993), pp. 519, 503.
6. Linda Hutcheon and Michael Hutcheon, '"Here's Lookin' at You, Kid": The Empowering Gaze in "Salome"', in *Profession* (1998), p. 16.
7. For further scholarship on Salomé's gaze, see Hutcheon, '"Here's Lookin' at You, Kid"', and Bucknell, 'On "Seeing" Salome'.
8. Dustin Friedman, *Before Queer Theory: Victorian Aestheticism and the Self* (Baltimore: Johns Hopkins University Press, 2019), p. 5.
9. Michel Foucault, *History of Sexuality Vol. 1: An Introduction*, trans. by Robert Hurley (New York: Vintage Books, 1980), p. 58.
10. *The Karma Sutra* was translated into English by Sir Richard Burton and published in 1883 for the Erotika Biblion Society by Leonard Smithers. *Psychopathia Sexualis* was translated into English in 1892 by Charles Gilbert Chaddock.
11. Joseph Bristow, 'Preface', and 'Introduction', *Oscar Wilde and Modern Culture: The Making of a Legend*, ed. by Joseph Bristow (Athens: Ohio University Press), 2009, pp. ix–xxx, 1–45 (pp. xii, 3–4). See also *Wilde Writings: Contextual Conditions*, ed. by Joseph Bristow (Toronto: University of Toronto Press, 2003). Other significant works by Bristow are noted in the Introduction.
12. 'From Depilation by Catamites' in *Priapeia sive diversorum poetarum in Priapum lusus or SPORTIVE EPIGRAMS ON PRIAPUS by divers poets in English verse and prose*, trans. and ed. by Leonard C. Smithers and Sir Richard Burton (Cosmopoli: Erotika Biblion Society (London: Leonard Smithers), 1890).

13. For a detailed history see, James G. Nelson, *Publisher to the Decadents: Leonard Smithers in the Careers of Beardsley, Wilde, Dowson. With an Appendix on Smithers and the Erotic Book Trade by Peter Mendes and a Checklist of Smithers's Publication by James G. Nelson and Peter Mendes* (University Park: The Pennsylvania State University Press, 2000).
14. Lisa Z. Sigel. *Governing Pleasures: Pornography and Social Change in England, 1815–1914* (New Brunswick, NJ: Rutgers University Press, 2002), pp. 27–8.
15. Merlin Holland's *The Real Trials of Oscar Wilde* (New York: Perennial, 2003) provides detailed transcripts of Prosecutor Edward Carson's questioning of Wilde and it is filled with details in which Carson tries to shock the jury with Wilde's choice to bring lower-class men to Paris or dine with them at the Savoy. The suggestion was that Wilde was a terrible influence on young men who had no place in these upper-middle class spaces. By subverting class, Wilde's subversion of sexuality was apparent.
16. Robert Gray and Christopher Keep, '"An Uninterrupted Current": Homoeroticism and Collaborative Authorship in *Teleny*', in *Literary Couplings: Writing Couples, Collaborators, and the Construction of Authorship*, ed. by Marjorie Stone and Judith Thompson (Madison: University of Wisconsin Press, 2006), pp. 193–208. See also Frederick D. King, 'British Aestheticism, Sexology, and Erotica: Negotiating Sexual Discourses in *Teleny*', *Victorian Review*, 41.1 (2015), pp. 163–79.
17. Sigel, *Governing Pleasures*, p. 61.
18. James. G. Nelson, *The Early Nineties*, p. 106; prices advertised in *Pall Mall Gazette*, 22 Feb. 1894. British Library Newspapers.
19. Sonya Petersson, 'The Counteractive Illustration and Its Metalanguage', *Word & Image*, 34.4 (2018), p. 349.
20. Petersson, 'The Counteractive Illustration', p. 352.
21. Petersson, 'The Counteractive Illustration', p. 352.
22. Linda C. Dowling, *Language and Decadence at the Victorian Fin de Siècle* (Princeton, NJ: Princeton University Press, 1986), p. 161.
23. Dowling, *Language and Decadence*, p. 163.
24. Natasha Hurley, *Circulating Queerness: Before the Gay and Lesbian Novel* (Minneapolis: University of Minnesota Press, 2018), p. 3.
25. Hurley, *Circulating Queerness*, p. 3.
26. Friedman, *Before Queer Theory*, p. 3.

27. Joseph Grigley, *Textualterity: Art, Theory, and Textual Criticism* (Ann Arbor: University of Michigan Press, 1995), p. 123.
28. Charles Ricketts, *Reflections on Wilde*, p. 51.
29. Richard Ellmann, *Oscar Wilde* (New York: Penguin Books, 1988), p. 353.
30. Matthew Sturgis, *Aubrey Beardsley: A Biography* (Hammersmith: HarperCollins, 1998), p. 121.
31. Robert Ross, *Aubrey Beardsley*, introduced by Matthew Sturgis (repr.; London: Pallas Athene, 2011), pp. 51–2.
32. Ross, *Aubrey Beardsley*, p. 52.
33. Layla Bloom, 'The Book Illustrators', *Fancy and Imagination: Beardsley and the Book Illustrators* (Leeds: The Stanley & Audrey Burton Gallery, University of Leeds, 2010), p. 28.
34. Layla Bloom, 'The Book Illustrators', p. 28.
35. Philip Gaskell, *A New Introduction to Bibliography: The Classic Manual of Bibliography* (New Castle: Oak Knoll Press, 1995), p. 271.
36. Gaskell, *A New Introduction to Bibliography*, p. 271.
37. Gaskell, *A New Introduction to Bibliography*, p. 271.
38. Gaskell, *A New Introduction to Bibliography*, p. 271.
39. Frankel, *Oscar Wilde's Decorated Books*, p. 69.
40. Walter Crane, *Of the Decorative Illustration of Books Old and New* (London: George Bell and Sons, 1896), p. 125.
41. Crane, *Of the Decorative Illustration*, p. 129.
42. Crane, *Of the Decorative Illustration*, pp. 218–21.
43. Crane, *Of the Decorative Illustration*, p. 174.
44. Crane, *Of the Decorative Illustration*, p. 174.
45. Frankel, *Oscar Wilde's Decorated Books*, p. 68.
46. Linda Gertner Zaitlin, *Aubrey Beardsley, Japonisme, and the Perversion of the Victorian Ideal* (New York: Cambridge University Press, 1997), p. 53.
47. James. G. Nelson, *The Early Nineties*, pp. 238–9.
48. Nicholas Frankel, *The Invention of Oscar Wilde* (London: Reaktion Books, 2021), p. 184.
49. G. A. Cevasco, *The Breviary of Decadence*, p. 112.
50. *The Complete Letters of Oscar Wilde*, ed. by Merlin Holland and Rupert Hart-Davis (New York: Henry Holt and Company, 2000), p. 587.
51. Austin, Harry Ransom Center, University of Texas, John Lane Company Records. Aubrey Beardsley 42. Underline in original.

52. Charles Ricketts, *Oscar Wilde: Recollections by Jean Paul Raymond & Charles Rickets* (repr.; London: Pallas Athene, 2011), p. 51.
53. Ricketts, *Oscar Wilde*, pp. 51–2.
54. Karl Beckson, *Aesthetes and Decadents of the 1890s: An Anthology of British Poetry and Prose*, rev. edition, ed. by Karl Beckson (Chicago: Academy Chicago Publishers, 1981), p. 194.
55. Ellmann, *Oscar Wilde*, p. 355.
56. Elliot L. Gilbert, '"Tumult of Images": Wilde, Beardsley, "Salome"', *Victorian Studies*, 26.2 (1983), p. 147.
57. Linda Gertner Zaitlin, *Aubrey Beardsley, Japonisme, and the Perversion of the Victorian Ideal* (New York: Cambridge University Press, 1997), p. 147.
58. Zaitlin, *Aubrey Beardsley*, p. 147.
59. Max Beerbohm, 'A Defence of Cosmetics', *The Yellow Book: An Illustrated Quarterly*, 1 (London: Elkin Mathews and John Lane, 1894), p. 71.
60. Ellmann, *Oscar Wilde*, p. 379.
61. Ellmann, *Oscar Wilde*, p. 379.
62. Ellmann, *Oscar Wilde*, p. 379.
63. Ellmann, *Oscar Wilde*, p. 380.
64. Qtd in Ellmann, *Oscar Wilde*, p. 380.
65. Ellmann, *Oscar Wilde*, p. 380.
66. Ellmann, *Oscar Wilde*, p. 380.
67. Qtd in Ellmann, *Oscar Wilde*, p. 381.
68. Frankel, *The Invention of Oscar Wilde*, pp. 162, 179.
69. *The Letters of Aubrey* Beardsley, ed. by Henry Mass, John Duncan and W. G. Good (Rutherford: Fairleigh Dickinson University Press, 1970), p. 54.
70. Sturgis, *Aubrey Beardsley*, p. 161.
71. Mass et al., *Letters of Aubrey Beardsley*, p. 56.
72. The British Library, London, Lady Eccles Oscar Wilde Collection RP 3196.
73. The British Library, London, Lady Eccles Oscar Wilde Collection RP 3196. Autograph Letter Signed to John Lane. Feb. 1893.
74. Holland and Hart-Davis, *Collected Letters of Oscar Wilde*, pp. 578–9.
75. Jerome McGann, 'Literature by Design since 1790', *Victorian Poetry*, 48.1 (2010), pp. 11–40.
76. McLean, *Thames and Hudson*, p. 112.
77. Max Nordau's *Degeneration* was translated into English from its original German and published in Britain in 1895.

78. Richard von Krafft-Ebing, *Psychopathia Sexualis: The Classic Study of Deviant Sex*, trans. by Franklin S. Klaf (New York: Arcade Publishing, 2011), pp. 329–30.
79. Pierre-Louis Mathieu, *The Symbolist Generation, 1870–1910* (New York: Skira Rizzoli, 1990), p. 25.
80. Joris-Karl Huysmans, *Against Nature (A rebours)* [1884], trans. by Margaret Mauldon and ed. by Nicholas White, Oxford World's Classics (New York: Oxford University Press, 1998), p. 46.
81. William Acton, *The Functions and Disorders of the Reproductive Organs in Childhood, Youth, Adult Age, and Advanced Life: Considered in Their Physiological, Social, and Moral Relations* (London: Churchill, 1862).
82. Nickie Roberts, *Whores in History: Prostitution in Western Society* (Hammersmith, London: HarperCollins, 1992), p. 224.
83. Cecily Hamilton, *Marriage as a Trade* (New York: Moffat, Yard and Company, 1909).
84. Krafft-Ebing, *Psychopathia Sexualis*, p. 329.
85. Sarah E. Maier, 'Symbolist Salomés and the Dance of Dionysus', *Nineteenth-Century Contexts*, 28.3 (2006), pp. 211–23, p. 211.
86. Maier, 'Symbolist Salomés', p. 222.
87. Jackson, *The Eighteen Nineties*, p. 63.
88. Oscar Wilde, *Salome: A Tragedy in One Act* (London: Elkin Mathews and John Lane, 1894), p. 18.
89. Wilde, *Salome*, p. 18.
90. Wilde, *Salome*, p. 18.
91. Wilde, *Salome*, p. 21.
92. Wilde, *Salome*, p. 22.
93. Wilde, *Salome*, p. 22.
94. Wilde, *Salome*, p. 22.
95. Wilde, *Salome*, p. 22.
96. S. I. Salamensky, *The Modern Art of Influence and the Spectacle of Oscar Wilde* (New York: Palgrave Macmillan, 2011), p. 47.
97. Rocha, Leon Antonio, 'Scientia Sexualis versus Ars Erotica: Foucault, van Gulik, Needham', *Studies in the History and Philosophy of Biological and Biomedical Sciences*, 42 (2011), p. 330.
98. Foucault, *History of Sexuality*, pp. 57–8.
99. Foucault, *History of Sexuality*, p. 57.
100. Rocha, 'Scientia Sexualis versus Ars Erotica', p. 333.
101. For an example of its more common usage, see John Addington Symonds's 'A Problem in Greek Ethics', printed as appendix A in

Havelock Ellis and John Addington Symonds, *Sexual Inversion: A Critical Edition*, ed. by Ivan Crozier (Basingstoke: Palgrave MacMillan, 2008), pp. 227–95.
102. Richard Burton, 'From Volume XX, From Terminal Essay, IV, Social Condition, D – Pederasty', *Lad's Love: An Anthology of Uranian Poetry and Prose*, ed. and intro. by Michael Matthew Kaylor (Kansas City: Valancourt Books, 2010), p. 161.
103. Joseph A. Boone, 'Vacation Cruises; Or, the Homoerotics of Orientalism', *PMLA. Publications of the Modern Language Association of America*, 110.1 (1995), p. 99.
104. Christopher Chitty, *Sexual Hegemony: Statecraft, Sodomy, and Capital in the Rise of the World System* (Durham, NC: Duke University Press, 2020), pp. 74–5.
105. Wilde, *Salome*, p. 3.
106. Wilde, *Salome*, p. 3.
107. Wilde, *Salome*, p. 3.
108. These two paragraphs and several other passages in this originally appeared in my 'Oscar Wilde's Salome and the Queer Space of the Book', chapter 8 of *Wilde's Wiles: Studies of the Influences on Oscar Wilde and His Enduring Influences in the Twenty-First Century*, ed. by Annette M. Magid (Newcastle upon Tyne: Cambridge Scholars Press, 2015), pp. 159–78. Published with the permission of Cambridge Scholars Publishing. I also acknowledge and thank Annette M. Magid for her editing work and encouragement when writing that original essay.
109. Lorraine Janzen Kooistra, *The Artist as Critic: Bitextuality in Fin-de-Siècle Illustrated Books* (Aldershot: Scolar Press, 1997), pp. 26, 132.
110. Ian Fletcher, *Aubrey Beardsley* (Boston: Twayne Publishers, 1987), p. 78.
111. Wilde, *Salome*, p. 68.
112. Wilde, *Salome*, p. 66.
113. Wilde, *Salome*, p. 68.
114. Wilde, *Salome*, p. 68.

Conclusion
Queer Books and Their Digital Afterlives

The recent digitisation of the periodical *The Pageant* (1896–7) for *The Yellow Nineties Online* (c. 1890s) brings scholars and students new access to aesthetic works not in general circulation for readers today. Under literary editor J. W. Gleeson White, and art editor Charles Haslewood Shannon, *The Pageant* features plays, poems, art reproductions, woodcuts and critical essays from multiple queer authors and artists including Michael Field, Laurence Housman, Lionel Johnson, Charles Ricketts and Paul Verlaine. Published by Henry & Company, the two published volumes were wrapped in beautiful claret-clothed boards with gold impressing by Ricketts (see Fig. C.2). While not as finely crafted as the queer books presented in previous chapters, it collects artifacts of queerness among other aesthetic curiosities demonstrating the ways in which queer lives emerged out of, and interacted within, heteronormative spaces.

The image 'Death and the Bathers' by queer author and artist Laurence Housman (1865–1959) is from the first volume of *The Pageant* (see Fig. C.1). Like the authors featured in this book, he produced many beautiful texts contributing both poetry and imagery. The image, inspired by the Narcissus myth, depicts a group of nude men bathing in a river. At first glance, the men appear to gaze at their reflections in the water, enamoured of the beauty that looks back at them. But only one man, to the left of the image, does that. Look closer and the man in the foreground is standing on another man's chest. At his feet is not a reflection, but a man floating on his back with his face and chest rising out of the water. This other man holds the foregrounded man's feet in his hands. The reference to Narcissus is a deflection that only applies to one

Figure c.1 'Death and the Bathers' by Laurence Housman from *The Pageant* (1896). Private collection.

of the men in the image. Most of the men in the image are looking at one another and enjoying the pleasure of each other's company. So where is this Death that Housman's title references? Is the man in the water going to pull the other man into the water and drown him? Perhaps, but the foregrounded figure is shrouded in shadow with hair adorned with flowers. The suggestion is that perhaps he is Death. Death is perhaps a reference to the potential threat to these men. Narcissus dies, not because he drowns, but because he cannot tear himself away from the reflection of his own beauty. Like Narcissus, the desire that these men have, extends Narcissus away from selfhood reflected and towards the same sex. These men enjoy a moment of queer relationality together in nature, with each other, and pleasure without consequence, at least in this secluded spot. To be discovered could have terrible consequences, certainly, but for now, in this queer space, they are free.

That space, exists in the pages of *The Pageant* and, once more, shows us how queer spaces emerge from within existing heteronormative structures. Published as a Christmas annual for middle-class readers, *The Pageant* only survived for two seasons, but it remains an archive of ideas and experiments that seemed important enough to preserve in the twenty-first century. The digital preservation records not only the content and the original published book, but the condition in which these volumes were found. As ex-library copies, they show foxing, tearing, white-inked spine numbers. With pages originally uncut, it was a set of books that no one read, undervalued and forgotten in a library archive until they were eventually discarded.[1]

The Pageant is but one example of the problem with library preservation and serves as an argument for the digitisation of historical texts. Books must be preserved, not just for their content, but for their material value. While a digital edition does not necessarily preserve that materiality, it mimics that materiality and recreates it in a manner that library storage does not always achieve. Books are stamped, marked, misplaced and mistreated even when stored in restrictive collections. The volumes of *Silverpoints* and *A House of Pomegranates* (see Figs 1.1 and 2.1) that I worked on from another library archive each had a sticker on the front of it that read 'for library use only' in bright red letters. That sticker was placed over the gold-impressed design, scaring the book's beauty. At one point, when I returned to follow up with the volume, they could not find it. It was small, thin and had nothing

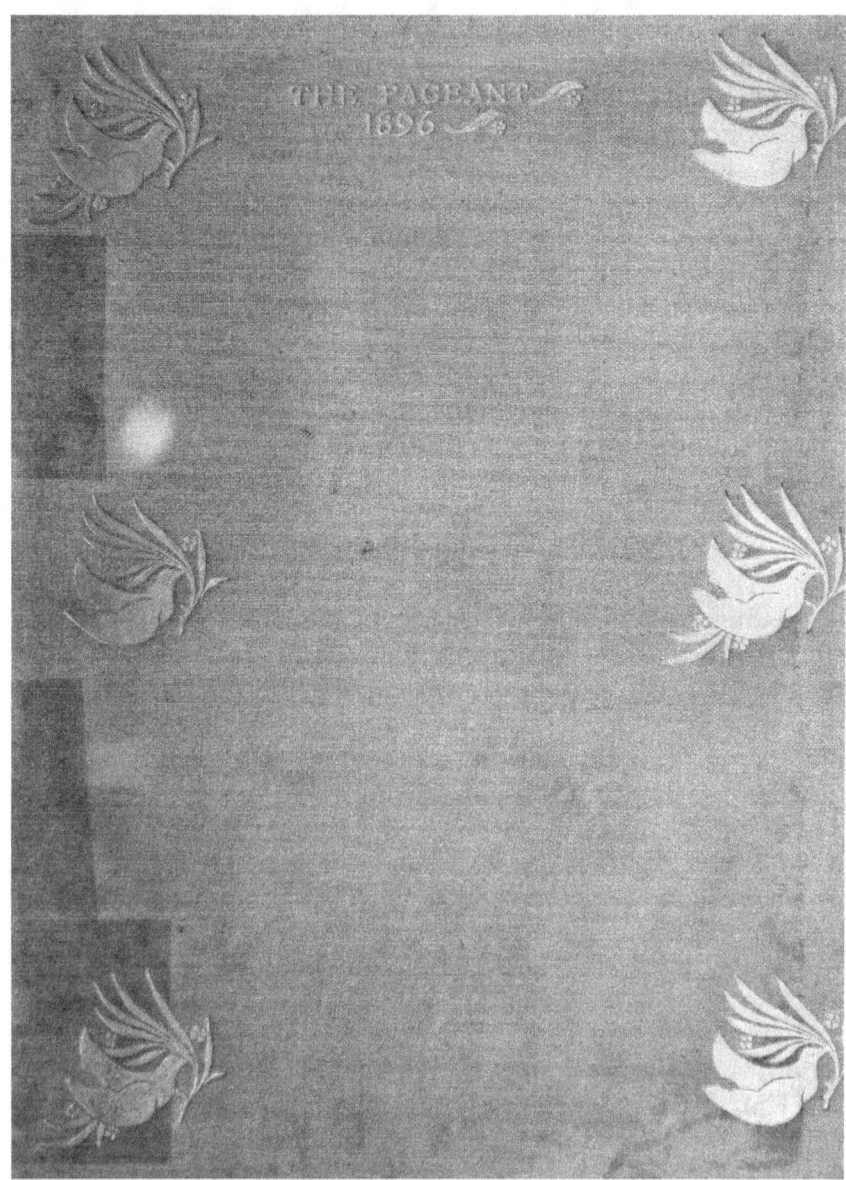

Figure c.2 Cover design for *The Pageant* (1896). Note the stains along the spine from the packing tape used by the library to hold the book together. Private collection.

written on the spine, but nothing was done to ensure its accessibility. They thought perhaps that it had been lost a long time before. It was only because of my insistence on my recent research-related access to it that they searched for it and eventually it was found. The library treated this precious little book not like an art object, certainly not like a rare example of queer space in late Victorian bibliographic history, but like a storage case for printed text, but ultimately content. Its value as a work of literature, let alone as an object of beauty was inconsequential. Carolyn Steedman notes that library archives of all kinds are choices as well as random accidents that were not necessarily conscious choices. I suspect that *The Pageant* is one of these accidents. Regardless, what is stored in the archive are meaningless artifacts until someone reads and interprets their contents.[2] What narratives emerge from the archive depend upon the researcher, and it is clear that libraries are storing books, not as artifacts or objects of art to be preserved, but as containers for units of information.

The state of our libraries is not necessarily the fault of our librarians who have evolved and adapted to the many changes and expectations researchers place on their holdings. Often it is a matter of budget and historical practices. I went to the Harry Ransom Centre at the University of Texas because much of the content that once belonged to the British Library had been sold years earlier to this well-endowed American institution. Back at the British Library, I could pour through the many photocopies of letters that remained, as if the text was what mattered and not the ephemeral document. It is also possible that the fact that these texts were queer contributed to their treatment since that history is not one that the heteronormative archived sought to preserve. Some works that were preserved carefully are also misunderstood. For example, when reading *Priapeia* and *White Stains* at the British Library, I was required to sit in a section of the reading room where I would be observed while studying the text. It was not because of the great delicacy of the texts – scholars reading delicate, hand-painted volumes centuries-old medieval manuscripts across the hall were not watched the same way. These books were policed because they were sexually explicit, describing not just sex, but homosexual sex. Their status was declared a century before when they were placed in the British Library's Private Case Collection and has never been changed: marginal works. Books that heterosexuals could recognise as queer were labelled *verboten* and stayed that way, a hidden and policed part of Britain's literary history and archival present.

Libraries are important, but imperfect archives and the methods of preservation, something archive theory has increasingly drawn attention to, are complicated by the archivist's methodologies and choices. Marlene Manoff notes how what archivists consider worthwhile contributions to a record is influenced by changes in archival science throughout history.[3] Take for example the fact that *The Pageant* was probably added to the library's collection when it was still new. They had more than one copy and were brought in as contemporary reading material. That means its archivists saw it as new work, another Christmas annual to add to the pile, and not something that deserved special consideration. That cognitive dissonance from how we look at work from the same period today is something that both researchers and archivists must reconsider. Manoff uses the recent interest in popular culture influencing new contributions to library collections as an example of how archival science has changed.[4] By extension, then, the continued study of queer textuality would also contribute to the preservation of these books. The issue is not individual employees. Everyone I have ever worked with at any of these institutions has been both professional and helpful. The issue is with the systemic process of archival practice. Joan M. Schwartz and Terry Cook argue that the

> refusal of the archival profession to acknowledge the power relations embedded in the archival enterprise carries a concomitant abdication of responsibility for the consequences of the exercise of that power, and, in turn, serious consequences for the understanding and carrying out the role of archives in an ever-changing present, or for using archive with subtlety and reflection in a more distant future.[5]

Digital scholarship and archival practice are important instigators of change in these long-standing practices.

The Yellow Nineties Online is not an archive, but a collection of digital editions of late Victorian periodicals, placing the critical edition of *The Pageant* in companionship with *The Yellow Book*, *The Savoy*, *The Venture* and other periodicals of the period. The collection suggests a broad audience for late Victorian periodical scholars, but it is also accessed by undergraduate university and high-school students to study literary and cultural history. Various representations are available that, before digitisation, may not have been as easily accessible. The digitisation of these texts not only broadens their audience to new readers who may not otherwise have discovered them but changes the audience. They are taken out of time and placed into the here and now.

This shift from the material to the digital means that there is an opportunity to broaden the influence of queer books and create new queer relations with the past, as outlined with Michael Field's *Long Ago*. That book placed late nineteenth-century queer lives together with the queer discourse of same-sex desire preserved in Sappho's fragments. These books and their sexual discourse are, in a sense, fragmented, and kept out of the hands of today's queer readers. By bringing them online, both the literature they contain and the physical presentation of the book, the queer textual intercourse of the queer book, is in part preserved for visual access via the digital interface.

Long Ago is the subject of its own digital humanities project and the changes to the text taken on by its editors suggest new approaches to digital engagement with the queer past. Sarah E. Kersh's project, *The Poems of Michael Field* (2015), makes available not just this volume, but *Sight and Song* (1892) as well as *Underneath the Bough* (1893). The project not only preserves the three texts but aligns texts with historical referents. For *Sight and Song*, ekphrastic poems exploring the women's sensual and aesthetic responses to various works of art, each poem is placed alongside the paintings and drawings that inspired their composition. Rather than offering selections or anthologised excerpts, Michael Field's work is once again accessible in the collected arrangement originally offered. What is missing is the tactile element of touch, but whether we read the project on our laptops, tablets or smartphones, touch is still a key part of reading digital texts – what we touch is the thing that has changed.

Both the digital edition of *The Pageant* and *Queer Books* grew from an interest in queer authors of the late nineteenth century. I discovered them originally in *The Yellow Book* with works by Housman, Henry James, Vernon Lee, Charlotte Mew and Frederick Rolfe. Before then, it was only Oscar Wilde that was generally discussed at an undergraduate level. Now, the *Yellow Nineties* is a site where students can interact with this periodical among others to engage with literature and the context of its publication, all guided by scholarly apparatus to enrich the learning experience. *Queer Books* is intended as a contribution to an understanding of a historical queer community of bibliophiles, designers, writers and collectors. Others will read the same texts that I did and find other communities and reasons to place books into conversation with one another. In that sense, *Queer Books* serves an archival purpose as well, collecting texts together to be read in a certain manner.

The premise of *Queer Books* is the idea of sexual discourse, intercourse between book design and literary content, as well as intercourse between book and reader. That terminology is intentionally lurid – not to be sensational, but to draw attention to the intimacy of reading as a critical practice. In the case of understanding queer experiences of the past, that intimacy is crucial because it requires the reader to step out of their experiences in the here and now and imagine alternate discourses, identities and terminology for same-sex desire that, while reminiscent of our own experience, is also entirely different due to the cultural contexts of the late nineteenth century.

The books studied here were publicly accessible, on a much smaller scale than digital texts today of course, but anyone with money in their pocket could have walked into the Bodley Head on Vigo St or another bookshop in 1890s London and purchased one of these works. That did not mean everyone accessed them, but they found audiences. Digital access means that accessibility to queer books is once more available. The digital shift in textual studies coincides with a splintering of mass cultural discourses. If the materiality of the book influences our interpretation, then it suggests that the digital distribution of texts would also influence and change meaning. They do not circulate or influence small coteries of queer authors, artists and readers as they would have in the late Victorian period. But there are similarities and relationships that should still be considered. Like the aesthetes, scholars of aestheticism and decadence are appealing to a coterie audience of readers who take pleasure and find intellectual value in the historical works that they read. Digitisation of these books means that, rather than describing texts to our students or showing pictures, we can ask students to read these books. We can create niche classes that speak to the issues students face today, including addressing issues of sexuality and gender. The aesthetes, as we see from their historical approach to queer relationality, have a cultural history that enriched the theoretical work of the late, great José Esteban Muñoz (1967–2013), and more recent interventions into British aestheticism and queer publishing history by Dustin Friedman and Natasha Hurley respectively. Digitisation also draws heightened attention to the material history of publishing and circulation by distancing the student from the experience through computer interfaces that can display, but not mimic, the codex book.

Queer space has moved to the Internet, so nineteenth-century queer books also moving there is not a surprise. The nightclub culture of the late twentieth century is gone, replaced by social media, dating apps, gaming spaces like Fortnite and Facebook's newly announced Metaverse, all spaces where queer people find and relate to one another. The architectural spaces lauded by Aaron Betsky are once more being replaced by media interface, digital today rather than print. Queer artists and authors are creating spaces in these new formats for community and the sharing of their desires and ideas. That sharing remains important because as much as we discuss advances in queer lives, much has remained the same. That is why the historically specific experiences of Aubrey Beardsley, Katharine Bradley, Edith Cooper, John Gray, Charles Ricketts, Charles Shannon and Oscar Wilde must be taken into account as new points of view emerge.

Like this historical artists and authors, many diverse LGBTQ2SIA+ people still must hide who they are, dealing not just with the laws of the land, but with the sexual discourses of their families and cultures that are not understanding of same-sex desire or trans* gender experience. Queer space needs to accommodate more people than ever. At the same time, we must not disconnect from past experiences that, while not specifically relatable to people today, help us empathise with new expressions that are equally alien. We may not call ourselves *Uranians* as some aesthetes did, but that does not mean our terminology will endure. *Queer* has come to replace the word *gay* for many youth today. Tomorrow, or a century from now, that language will continue to change. By linking our histories together, and despite the changing language, we can still access history and collect an archive of identities that fall into a common discourse of same-sex desire.

Much of this book has been focused on utopian ideals of queer relationality, but those ideals are motivated by the lack of utopia that surrounds queer lives daily. The lives of the artists and authors behind the books studied here are not lives that any queer youth should romanticise or celebrate. Oscar Wilde's imprisonment and early death are only one man's example. The utopia that the aesthetes of the *fin de siècle* sought was never realised. It was a dream. It continues to be a dream for many and that should be recognised when considering these works. That is the point of utopian thinking and queer relationality – to form relationships, bonds and collect our historical documents for pleasure in the present, and in hopes of better times to come.

In one sense, the book is a material experience. Purchasing, collecting and reading these books in the privacy of one's home or sharing with intimate friends is an essential part of how queer discourses circulated in the late nineteenth century. It was covert, it was hidden in plain sight, and an unspoken knowledge that many shared to form community in the space of the material book. The old codes are outdated, but they can inspire new ones. Queer lives can be remembered, just as Katharine Bradley ensured that Michael Field would be remembered when she paid to publish *Whym Chow*. Despite John Gray's rejection of his decadent pose as a poet, that identity was preserved when Ricketts embodied his performance in the creation of *Silverpoints*. The queer book still has value, it is just circulated increasingly through digital platforms and socially distanced online communities. New languages and different languages will develop that integrate the experiences and cultures of its contributors. The queer books I seek to preserve in the discourse of Victorian studies with this book are texts that demonstrate a history of disavowing social ideologies of heteronormativity in sex and gender. Within the realm of scholarship on late Victorian literature and culture, what we need to better understand still is not just how readers in the nineteenth century interacted through print culture, but how our students interact with these texts.

One consideration is to understand the historical text as an artifact, an object that is a part of what we are teaching. *Queer Books*' focus on the material meaning of literature is an important consideration that goes beyond the queer experience, just in different ways. The past must be in conversation with the present. Wilde's *Salome* placed *fin de siècle* sexual mores into conversation with biblical history and the mythos of western Christian culture. Michael Field turned to the ancients and repositioned lesbian and homosexual desire, as well as paganism, as the centre of western art and aesthetic theory. John Gray equated queer sexual desire with the spiritual ecstasy he found in his Catholic faith. Ricketts and Shannon looked at Wilde's fairy tales as an opportunity to challenge Victorian neo-medievalism and recentre Renaissance bookmaking practices that aligned with the rediscovery of the ancient world. History and the past were alive for these artists and authors, often accused of anachronism, but it is that historical context that is the spirit of engagement that is reflected in the digital rerelease of queer books.

There is no reason to resist the inevitable difference that is going to arise when transferring a book into a new medium. First, we are preserving the original experience, at least the memory of that experience in its digital realisation. Second, we are wrestling with the differences and announcing our dependence upon the codex for regulating a normalised book-reading experience. One tool that shows a great deal of promise is Dino Felluga's *Cove Collective*, where professors and students can create shared spaces to interact, not just through lectures and seminars, but through digital editing tools. That means that by reading these books online, we elicit new reading practices and engage in a disruption of the codex that acknowledges the past but is dependent upon a new language all its own, unavailable to literary print culture.

The radical change in bibliographic culture from the circulation of codex texts to the digital devices of today aligns with radical changes in queer culture. Our sexual discourses have changed, influenced by a shift from sexuality to gender identity in trans* discourses of today. It allows us an opportunity to rediscover the past in new ways by seeing how the language and terminology of today emerged from the past. Queer itself is a word whose meaning went from defining the strange and curious in the nineteenth century to an angry homophobic slur in the twentieth century to being transformed by critical theory in gay and lesbian studies in the 1980s and 1990s, to being embraced as a proud identity for many millennials and Gen Z LGBT2SQIA+ persons. Specifically, theories of trans* gender and identity imagine a future where gender rules are no longer naturalised, and the imposition of heteronormativity is identified for the often-damaging effects it has on queer individuals who desire the same sex or desire a non-binary relationship to gender roles and cultural practices of masculinity and femininity.

Scepticism that such a future is possible is important, but it is in this queer utopian space where trans* culture aligns with José Esteban Muñoz's concept of queer futurity – as young people still hopeful about the future, trans* expressions imagine a future that may not yet be realised in day-to-day life but is imagined and hoped for as a possible means of future relations. In that sense, its queer beauty is both refreshing and with potential for deep historicity. By acknowledging the past and facing the blurred lines between same-sex desire and self-relations with gender, the trans* community doesn't just imagine a future but embraces a queer past.

Notes

1. Frederick D. King, 'The Pageant (1896–1897): An Overview', Pageant Digital Edition, Yellow Nineties 2.0, ed. by Lorraine Janzen Kooistra, Ryerson University Centre for Digital Humanities, 2019, par. 13. https://1890s.ca/pageant_overview/.
2. Carolyn Steedman, Dust: The Archive and Cultural History (New Brunswick, NJ: Rutgers University Press), p. 68.
3. Marlene Manoff, 'Theories of the Archive from across the Disciplines', portal: Libraries and the Academy, 4.1 (2004), p. 14.
4. Manoff, 'Theories of the Archive', p. 14.
5. Joan M. Schwartz and Terry Cook, 'Archives, Records, and Power: The Making of Modern Memory', Archival Science 2 (2002), pp. 5–6.

Bibliography

Acton, William, *The Functions and Disorders of the Reproductive Organs in Childhood, Youth, Adult Age, and Advanced Life: Considered in Their Physiological, Social, and Moral Relations* (London: Churchill, 1862).

Adams, James Eli, *Dandies and Desert Saints: Styles of Victorian Manhood* (Ithaca, NY: Cornell University Press, 1995).

'A House of Pomegranates by Oscar Wilde' (review), *The Spectator* (19 Mar. 1892), p. 408. Periodicals Archive Online. proquest.com/pao.

Altick, Richard, *The English Common Reader: A Social History of the Mass Reading Public, 1800–1900*, 2nd edition with foreword by Jonathan Rose (Columbus: Ohio State University Press, 1998).

'The Arts and Crafts Exhibition' (review), *The Spectator* (28 Oct. 1893), p. 580. *Periodicals Archive Online*. proquest.com/pao.

Barbier, Frédéric, 'The Publishing Industry and Printed Output in Nineteenth-Century France', in *The History of the Book in the West: 1800–1914, Volume IV*, ed. by Stephen Colclough and Alexis Weedon (Burlington, VT: Ashgate, 2010), pp. 13–44.

Barolini, Helen, *Aldus and his Dream Book* (New York: Italica Press, 1992).

Beckson, Karl, ed., *Aesthetes and Decadents of the 1890s: An Anthology of British Poetry and Prose* (Chicago: Academy Chicago Publishers, 1981).

Beerbohm, Max, 'A Defence of Cosmetics', *The Yellow Book: An Illustrated Quarterly*, 1 (London: Elkin Mathews and John Lane, 1894), pp. 65–82.

Betsky, Aaron, *Queer Space: Architecture and Same-Sex Desire* (New York: William Morrow and Company, 1997).

'Binding Design: Poems (1870) [1], Dante Gabriel Rossetti, 1870', *The Rossetti Archive*. Retrieved from http://www.rossettiarchive.org/docs/sa122.1-1870.rap.html.

Bloom, Layla, 'The Book Illustrators', in *Fancy and Imagination: Beardsley and the Book Illustrators* (Leeds: The Stanley & Audrey Burton Gallery, University of Leeds, 2010), pp. 24–31.
Boone, Joseph A., 'Vacation Cruises; Or, the Homoerotics of Orientalism', *PMLA. Publications of the Modern Language Association of America*, 110.1 (1995), pp. 89–107.
Bringhurst, Robert, *The Elements of Typographic Style* (Vancouver: Hartley and Marks, 1992).
Bristow, Joseph, 'Introduction', in *The Fin-de-Siècle Poem: English Literary Culture and the 1890s*, ed. by Joseph Bristow (Athens: Ohio University Press, 2005), pp. 1–46.
——, *Oscar Wilde and Modern Culture: The Making of a Legend*, ed. by Joseph Bristow (Athens: Ohio University Press, 2009).
——, *Oscar Wilde on Trial: The Criminal Proceedings from Arrest to Imprisonment* (New Haven, CT: Yale University Press, 2023).
——, *Sexuality* (London: Routledge, 1990).
——, *Writings: Contextual Conditions*, ed. by Joseph Bristow (Toronto: University of Toronto Press, 2003).
British Library, London, Chiswick Press Papers Vol. CXV 1880–1890, 1898–1899, Add MS50913, MS50917.
——, Lady Eccles Oscar Wilde Collection RP3196.
Bucknell, Brad, 'On "Seeing" Salome', *ELH: English Literary History*, 60.2 (1993), pp. 503–26.
Burton, Sir Richard, ed. and trans., *The Karma Sutra* (London: Erotika Biblion Society (Leonard Smithers), 1883).
——, 'From Volume X, From Terminal Essay, IV, Social Condition, D – Paederasty', in *Lad's Love: An Anthology of Uranian Poetry and Prose*, ed. and intro. by Michael Matthew Kaylor (Kansas City: Valancourt Books, 2010), pp. 160–78.
Burton, Sir Richard, and Leonard C. Smithers, trans. and ed., *Priapeia sive diversorum poetarum in Priapum lusus or SPORTIVE EPIGRAMS ON PRIAPUS by divers poets in English verse and prose* (Cosmopoli: Erotika Biblion Society (London: Leonard Smithers), 1890).
Butler, Judith, *Bodies That Matter: On the Discursive Limits of Sex* (London: Routledge, 2011).
Carlyle, Thomas. *Past and Present*, ed. by Richard Altick (New York: New York University Press, 1977).
Castle, Terry, *The Apparitional Lesbian* (New York: Columbia University Press, 1993).
Cevasco, G. A., *The Breviary of Decadence: J-K Huysmans's A Rebours and English Literature* (New York: AMS Press, 2001).

—, 'John Gray's *Silverpoints* and the Gallic Impress', *Cahiers victoriens et* édouardiens, 36 (1992), pp. 103–20.
Chatterjee, Ronjaunee, Alicia Mireles Christoff and Amy R. Wong, 'Introduction: Undisciplining Victorian Studies', *Victorian Studies*, 62.3 (2020), pp. 369–91.
Chitty, Christopher, *Sexual Hegemony: Statecraft, Sodomy, and Capital in the Rise of the World System* (Durham, NC: Duke University Press, 2020).
Clark, Petra, '"Cleverly Drawn": Oscar Wilde, Charles Ricketts, and the Art of the *Woman's World*', *Journal of Victorian Culture*, 20.5 (2015), pp. 375–400.
Coleman, D. C., *The British Paper Industry, 1495–1860: A Study in Industrial Growth* (Oxford: Clarendon Press, 1958).
Crane, Walter, *Of the Decorative Illustration of Books Old and New* (London: George Bell and Sons, 1896).
Crowley, Aleister, *White Stains* (London: Leonard Smithers, 1898).
Davies, Martin, *Aldus Manutius: Printer and Publisher of Renaissance Venice* (Tempe: Arizona Center for Medieval and Renaissance Studies, 1999).
Dellamora, Richard, *Masculine Desire: The Sexual Politics of Victorian Aestheticism* (Chapel Hill: University of North Carolina Press, 1990).
Denisoff, Dennis, *Decadent Ecology in British Literature and Art, 1860–1910* (Cambridge: Cambridge University Press, 2021).
Dever, Carolyn, '"Modern" Love and the Proto-Post-Victorian', *PMLA. Publications of the Modern Language Association of America*, 12.2 (2009), pp. 370–4.
Donahue, Joseph, 'Distance, Death and Desire in *Salome*', in *The Cambridge Companion to Oscar Wilde*, ed. by Peter Raby (Cambridge: Cambridge University Press, 1997), pp. 118–42.
Dowling, Linda, *Language and Decadence at the Victorian Fin de Siècle* (Princeton, NJ: Princeton University Press, 1986).
—, 'Nature and Decadence: John Gray's "Silverpoints"', *Victorian Poetry*, 15.2 (1977), pp. 159–69.
Drucker, Johanna, 'Distributed and Conditional Documents: Conceptualizing Bibliographical Alterities', *MATLIT: Revista do Programa de Doutoramento em Materialidades da Literatura*, 2.1 (2014), pp. 11–29.
—, *The Visible Word: Experimental Typography and Modern Art, 1909–1923* (Chicago: University of Chicago Press, 1994).
Dumpert, Dawn (project manager), *The Diaries of Michael Field*. https://michaelfielddiary.dartmouth.edu/home.

Dytor, Frankie, '"The Eyes of an Intellectual Vampire": Michael Field, Vernon Lee and Female Masculinities in Late-Victorian Aestheticism', *Journal of Victorian Culture*, 26.4 (2021), pp. 582–95.
Ehnenn, Jill, *Michael Field's Revisionary Poetics*, Nineteenth-Century and Neo-Victorian Cultures (Edinburgh: Edinburgh University Press, 2023).
—, *Women's Literary Collaboration, Queerness, and Late-Victorian Culture*, The Nineteenth Century Series (Farnham: Ashgate Publishing Ltd., 2008).
Elliott, Patricia, *Debates in Transgender, Queer, and Feminist Theory: Contested Sites* (London: Ashgate Publishing, 2010).
Ellmann, Richard, *Oscar Wilde* (New York: Penguin Books, 1988).
Engels, Friedrich, *The Condition of the Working Class in England* (1845), ed. by Victor Kiernan (London: Penguin, 2009).
Evangelista, Stefano, *British Aestheticism and Ancient Greece: Hellenism, Reception, Gods in Exile* (New York: Palgrave MacMillan, 2009).
Field, Michael, *Long Ago* (London: George Bell and Sons, 1889).
—, *Whym Chow: Flame of Love* (London: Eragny Press, 1914).
Fletcher, Ian, *Aubrey Beardsley* (Boston: Twayne Publishers, 1987).
Fone, Byrne R. S., *A Road to Stonewall, 1750–1969: Male Homosexuality and Homophobia in English and American Literature* (New York: Twayne Publishers, 1994).
Foucault, Michel, *The History of Sexuality an Introduction. Volume I*, trans. by Robert Hurley (New York: Vintage, 1980).
Frankel, Nicholas, 'Introduction', in *The Picture of Dorian Gray: An Annotated, Uncensored Edition*, ed. by Nicholas Frankel (Cambridge, MA: The Belknap Press of Harvard University Press, 2011).
—, *The Invention of Oscar Wilde* (London: Reaktion Books, 2021).
—, *Masking the Text: Essays on Literature and Mediation in the 1890s* (High Wycombe: Rivendale Press, 2009).
—, *Oscar Wilde's Decorated Books* (Ann Arbor: University of Michigan Press, 2000).
Freedman, Joseph, *Professions of Taste: Henry James, Aestheticism, and Commodity Culture* (Stanford, CA: Stanford University Press, 1990).
Friedman, Dustin, *Before Queer Theory: Victorian Aestheticism and the Self* (Baltimore: Johns Hopkins University Press, 2019).
Gannon, Patricio, 'John Gray', *The Aylesford Review*, 4.2 (1961), pp. 47–8.
Gaskell, Philip, *A New Introduction to Bibliography: The Classic Manual of Bibliography* (New Castle, DE: Oak Knoll Press, 1995).
Genette, Gerard, *Paratexts*, trans. by Jane E. Lewin (Cambridge: Cambridge University Press, 1987).

Genz, Marcella D., *A History of the Eragny Press, 1894–1914* (London: Oak Knoll Press, 2003).

'"George Bell and Sons." British Library Publishing Houses, 1820–1880', *Dictionary of Literary Biography Complete Online* ed. by Patricia Anderson and Jonathan Rose, 106 (1991), 21–31.

Gilbert, Elliot L., '"Tumult of Images,": Wilde, Beardsley, "Salome"', *Victorian Studies* 26.2 (1983), 133–159.

Gray, John, *The Poems of John Gray*, ed. by Ian Fletcher (Greensboro, NC: ELT Press, 1988).

——, *Silverpoints* (London: John Lane and Elkin Mathews, 1893).

Gray, Robert, and Christopher Keep, '"An Uninterrupted Current": Homoeroticism and Collaborative Authorship in *Teleny*', in *Literary Couplings: Writing Couples, Collaborators, and the Construction of Authorship*, ed. by Marjorie Stone and Judith Thompson (Madison: University of Wisconsin Press, 2006), pp. 193–208.

Grigley, Joseph, *Textualterity: Art, Theory, and Textual Criticism* (Ann Arbor, MI: University of Michigan Press, 1995).

Guy, Josephine, and Ian Small, *Oscar Wilde's Profession: Writing and the Culture Industry in the Late Nineteenth Century* (Oxford: Oxford University Press, 2000).

Haefele-Thomas, Ardel, 'Introduction: Trans Victorians', *Victorian Review*, 44.1 (2018), pp. 31–6.

Hager, Lisa, 'A Case for a Trans Studies Turn in Victorian Studies: "Female Husbands" of the Nineteenth Century', *Victorian Review*, 44.1 (2018), pp. 37–54.

Hall, Donald E., *Reading Sexualities: Hermeneutic Theory and the Future of Queer Studies* (New York: Routledge, 2009).

Halperin, David, *How to do the History of Homosexuality* (London: University of Chicago Press, 2002).

Hamilton, Cecily, *Marriage as a Trade* (New York: Moffat, Yard and Company, 1909).

Hanson, Ellis, *Decadence and Catholicism* (Cambridge, MA: Harvard University Press, 1997).

Harvey, Charles, and Jon Press, 'The Business Career of William Morris', in *William Morris: Art and Kelmscott*, ed. by Linda Parry, Occasional Papers of the Society of Antiquaries of London 18 (London: The Boydell Press, 1996).

Hatt, Michael, 'The Book Beautiful: Reading, Vision, and the Homosexual Imagination in Late-Victorian Britain', in *Illustrations, Optics and Objects in Nineteenth-Century Literary and Visual Cultures*, ed. by Luisa Calè, P. Di Bello and Patrizia Di Bello (Basingstoke: Palgrave Macmillan, 2010).

Helsinger, Elizabeth K., *Poetry and the Pre-Raphaelite Arts: Dante Gabriel Rossetti and William Morris* (New Haven, CT: Yale University Press, 2008).

Hildebrand, R. Jayne, 'News from Nowhere and William Morris's Aesthetics of Unreflectiveness: Pleasurable Habits', *English Literature in Transition, 1880–1920*, 54.1 (2011), pp. 3–27.

Holland, Merlin, ed., *The Real Trial of Oscar Wilde* (New York: Perennial, 2003).

Hunt, John Dixon, 'The Plot of *Hypnerotomachia Poliphili* and Its Afterlives', *Word & Image: A Journal of Verbal/Visual Enquiry*, 31.2 (2015), pp. 129–39.

Hurley, Natasha, *Circulating Queerness: Before the Gay and Lesbian Novel* (Minneapolis: University of Minnesota Press, 2018).

Hutcheon, Linda, and Michael Hutcheon, '"Here's Lookin' at You, Kid": The Empowering Gaze in "Salome"', *Profession* (1998), 11–22.

Huysmans, Joris-Karl, *Against Nature (A rebours)* [1884], trans. by Margaret Mauldon and ed. by Nicholas White, Oxford World's Classics (New York: Oxford University Press, 1998).

Iser, Wolfgang, *The Act of Reading: A Theory of Aesthetic Response* (Baltimore: Johns Hopkins University Press, 1978).

—, *Walter Pater: The Aesthetic Moment* (Cambridge, MA: Cambridge University Press, 1987).

Jackson, Holbrook, *The Eighteen Nineties: A Review of Art and Ideas at the Close of the Nineteenth Century* [1913], new illustrated edition with an intro. by Christophe Campos (Brighton, UK: The Harvester Press, 1976).

John Lane Company Records, Harry Ransom Center, University of Texas, Austin.

Johnson, Marguerite, 'Sappho 600 B.C.E.–500 B.C.E.', in *The Literary Encyclopedia. Volume 1.1.1: Greek Writing and Culture: Archaic, Classical, Hellenistic and Imperial, 800–100*, ed. by Vaios Liapis (Latsia: Open University of Cyprus, 2010).

Jones, Justin T., 'Morality's Ugly Implications in Oscar Wilde's Fairy Tales', *Studies in English Literature 1500–1900*, 51.4 (2011), pp. 883–903.

Joyce, Simon, *LGBT Victorians: Sexuality and Gender in the Nineteenth-Century Archives* (Oxford: Oxford University Press, 2023).

—, 'Two Women Walk into a Theatre Bathroom: The Fanny and Stella Trials as Trans Narrative', *Victorian Review*, 44.1 (2018), pp. 83–98.

Kains-Jackson, Charles, 'The New Chivalry', in *Nineteenth-Century Writings on Homosexuality: A Sourcebook*, ed. by Chris White (London: Routledge, 1999), pp. 154–8.

King, Frederick D., 'British Aestheticism, Sexology, and Erotica: Negotiating Sexual Discourses in *Teleny*', *Victorian Review*, 41.1 (2015), pp. 163–79.

——, 'Oscar Wilde's *Salome* and the Queer Space of the Book', in *Wilde's Wiles: Studies of the Influences on Oscar Wilde and His Enduring Influences in the Twenty-First Century*, ed. by Annette M. Magid (Newcastle upon Tyne: Cambridge Scholars Press, 2015), pp. 159–78.

——, 'The *Pageant* (1896–1897): An Overview', *Pageant Digital Edition, Yellow Nineties 2.0*, edited by Lorraine Janzen Kooistra, Ryerson University Centre for Digital Humanities, 2019, https://1890s.ca/pageant_overview/.

King, Frederick D., and Alison Lee, 'Bibliographic Metafiction: Dancing in the Margins with Alasdair Gray', *Contemporary Literature*, 57.2 (2016), pp. 216–44.

Kooistra, Lorraine Janzen, *The Artist as Critic: Bitextuality in Fin-de-Siècle Illustrated Books* (Aldershot: Scolar Press, 1997).

——, *Poetry, Pictures, and Popular Publishing: The Illustrated Gift Book and Victorian Visual Culture* (Athens, OH: Ohio University Press, 2011).

——, 'Wilde's Legacy: Fairy Tales, Laurence Housman, and the Expression of "Beautiful Untrue Things"', in *Oscar Wilde and the Cultures of Childhood*, ed. by Joseph Bristow, Palgrave Studies in Nineteenth-Century Writing and Culture (Basingstoke: Palgrave Macmillan, 2017), pp. 89–118.

Krafft-Ebing, Richard von, *Psychopathia Sexualis with especial reference to Contrary Sexual Instince: A Medio-Legal Study*, 7th edition, trans. by Charles Gilbert Chaddock (London: F. J. Rebman, 1894).

——, *Psychopathia Sexualis: The Classic Study of Deviant Sex*, trans. by Franklin S. Klaf (New York: Arcade Publishing, 2011).

Leighton, Mary Elizabeth, and Lisa A. Surridge, 'The Plot Thickens: Toward a Narratological Analysis of Illustrated Serial Fiction in the 1860s', *Victorian Studies*, 51.1 (2008), pp. 65–101.

Mackie, Greg, *Beautiful Untrue Things: Forging Oscar Wilde's Extraordinary Afterlife* (Toronto: University of Toronto Press, 2019).

Mahoney, Kristin, 'Michael Field and Queer Community at the *Fin de Siècle*', *Victorian Review*, 41.1 (2015), pp. 35–40.

Maier, Sarah E., 'Symbolist Salomés and the Dance of Dionysus', *Nineteenth-Century Contexts*, 28.3 (2006), pp. 211–23.

Mak, Bonnie, *How the Page Matters* (Toronto: University of Toronto Press, 2011).

Manoff, Marlene, 'Theories of the Archive from across the Disciplines', *portal: Libraries and the Academy*, 4.1 (2004), pp. 9–25.

Markey, Anne, *Oscar Wilde's Fairy Tales: Origins and Contexts* (Portland, OR: Irish Academic Press, 2011).

Marx, Karl, and Friedrich Engels, *The Communist Manifesto* (London: Penguin, 2002).

Mass, Henry, John Duncan and W. G. Good, eds, *The Letters of Aubrey Beardsley* (Rutherford, NJ: Fairleigh Dickinson University Press, 1970).

Masten, Jeffrey, *Textual Intercourse: Collaboration, Authorship, and Sexualities, in Renaissance Drama* (Cambridge: Cambridge University Press, 1997).

Mathieu, Pierre-Louis, *The Symbolist Generation, 1870–1910* (New York: Skira Rizzoli, 1990).

McCormack, Jerusha Hull, *John Gray: Poet, Dandy, Priest* (Waltham, MA: Brandeis University Press, 1991).

McGann, Jerome, *A New Republic of Letters: Memory and Scholarship in the Age of Digital Reproduction* (Cambridge, MA: Harvard University Press, 2014).

——, 'Literature by Design since 1790', *Victorian Poetry*, 48.1 (2010), pp. 11–40.

McKitterick, David, ed., *The Cambridge History of the Book in Britain. Volume VI: 1830–1914* (New York: Cambridge University Press, 2009).

McLean, Ruari, *The Thames and Hudson Manual of Typography: With 188 Illustrations* (London: Thames & Hudson, 1980).

——, *Victorian Book Design and Colour Printing* (London: Faber & Faber, 1963).

Meyers, Terry L., ed., Letter from Michael Field to A. C. Swinburne, May 27, 1889. Reprinted in *Uncollected Letters of Algernon Charles Swinburne*, vol. 2 (London: Pickering and Chatto, 2005), p. 475.

Michael Field's 'Long Ago' (review), *The Spectator*, 63.3187 (27 July 1889), p. 119. Periodicals Archive Online. proquest.com/pao.

Miller, Elizabeth Carolyn, *Slow Print: Literary Radicalism and Late Victorian Print Culture* (Stanford, CA: Stanford University Press, 2013).

Miller, sj, 'Gender Identity Complexities Turn', *GLQ: A Journal of Lesbian and Gay Studies*, 26.2 (2020), pp. 239–42.

Muñoz, José Esteban, *Cruising Utopia: The Then and There of Queer Futurity* (New York: New York University Press, 2009).

Morris, William, *The Collected Letters of William Morris*, vol. III, *1889–1892* and vol. IV *1893–1896*, ed. by Norman Kelvin (Princeton, NJ: Princeton University Press, 1996).

——, *The Decorative Arts, their Relations to Modern Life, and Progress (Reprint of the Edition 1878): The Aims of Art (Reprint of the*

Edition 1887), ed. by Friedrich Adolf (Osnabrück, Germany: Schmidt-Künsemüller, Proff & Co. KG, Bad Honnef a. Rhein, 1975).

——, *The Ideal Book: Essays and Lectures on the Art of the Book by William Morris*, intro. by David S. Peterson (Berkely and Los Angeles: University of California Press, 1982).

——, *Notes on Early Wood-Cut Books* (New York: Elston Press, 1902).

——, *The Unpublished Lectures of William Morris*, ed. by Eugene D. Lemire (Detroit: Wayne State University Press, 1969).

Morris, William, and Emery Walker, *Printing: An Essay by William Morris and Emery Walker. From Arts and Crafts Essays by Members of the Arts and Crafts Society* (Park Ridge, IL: Village Press, 1903).

Nelson, James G., *The Early Nineties: A View from the Bodley Head* (Cambridge, MA: Harvard University Press, 1971).

——, *Publisher to the Decadents: Leonard Smithers in the Careers of Beardsley, Wilde, Dowson. With an Appendix on Smithers and the Erotic Book Trade by Peter Mendes and a Checklist of Smithers's Publication by James G. Nelson and Peter Mendes* (University Park: The Pennsylvania State University Press, 2000).

Noble, J. Bobby, 'Refusing to Make Sense: Mapping the In-Coherences of "Trans"', *Journal of Lesbian Studies*, 11.1/2 (2007), pp. 167–75.

Nordau, Mas, *Degeneration*, 7th edition, trans. from the original German (New York: D. Appleton and Company, 1895).

Oetinger, April, 'The *Hypnerotomachi Poliphili*: Art and Play in a Renaissance Romance', *Word & Image*, 27.1 (2011), pp. 15–30.

Pall Mall Gazette, 22 Feb. 1894. British Library Newspapers.

Parker, Sarah, and Ana Parejo Vadillo, eds, *Michael Field: Decadent Moderns* (Athens: Ohio University Press, 2019).

Pater, Walter, *Marius the Epicurean: His Sensations and Ideas*, ed. by Gerald Monsman (Kansas City: Valancourt Books, 2008).

——, *The Renaissance*, ed. by Adam Philips (Oxford: Oxford University Press, 1986).

——, *Studies in the History of the Renaissance* (London: MacMillan and Co., 1873).

Peterson, David S., 'Introduction', in *The Ideal Book: Essays and Lectures on the Arts of the Book by William Morris* (Berkeley and Los Angeles: University of California Press, 1982).

Petersson, Sonya, 'The Counteractive Illustration and Its Metalanguage', *Word & Image*, 34.4 (2018), pp. 349–62.

Potolsky, Matthew, *The Decadent Republic of Letters: Taste, Politics, and Cosmopolitan Community from Baudelaire to Beardsley* (Philadelphia: University of Pennsylvania Press, 2013).

Primamore, Elizabeth. 'Michael Field as Dandy Poet', in *Michael Field and Their World*, ed. by Stetz, Margaret D. and Cheryl A. Wilson (High Wycombe: The Rivendale Press, 2007), pp. 137–46.
Raffalovich, Marc-André, 'To One of My Readers', in *Cyril and Lionel and Other Poems: A Volume of Sentimental Studies* (London: Keagan Paul, Trench & Co, 1884), p. 87.
——, *Uranisme et sexualité: etude sur différentes manifestations de l'instinct sexuel*, Bibliothèque de criminology (Paris: A. Maloine, Éditeur, 1896).
Richardson, LeeAnne M., *The Forms of Michael Field* (Basingstoke: Palgrave Macmillan, 2021).
Ricketts, Charles, *A Defence of the Revival of Printing* (London: Ballantyne Press, 1899).
——, *Reflections of Oscar Wilde* [reprint of 1932 limited edition] (London: Pallas Athene, 2011).
Ricketts & Shannon Papers, British Library, London, Add MS 58085-58118, 61713-61724.
Roberts, Nickie, *Whores in History: Prostitution in Western Society* (Hammersmith, London: HarperCollins, 1992).
Rocha, Leon Antonio, 'Scientia sexualis versus ars erotica: Foucault, van Gulik, Needham', *Studies in the History and Philosophy of Biological and Biomedical Sciences*, 42 (2011), pp. 328–43.
Roden, Frederick S., *Same-Sex Desire in Victorian Religious Culture* (Basingstoke: Palgrave Macmillan, 2002).
Ross, Robert, *Aubrey Beardsley* [reprint of 1909 John Lane edition], intro. by Matthew Sturgis (London: Pallas Athene, 2011).
Salamensky, S. I., *The Modern Art of Influence and the Spectacle of Oscar Wilde* (New York: Palgrave Macmillan, 2011).
Schwartz, Joan M., and Terry Cook, 'Archives, Records, and Power: The Making of Modern Memory', *Archival Science*, 2 (2002), pp. 1–19.
Sedgwick, Eve Kosofsky, *Between Men: English Literature and Male Homosocial Desire* (New York: Columbia University Press, 1895).
——, *Tendencies* (Durham, NC: Duke University Press, 1993).
Sewell, Brocard, *In the Dorian Mode: A Life of John Gray, 1866–1934* (Padstow, Cornwall: Tabb House, 1983).
——, *Footnote to the Nineties: A Memoir of John Gray and André Raffalovich* (London: Cecil and Amelia Woolf, 1968).
Shillingsburg, Peter L., *From Gutenberg to Google: Electronic Representations of Literary Texts* (Cambridge: Cambridge University Press, 2006).

Sigel, Lisa Z., *Governing Pleasures: Pornography and Social Change in England, 1815–1914* (New Brunswick, NJ: Rutgers University Press, 2002).

Simonsen, Rasmus, 'Dark Avunculate: Shame, Animality, and Queer Development in Oscar Wilde's "The Star-Child"', *Children's Literature*, 42.1 (2014), pp. 20–41.

Small, Ian, and R. K. R. Thornton, 'Introduction', in *John Gray: Silverpoints (1893), Spiritual Poems (1896)*, ed. by R. K. R. Thornton and Ian Small (Oxford: Woodstock Books, 1994), unpaginated.

Smith, Shannon R., and Ann M. Hale, eds, *Victorian Periodicals Review*, special issue: Moments of Challenge and Change, 49.4 (2016), pp. 539–736.

Smith, Timothy d'Arch, *Love in Earnest: Some Notes on the Lives and Writings of English Uranian Poets from 1889 to 1930* (London: Routledge & Kegan Paul, 1970).

Snodgrass, Chris, 'Decadent Mythmaking: Arthur Symons, Aubrey Beardsley and *Salome*', *Victorian Poetry* 28.3–4 (1990) 61–109.

Steeden, Kathleen, 'Evans, Edmund', in *The Oxford Companion to the Book*, Volume 2 D–Z, ed. by Michael F. Suarez and H. R. Woudhuysen (New York: Oxford University Press, 2010), pp. 707–8.

Steedman, Carolyn, *Dust: The Archive and Cultural History* (New Brunswick, NJ: Rutgers University Press, 2002).

Sturgeon, Mary, *Michael Field* (New York: The Macmillan Company, 1922).

Sturgis, Matthew, *Aubrey Beardsley: A Biography* (Hammersmith: HarperCollins, 1998).

Swinburne, Algernon Charles, 'Anactoria', in *Poems and Ballads, First Series* (1866) (London: Chatto & Windus, 1910), pp. 64–74.

Symonds, John Addington, 'A Problem in Greek Ethics', in Havelock Ellis and John Addington Symonds, *Sexual Inversion: A Critical Edition*, ed. by Ivan Crozier (Basingstoke: Palgrave MacMillan, 2008), pp. 227–95.

Symons, Arthur, 'The Decadent Movement in Literature', in *Aesthetes and Decadents: An Anthology of British Poetry and Prose*, intro. and notes by Karl Beckson (Chicago: Academy Chicago Publishers, 1981), pp. 134–51.

Thain, Marion, 'Introduction', in *Michael Field, The Poet. Published and Manuscript Materials,* ed. by Marion Thain and Ana Parejo Vadillo (Peterborough: Broadview Press, 2009), pp. 23–51.

——, *'Michael Field': Poetry, Aestheticism and the Fin de Siècle* (Cambridge: Cambridge University Press, 2007).

Thompson, Paul, *The Work of William Morris* (New York: Oxford University Press, 1991).
Trippe, Rosemary, 'The "Hypnerotomachia Poliphi", Image, Text, and Vernacular Poetics', *Renaissance Quarterly*, 55.4 (2002), pp. 1222–58.
Tudor, Alyosxa, 'Im/possibilities of Refusing and Choosing Gender', *Feminist Theory*, 20.4 (2019), pp. 361–80.
Ulrichs, Karl Heinrich, *The Riddle of Man-Manly Love: The Pioneering Work on Male Homosexuality*, trans. by Michael A. Lombardi-Nash (New York: Prometheus Books, 1994).
Walsh, John A., 'An Introduction to Algernon Charles Swinburne', *The Algernon Charles Swinburne Project* (14 May 2017), http://swinburnearchive.indiana.edu/swinburne/view#docId=swinburne/acs0000503- 01.xml;outputAsDiv=true;anchor=df012d.
Watry, Maureen, ed., *The Vale Press: Charles Ricketts, a Publisher in Ernest* (London: Oak Knoll Press, The British Library, 2004).
Weinroth, Michelle, 'Redesigning the Language of Social Change: Rhetoric, Agency, and the Oneiric in William Morris's *A Dream of John Ball*', *Victorian Studies*, 53.1 (2010), pp. 37–63.
Wharton, Henry Thornton, ed., *Sappho: Memoir, Text, Selected Rendering and A Literal Translation*, 2nd edition (London: David Scott, 1887).
Wilde, Oscar, *The Complete Letters of Oscar Wilde*, ed. by Merlin Holland and Rupert Hart-Davis (New York: Henry Holt and Company, 2000).
—, 'The Decay of Lying', *The Artist as Critic: Critical Writings of Oscar Wilde*, ed. by Richard Ellmann (Chicago: University of Chicago Press, 1982).
—, *A House of Pomegranates* (London: Osgood McIlvaine, 1891).
—, *Salome: A Tragedy in One Act* (London: Bodley Head, 1894).
Yeats, William Butler, *Autobiography of William Butler Yeats* (New York: Macmillan, 1938).
Zaitlin, Linda Gertner, *Aubrey Beardsley, Japonisme, and the Perversion of the Victorian Ideal* (New York: Cambridge University Press, 1997).

Index

Acton, William, 203
Adams, James Eli, 5
advertisement, 82
aesthetes, 3, 122, 134–5, 137, 142, 147, 157, 208, 230
aesthetic discourse, 11, 44, 65, 80
aestheticism, 3–4, 7–8, 10, 13, 15–17, 21, 34, 37, 44, 49, 56, 69, 121, 134, 136, 170, 179, 186, 204, 231
agency, 175, 178, 214
Aldine Edition of British Poets, 147
Aldine italics *see* italics
Aldine Press, 39, 59–60
Aldino *see* italics
ambiguity, 133, 146, 178, 212
anachronism, 27, 95, 179, 186, 233
Anglo-Germanic heritage, 89–90, 95, 209
antiquarians, 185
appropriation, 192
Apuleius, Lucius, 47
archive theory, 228
archives, 227–8, 230
ars amatoria, 208

ars erotica, 26, 179, 181, 202, 208
artificiality, 15, 20, 46, 51, 57–8, 61, 65–6, 107, 112, 121, 136, 195, 197, 212
Artist and Journal of Home Culture, The, 68
Arts and Crafts movement, 77, 80, 87, 91, 190, 212
Athenaeum, The, 131
Atthis, 157
author, 77, 79, 124, 131, 179, 181, 196, 216, 231, 233
authorial supremacy, 198
autocratic practice, 90
Aylesford Review, The, 39

Bacchus, 162
Barbier, Frédéric, 81
Barolini, Helen, 55
bastard title, 158
Batchelor & Arnold, 67
Batchelor & Son, 94
Baud, Henry, 95
Beardsley, Aubrey, 8, 15, 26–7, 175–82, 185–201, 204–6, 210, 213–16, 231
'Black Cape, The', 196

Beardsley, Aubrey (*cont.*)
   'Climax, The', 213–14
   'Death of Salome, The', 204, 215–16
   'Enter Herodias', 189
   'Eyes of Herod, The', 206
   'J'ai Baisé Ta Bouche Iokanaan', 192
   'John and Salome', 198
   'Morte Darthur', 187
   'Rape of the Lock', 187
   'Salome's Toilette', 198
   'Stomach Dance, The', 27, 177–8
   'Title Page', 177
Beardsley, Ellen, 194
Beckson, Karl, 194
Beerbohm, Max, 196
   'Defence of Cosmetics, A', 196
Bell, Edward, 147
belle lettres, 22, 190
Betsky, Aaron, 22, 78, 231
Bible, 175, 179, 192, 208
bibliographic code, 24
bibliographic content or design *see* bibliography
bibliography, 12, 25, 80, 84–7, 96, 100, 104, 117, 124, 137, 140, 149, 162, 180–1, 186, 192, 200, 204, 216, 227, 230, 233
binaries, 48, 80, 132, 137–8, 155, 157, 169, 178, 180, 184
binders *see* binding
binding, 9, 26, 82, 88, 91, 97–8, 104, 141, 157, 162, 188, 195–6, 200–1
bisexual/pansexual desire, 151
Blaikie, Walter, 9
Blake, William, 196
Bloom, Layla, 188

Bodley Head, The, 17, 78, 175, 185, 187, 198–9, 204
bodies, 135, 183, 186, 204–6, 210
Bogue and Company, 18
book dealers, 185
Book of the Thousand Nights and One Night, The, 209
bookmaking, 77, 79–81, 84, 94, 98, 100, 103–4, 189–90, 192, 233
booksellers, 185
Boone, Joseph A., 210
Bradley, Katharine *see* Field, Michael
Bringhurst, Robert, 62
Bristow, Joseph, 5, 40, 181–2
British aestheticism *see* aestheticism
British Library, 139, 158, 199, 227
British Museum, 147
Brown, Ford Maddox, 87, 91
Browning, Elizabeth Barrett, 136
Browning, Robert, 131–2, 136, 158
   'Rabbi Ben Ezra', 158
Buchanan, Robert, 109
Bucknell, Brad, 178
Burne-Jones, Edward, 87, 92
Burton, Richard, 180, 182–3, 209–10
   'Terminal Essay', 209
Butler, Judith, 28, 76, 208

Cahiers victoriens et édouardiens, 40
Campbell, Mrs Patrick, 194
capitalism, 20, 81, 87, 124
Cards of Freedom, 94
Castle, Terry, 134
catamite, 182–3

Catholicism, 23, 26, 37, 40, 57, 61, 111, 138, 158, 160–1, 164–5, 167, 169–70, 232
cellulose fibres, 94
Cevasco, G. A., 40, 56, 193
chancery hand, 55
Chatterjee, Ronjaunee, 28
children, 74, 101, 105, 113, 119
children's books, 22, 99, 102
Christmas annual, 225, 228
Chiswick Press, 9, 27, 96–7, 100, 147
Chitty, Christopher, 210
Christ, 205, 208
Christoff, Alicia Mireles, 28
circuits, 186
circulation, 7, 21–2, 28, 29, 79, 166, 176, 180, 183, 186, 207, 230–3
cis-gender, 157
Clark, Petra, 59
classicism, 5
closet drama, 7
co-author *see* author
codex, 29
codices *see* codex
Coleman, D. C., 94
collaboration, 79, 90, 91, 99, 133–4, 136, 140, 161, 179–82, 185, 189–90, 192, 199, 216
collective culture, 91
Collins, Wilkie, 82
  Hide and Seek, 82
colonialism, 179, 210
colophon, 201
commemoration, 138, 161
commodification, 21, 99, 204
compromise, 188
comradeship, 3
consolation, 166

conversion, 165
Cook, Terry, 228
Cooper, Edith *see* Field, Michael
Cosmopoli, 7
Cosmopolitanism, 190–2, 208
Cove Collective, 233
Crane, Walter, 81, 189–90
Cranstoun, James, 182
critical theory, 140
Crowley, Aleister, 23
  'Ballad of Passive Pederasty, The', 23
  White Stains, 23, 227
cultural materialism *see* material culture

dandies, 134–5
Day, Fred Holland, 100–1
death, 138, 158, 212–14, 225, 231
decadence, 2, 8, 10, 13, 14, 16, 34, 44, 111–15, 125, 136, 155, 167, 175, 186–7, 192, 195, 200, 203–4, 208, 212–13, 216, 230, 232
decadents *see* decadence
degeneration, 90, 92, 96, 207, 209
Dellamora, Richard, 5
Delphi, 164
Denisoff, Dennis, 164
Dever, Carolyn, 133–4
diaries, 133
digital edition, 158, 223, 225, 228–31, 233
digital humanities, 27, 228–9
digital interface (media interface), 12, 27, 229, 231
digital platforms, 232
Dionysus, 162
dog, 138, 158, 161, 163–5, 169

Douglas, Lord Alfred (Bosie), 37, 197
Dowling, Linda, 40, 185
dramatic monologues, 136
drawings, 180, 187, 191, 194, 205–6
Drucker, Johanna, 8 26
Dytor, Frankie, 133

editor, 23
education, 137
Egerton, George (Mary Chavelita Dunne Bright), 132
Ehnenn, Jill, 133
Eliot, George, 139
Elliot, Patricia, 142
Ellis, Havelock, 24, 131, 133
Ellmann, Richard, 187, 194
empiricist ethos, 192
Engels, Friedrich, 90
ennui, 14
Eragny Press, 138, 158, 160
eros, 3, 6, 76
erotica, 182–5
Erotika Biblion Society, 180, 182–3
Et in Arcadia Ego, 183
Evangelista, Stephano, 5, 10, 51
Evans, Edmund, 82
Examiner of Plays, 198

fairy tales, 6, 74, 79, 101, 105, 232
Falkner, Charles, 87
family, 78, 85, 162
Felluga, Dino, 233
female desire, 150, 154, 169, 204
female orgasm, 155
femininity, 146, 167, 178, 233
feminism, 28, 135, 139, 143
femme fatale, 204, 212, 216

Fénéon, Félix, 34, 54
Field, Michael, 2, 8, 9, 26, 131–70, 229, 231–2
  Callirrhoë, 136
  Equal Love, 139
  Fair Rosamund, 136
  Long Ago, 9, 26, 132–3, 135–8, 143–4, 146–58, 170, 229
  'Maids, not to you my mind doth change', 153
  Mystic Trees, 158
  Sight and Song, 133
  'Trinity', 162–3
  Underneath the Bough, 229
  Whym Chow, 9, 26, 132–3, 135, 137–8, 143–4, 158–70, 232
fine press movement, 81
Flaubert, Gustave, 187, 194
  Salammbô, 194
  Temptation of Saint Anthony
  Trois Contes, 187, 194
Fletcher, Ian, 68, 212
Folkards, 37
footnotes, 184
Fortex, Emily, 158
Foucault, Michel, 4, 179–80, 202, 208
foxing, 225
Frankel, Nicholas, 8, 11, 99, 117, 189, 191, 193, 198
Freedman, Joseph, 21
Friedman, Dustin, 21, 29, 179, 181, 186, 231
frontispiece, 149
futurity *see* queer futurity

Gannon, Patricio, 40
Gaskell, Philip, 188
gaze, 178, 202, 205–6, 210, 212, 214

gender, 6, 75–6, 119, 132–4, 136, 139–42, 144, 146–7, 151, 155, 157–8, 178, 182, 186, 203, 231, 233–4
Genette, Gérard, 8
genitals, 178
George Bells & Sons, 147
Gilbert, Elliot L., 194
Gillot, Firmin, 188
Godwin, E. W., 196
gothic, 88, 92, 189
Gray, Alasdair, 59
Gray, John, 1, 2, 8, 9, 10, 25, 34, 37–41, 50–6, 60–9, 135, 162, 231–2
  'Barber, The', 62–5
  'Chevalier Malheur, Le', 56–7
  'Did we not, Darling', 66–8
  'Lean back and press the pillow deep', 66
  'Mishka', 58
  Silverpoints, 1, 9, 10, 25, 36, 37–41, 50–6, 60–8, 225, 232
  'Summer Past', 51–2
Gray, Richard, 184
green carnation, 204
grief, 168
Grigley, Joseph, 186–7
Gutenberg, Johann, 77, 81
Guy, Josephine, 11, 103

Hades, 74
Hager, Lisa, 141
Hall, Donald, E., 101, 144
Halperin, David, 10, 50
Hamilton, Cecily, 203
hand press, Albion, 96
Hanson, Ellis, 40
Harry Ransom Center, 227
Harvey, Charles, 98

Hatt, Michael, 40
Haefele-Thomas, Ardel, 141
Hellenism, 10, 21, 36, 38, 50
Helsinger, Elizabeth, 11, 85–6
Hentschel, Carl, 189
Hera, 155
Herod, King, 175
Herodian, 151
hermaphroditic figure, 177–8, 186
hetero-beautiful, 25, 27, 80, 87, 124
heteronormativity, 22, 39, 48, 61, 74, 76, 78–81, 85, 91, 99, 102, 111, 117–18, 123–4, 150, 153, 178–9, 181, 197, 199–201, 205, 214, 232–3
heterosexuality, 78, 153, 199, 202, 227
Hildebrand, R. Jayne, 91
history, 76, 79, 133, 138, 144–6, 149, 151–2, 154, 158, 170, 180–3, 186–7, 190, 207, 209–10, 227–31
historical documents, 232
historical literature, 140
Holy Trinity, 164
homoeroticism, 1, 20, 44, 48, 74, 76, 152
homogeneity, 91
homosexuality, 42, 150–1, 180, 192, 204, 207, 209, 227, 232
homosociality, 42, 150
Housman, Laurence, 223–4, 229
  'Death and the Bathers', 223–4
Hunt, John Dixon, 59
Hurley, Natasha, 181, 186
Hutcheon, Linda, 178
Hutcheon, Michael, 178

Huysmans, Joris-Karl, 31n, 41–2, 203
A rebours, 41–2, 203
Hypnerotomachia Poliphili, 59–61
hysteria, 14, 192, 202–4

iconotext, 179, 185, 188
Ideal Book, Morris's, 77, 80, 87, 105
identity, 134–7, 139, 142, 149, 153, 182, 233
illustration, 9, 12, 82–4, 88, 93, 111, 116, 122, 176, 181–2, 185, 188–91, 193–4, 196, 200, 206, 210
  illustrative process, 12
  Japanese illustration, 193
imperial supremacy, 192
impressing, 103, 223, 225
incest, 162
incoherence, 141
indeterminacy, 80, 140
ink, 9, 12, 25, 88, 95–6, 98, 149, 157, 178, 188, 190–1
Iokanaan, 175, 179, 186, 195, 198, 205–6, 213, 215
Iser, Wolfgang, 17
Italian Renaissance *see* Renaissance
italics, 51, 54, 55, 65

Jackson, Holbrook, 39
James, Henry, 229
James R. Osgood McIlvaine & Co., 80, 99
japonisme, 187, 190–2
Jekyll, Thomas, 196
Jenson, Nicholas, 77
John the Baptist *see* Iokanaan
Johnson, Lionel, 223

Jones, Justin T., 113, 119
Joyce, Simon, 141

Kains-Jackson, Charles, 49, 61
Karma Sutra, 179
Keep, Christopher, 184
Kelmscott Press, 25, 27, 77, 79, 81, 87–91, 93–4, 96–9, 125, 149, 193
  Works of Chaucer, The, 88, 93
Kersh, Sarah E., 229
Kooistra, Lorraine Janzen, 11, 83, 212

Lady's Pictorial, The, 102
Laforgue, Jules, 34, 54, 67
Lane, John, 17, 27, 34, 186, 192, 194, 197, 199–200, 207
Lee, Veron (Violet Paget), 42, 132, 139, 229
Le Gallienne, Richard, 42
Leigh, Arran, 131
Leighton, Mary Elizabeth, 82
lesbian, 26, 131, 134–5, 137, 144, 152, 154–5, 157, 170
lesbian haunting, 134, 143–4
Lesbos, 146, 157–8
letterpress intaglio, 200
Leverson, Ada, 63
limited editions, 9
line-block printing 188–91, 200
linseed oil, 95
Lippincott's Magazine, 43
literary marketplace, 11, 76, 78–9, 81, 86–7, 90, 124, 177, 180, 182, 216
lithography, 188
Louÿs, Pierre, 34, 187
lyric poetry, 7

McCormack, Jerusha, 40, 67
McGann, Jerome, 12, 200
Mackie, Greg, 181
Mackmurdo, Arthur, 196
McLean, Ruari, 82, 94
Maeterlinck, Maurice, 193
Maier, Sarah E., 204
Mak, Bonnie, 63
male supremacy, 91
Mallarmé, Stéphane, 193
Manoff, Marlene, 228
Manutius, Aldus, 38–9, 41, 54, 77
marginalia, 96, 149
margins, 25, 77, 96, 158
Markey, Anne, 102–3
marriage, 134
Marshall, Peter Paul, 87
Martial, 182–3
Marx, Karl, 90
masculinity, 92, 119, 133, 155, 167, 233
Masten, Jeffrey, n32
material book, 12, 132, 160, 186, 196, 207, 213, 232
material culture, 10, 11, 160
Mathews, Elkin, 17, 34, 38, 200
medallions, 109–10, 116, 118, 122
media archaeology, 12
media history *see* media archaeology
media studies, 12
Medievalism, 91, 105, 123
memory, 167
Merrill, Stuart, 187
metaphysical conceit, 167
Mew, Charlotte, 229
millboard, 97
Miller, Elizabeth Carolyn, 11, 81
Miller, sj, 29, 140
monologue, 214

Moore, George, 42
Moreau Gustave, n31, 194, 203
Morris & Co., 87, 94
Morris, Marshal, Faulkner & Co., 87
Morris, William, 8, 9, 25, 77–8, 80–2, 87, 89, 91–2, 97–8, 100–1, 105, 122–3, 147, 149, 188–9, 193, 199–200, 212
  Defence of Guenevere, The, 147
  Dream of John Ball, A, 88
  Earthly Paradise, 8, 88, 92, 98
  Story of Gunnlaug, The, 97
  Story of the Glittering Plain, The, 87, 94
mosaic, 131, 135
multimedial art, 3, 10, 13, 80, 123, 132, 186, 213
multisensory *see* multimedial art
Muñoz, José Esteban, 20–1, 23, 25, 29, 39, 43, 79, 124, 230, 233
mustard-plaster books *see* yellow-back novels

Narcissus, 223, 225
nature, 53
necrophilia, 213
Nelson, James G., 18, 54, 64
neoclassicism, 92
Neo-Platonism, 5
'New Chivalry', the, 6, 49
New Woman, 15
Newnham College, 136
newspapers, 93
Nichols, Harry Sidney, 180
Noble, J. Bobby, 141
non-binary, 109, 133, 135, 233
non-realist, 21
Nordau, Max, 13–14, 20, 202

octavo, 161
O'Hara, Frank, 20–1
online communities, 232
orgasm, 214–15
Ovid, 208

paganism, 26, 57, 118, 138, 151, 162, 165–7, 169–70, 232
page layout, 9, 132, 149, 200
Pageant, The, 9, 27, 104, 139, 223, 225, 229
Pall Mall Gazette, 99
paper, 9, 12, 37, 82, 94–5, 122, 178, 191, 199
  Bolognese paper, 94
  Van Gelder paper, 37
  Whatman paper, 191
papermakers, 91, 98
paratextuality, 24, 141
Paris Ilustré, 102
Parker, Sarah, 134, 147
Pater, Walter, 5, 10, 16, 25, 36, 41–2, 46–8, 60, 121, 135–6
  Marius the Epicurean, 25, 41–2, 46–8, 49
  Studies in the History of the Renaissance, 5, 10, 16, 17, 60, 121, 136
paterfamilias, 84, 91
pathology, 14, 24, 151, 202
pederasty, 209
penny magazines, 93
performance artist, 182
performativity, 38, 57
periodicals, 7, 84, 102, 143, 223, 228
Persephone, 74, 76, 80, 105
persona, 133, 135, 182
pet *see* dog
Petersson, Sonya, 185
Phaon, 156, 158

photo-engraving, 188–9, 193
photographic reproduction, 188, 190
photomechanical illustrative process, 25, 200
Pissarro, Esther, 161
Pissarro, Lucien, 161
Platonism, 20
Poems of Michael Field, The, 229
Pope, Alexander, 187
pornography *see* erotica
posters, 188
postmodern, 12
Potolsky, Matthew, 48
pre-Raphaelites, 4, 11, 85–7, 109
presentism, 29, 139
preservation, 225
Press, Jon, 98
Priapeia, 182–5, 227
Primamore, Elizabeth, 134
print culture, 8, 11, 22, 69, 180, 190–1, 232–3
  Japanese printmaking, 191
printers, 91, 200–1
printing technology, 79, 187–91, 193
private circulation *see* circulation
private publication, 167
pronouns, 147, 149
prose poems, 7
prostitution *see* sex work
publisher, 77, 138, 183, 191, 199
publishing industry, 81, 180–1, 187, 193, 231
Puvis de Chavannes, Pierre, 203

queer, 4, 9, 133–4, 139, 153, 155, 181, 200–1, 205, 212
queer books, 1, 2, 8, 10, 13, 15, 21, 23, 25, 29, 50, 63, 69, 76, 79–81, 90, 99, 109, 123,

134, 179, 204, 206, 216, 223, 232
queer community, 166, 230
queer futurity, 20–2, 29, 39, 76, 79, 81, 133, 144, 234
queer literary studies, 208
queer relationality, 20–1, 24, 29, 39, 58, 158, 181, 230–2, 234
queer space, 23, 24, 29, 48, 77–8, 138, 145, 157, 176–7, 180, 186, 192, 196, 199, 208–9, 212, 214, 225, 231
queer theory, 12, 20–1, 28, 135, 179
queerness, 18, 22, 24, 207
quire, 157

Rachilde (Marguerette Vallette-Eymery), 43
 Monsieur Venus, 43
race (racialisation, racism), 14, 27, 91, 179, 208–10
rag (cotton, linen), 93–5
Raffalovich, Marc-André, 34, 40, 56–7, 136
readability, 77
reader response theory, 17
readers, 23, 24, 74, 101, 104, 111, 119, 124, 132–3, 150, 168, 178–80, 183, 185–6, 192, 195–6, 201–2, 205–6, 210–13, 215, 229–30, 232
realism, 6
Renaissance, 5, 39, 77, 81, 88, 90, 189–90, 233
Retté, Adolphe, 187
Revival of Printing, 9, 76–7, 80, 83, 85, 193
Rhymer's Club, 34
Richardson, LeeAnne, 133

Ricketts, Charles, 2, 8, 11, 25, 27, 34, 38–9, 53, 60–1, 74, 77–9, 90, 99–104, 108–18, 122–3, 125, 136, 138, 191, 193–4, 198–9, 223, 231–2
 Defence of the Revival of Printing, The, 77
 Recollections of Oscar Wilde, 194
Ricketts and Shannon Papers, 139
Roberts, Nickie, 203
Rocha, Leon Antonio, 208–9
Roden, Frederick D., 40
Rolfe, Frederick, 229
Rothenstein, Will, 198
Ross, Robbie, 188–9, 193, 197
Rossetti, Dante Gabriel, 81, 85, 87, 109
Ruggaber, Michelle, 101
Ruskin, John, 88, 93
 Nature of Gothic, The, 88, 93

sacrilege, 167
sadomasochism, 152
Salamensky, S. I., 207
Salomé (cultural and fictional figure), 177–9, 186–7, 193, 196, 198, 202–7, 210, 213–15
same-sex desire, 4, 7, 10, 13, 17, 21–2, 25–6, 44, 61, 69, 80, 119, 139, 144, 153, 181, 184, 209, 231, 233–4
Sappho, 3, 26, 132–3, 141, 146–53, 156–8
 fragments of, 148–57
Savoy, The, 182, 187, 228
Schoeffer, Peter, 96
Schwab, Marcel, 187
Schwartz, Joan M., 228
scientia sexualis, 184, 202

scientific racism, 27, 210
sculpsit, 189
serialised novels, 82
sex worker, 202, 207, 210
sex work, 203–4, 210
sexology, 2, 3, 57
Sedgwick, Eve Kosofsky, 28, 42, 63
Sewell, Brocard, 40
sexual discourse, 2–3, 6, 9–10, 21–3, 27, 29, 46, 75, 99, 105, 178–81, 184–6, 197, 201, 204, 207–8, 216, 231, 233
sexual dissidence, 6, 74
sexual inversion, 204
sexual orientation, 6, 135
Shannon, Charles, 8, 9, 25, 27, 34, 74, 78–9, 90, 99–100, 103–4, 112, 116, 122–3, 125, 136, 191, 223, 231–2
  'The Wounded Amazon', 104
short stories, 6
Shillingsburg, Peter, 8, 12, 38
Sigel, Lisa Z., 183
Simonsen, Rasmus, 119
Small, Ian, 11, 103
Smith, Elder & Co., 82–3
Smithers, Leonard, 23, 97, 180, 182–3, 187
Snodgrass, Chris, 177–8
social Darwinism, n32, 209
Socialism, 11, 81
sodomy, 2, 4, 207
sotadic zone, 209–10
Spectator, The, 91, 106, 147, 155
spectrums, 183
Spencer, Herbert, n32
Strand Theatre, 142
Studio, 192

studiolo, 61
Sturgeon, Mary, 158
Sturgis, Matthew, 187
subscribers, 184
subtitle, 23
Surridge, Lisa, 82
Swinburne, Algernon Charles, 136, 151–2
  'Anactoria', 151–2
  Poems and Ballads, First Series, 152
Swinburnian, 105
Symbolist poets, 175, 187, 191, 198
Symbolism, 177, 193, 195, 210, 216
Symonds, John Addington, 5, 137, 149, 150–1
Symons, Arthur, 13, n31, 34

T&A Constable, 200–1
tactile reading, 22, 229
Teleny, 184
textual scholarship *see* textual studies
textual body *see* textuality
textual studies, 7, 12, 185
textuality, 4, 131, 135, 142, 179
textual intercourse, 25, 38, 79, 100, 117, 122, 131, 133–4, 140, 151, 162, 179, 186–7, 193, 196, 216
textual interdisciplinarity, 6
textualterity, 186
Thain, Marion, 142
Thompson, Paul, 97
Tiresias, 154–5, 158
title page, 141, 158, 177
Toulouse-Lautrec, Henri, 191
tombstone, 144

trans*, 26, 134–5, 137, 139, 141–2, 149, 167, 170, 231, 233–4
trans-textuality, 134–5, 138, 143, 145, 149, 154
transing, 143–4
transgender theory, 28, 135, 139, 142
translation, 137, 150, 187, 197, 200
trinity, 138, 162, 164, 166
Trinity College, 147
Tudor, Alyosxa, 29, 143
type *see* typography
typographer *see* typography
typography, 9, 12, 25, 41, 54, 60, 62, 64, 69, 77, 82, 91, 96, 117, 157, 160, 200
typesetters, 200

Ulrichs, Karl Heinrich, 5, n33
unity, 139, 148
unity of design, 87–8, 98, 101, 190, 200–1
unutterability topos, 185, 186
Uranians, 231
Utopian thinking, 232

Vadillo, Ana Parejo, 134, 147
Vale Press, The, 78, 143
vellum, 26, 95, 97–8
Venture, The, 228
Verlaine, Paul, 37, 56, 223
Victorian Review, 141
von Krafft-Ebing, Richard, 24, 180, 202, 204

Walker, Emery, 81
Warhol, Andy, 20, 79
Webb, Philip, 87
Weinwroth, Michelle, 89

Wharton, Henry Thornton, 137, 148–51, 154
Sappho, A Memoir and Translation, 148, 151
Whistler, James McNeill, 191
White, J. W. Gleeson, 9, 27, 139, 223
white space, 8, 51, 96, 150, 191
white supremacy *see* racial supremacy
Wilde, Constance Mary, 102
Wilde, Oscar, 1, 3, 5, 8, 9, 11, 17, 18, 20, 26, 34, 41–2, 44, 51–2, 54, 56, 63, 74–6, 79–80, 99–102, 105–25, 135–6, 142, 175–83, 186–7, 192–201, 204, 206–8, 210–11, 213–16, 229, 231–2
Ballad of Reading Gaol, The, 182
'Birthday of the Infanta, The', 102, 111–16, 123
'Decay of Lying, The', 18, 51
'Fisherman and his Soul, The', 102, 117–19
'Hélas!', 1, 3, 18
House of Pomegranates, A, 8, 9, 26, 74–6, 79–80, 99–102, 104, 106–25, 225
Importance of Being Earnest, The, 182
Lady Windermere's Fan, 182
Picture of Dorian Gray, The, 10, 25, 34, 41–2, 44–6, 49, 51
Poems, 17
Salome, 6, 9, 26–7, 100, 175–82, 185, 188, 190, 192, 194–201, 206–8, 210–11, 213–16, 232
Sphinx, The, 11

Wilde, Oscar (*cont.*)
   'Star Child, The', 102, 119–23
   Woman's World, The, 59
   'Young King, The', 102, 106–11, 119, 121
Winckelmann, Johann Joachim, 51
Wong, Amy R., 28
wood pulp, 93, 94
woodcuts, 188, 193, 223
Wratislaw, Theodore, 55, 68

yellow-back novels, 82–3
Yellow Book, The, 6, 15, 100, 142–3, 228–9
Yellow Nineties Online, The, 223, 229

Zaitlin, Linda Gertner, 191, 196
zinc plates, 188–9, 200
zincography, 188

EU representative:
Easy Access System Europe
Mustamäe tee 50, 10621 Tallinn, Estonia
Gpsr.requests@easproject.com

www.ingramcontent.com/pod-product-compliance
Lightning Source LLC
Chambersburg PA
CBHW070321240426
43671CB00013BA/2326